SHEFFIELD HALLAM UNIVERSITY
LEARNING & IT SERVICES
ADSETTS CENTRE CITY CAMPUS
SHEFFIELD S1 1WB

SHEFFIELD H
LEARNI
WITHDRAWN

T H E   L I S

T E

Jean Brewster and Gail Ellis
with Denis Girard

PENGUIN ENGLISH

Pearson Education Limited
Edinburgh Gate
Harlow
Essex CM20 2JE, England
and Associated Companies throughout the world.

ISBN 978-0-582-44776-9

First edition published in French 1991, and in English 1992
This edition published 2002
Text copyright Jean Brewster, Gail Ellis and Denis Girard, 1991, 1992, 2002

Fourteenth impression 2012

Design and typesetting by Ferdinand Pageworks
Illustrations by Celia Hart
Printed in China
SWTC/14

All rights reserved; no part of this publication may be reproduced, stored in a retrieval system, or transmitted in any form or by any means, electronic, mechanical, photocopying, recording or otherwise, without the prior written permission of the Publishers.

Acknowledgements
The publishers make grateful acknowledgement to the following for permission to reproduce copyright material:

Page [38], Fig. 3 A cyclical model of teacher thinking and learning is adapted from The First Years at School, Angela Anning, Open University Press, 1988/1991; page [46], Fig. 5 A framework for task-based learning is from A Framework for Task-Based Learning, Jane Willis, Longman, 1996; page [134], Fig. 23 A mind map for planning a topic is from Portfolio Topic Book, Heroes, C. Nihlen et al., Almqvist & Wiksell, 1999; page [142], Fig. 25 Developing and using key visuals is adapted from Enriching Literacy- Text, Talk and Tales in Today's Classroom: A practical handbook for multilingual schools, Brent Language Service, Trentham Books, 1999; page [247], Fig. 47 The teaching and assessment cycle is adapted from The Practice of Foreign Language Teaching, W. Cajkler and R. Addleman, David Fulton Publishers, 2000

Every effort has been made to trace copyright holders in every case. The publishers would be interested to hear from any not acknowledged here.

Published by Pearson Education Limited in association with Penguin Books Ltd, both companies being subsidiaries of Pearson plc.

For a complete list of the titles available in the Penguin English please write to your local Pearson Education office or to: Penguin English Marketing Department, Pearson Education, Edinburgh Gate, Harlow, Essex CM20 2JE.

Contents

Introduction

The first edition of this guide in English was published in 1992 – a time when for many teachers all over the world the introduction of foreign languages into the primary curriculum was a new venture. When we wrote the first edition we were lucky enough to benefit from our collaboration with one of Europe's most respected and influential figures in the field of primary language teaching, Denis Girard.

At that time, there was a general feeling of excitement but also some apprehension at bringing together primary and secondary teachers, teacher trainers and inspectors for the fusion of ideas and resources. Ten years on, we have witnessed a decade of rapid change with the development of new materials and resources, new research, new applications of language learning theories and approaches, and a much greater awareness of issues such as globalization, multiple intelligences, and citizenship. This new edition takes these developments into account and includes completely revised and updated chapters on language learning at primary level, how children think and learn, teaching methodologies, learning to learn, development of the four skills including pronunciation, vocabulary and grammar, English accross the curriculum, resources, and management skills for teachers. It also includes brand new chapters on teaching culture, the role of technology in the classroom, record keeping and assessment, and parental involvement.

The teacher of foreign languages to children has become a highly skilled professional who can combine their knowledge, skills and sensitivities of a teacher of children with those of a teacher of language and balance the two. This guide caters for practising teachers of foreign languages to children between the ages of approximately five to eleven, as well as teacher trainers and trainees. Wherever possible, we have included examples from real classrooms to illustrate and support our points. We would like to encourage you to take on a reflective and analytical role so that you may make informed choices about what will work best in your own context and modify our suggestions as appropriate.

We hope you enjoy using this guide as much as we have enjoyed writing it. We would like to take this opportunity to thank our colleagues and students from whom we have learned so much and to whom we owe so much.

Jean Brewster and Gail Ellis
February 2002

THE YOUNG LANGUAGE LEARNER   **PART**

1 Foreign language learning at primary level

The world seems to be shrinking very rapidly as international barriers break down and people can more easily come into contact with other cultures and languages through travel, communication or new technology. This so-called globalization of the world is a modern and sometimes controversial trend which looks as though it may be here to stay, at least for the time being. In this chapter we will consider one aspect of this globalization – the growing trend for using English as a world language. This has led to the introduction of English language learning by many children in many countries all over the world. Let us examine this in a little more detail.

First, if English truly has the role of a global language, governments are keen to encourage their citizens to have English language competence for their country's economic benefit. English now has official status in sixty countries and a prominent position in twenty more countries. Pressure to introduce early English learning has often come from parents who strongly believe that having English as a tool will benefit their children greatly by giving them more opportunities to gain economic, cultural or educational advantages. Until recently, however, English language learning in many countries did not begin until secondary school. This brings us to the next trend, the lowering of the age at which children learn a foreign language.

Governments and private schools all over the world have decided to introduce English at primary level, because there is a strong 'folk' belief, a sort of 'act of faith', that young children learn languages better and more easily than older children. This means there is a widespread belief that there are definite advantages to introducing language learning early on in life which outweigh the disadvantages. This very controversial issue will be examined in detail in the next chapter.

A worldwide survey of teaching English to young children shows that educationalists all over the world have recognized the need for English language learning at primary level and are doing whatever they can to promote it (see website www.britishcouncil.org/english/eyl/index.htm). This chapter will examine the most common aims and objectives of primary level foreign language learning and also some important considerations of this trend for foreign language learning in secondary schools.

English language learning as a global phenomenon

In a book on the impact of global English on different parts of the world, McArthur (in Graddol and Meinhof 1999:5) writes that East Asia is a particularly good example. He writes that here 'the entire middle class seem to want English for their children as an international vehicle which they can then use with the rest of the world'. Many countries have now started teaching English in the state primary sector. Where primary ELT in the state sector is not yet widespread, or parents wish to supplement the work of state schools for whatever reason, private schools flourish. Greece and Taiwan are only two examples of the many countries where parents' wishes have created a rapid growth in private schools for English at primary and secondary levels. In Taiwan, for example, parents say they are only too aware of how competitive the educational climate is. Their children's attendance at private schools is seen as a way of guaranteeing a head start for their sons and daughters. In countries where educational competition is very strong, many young pupils are faced with a constant round of tests and examinations for English language. Their commitment to and motivation for learning English seems impressively high, although we may sometimes wonder how long this will continue in these conditions.

Within the European Union, 2001 was designated the European Year of Languages, during which many activities were organized to raise the profile of foreign language learning. Its aims were to celebrate the diversity of languages, to encourage lifelong learning and to provide information about the teaching and learning of languages. (See website http://culture.coe.fr/lang/ for the Modern Languages Division of the Council of Europe.) Here and in other parts of the world there is now increasing concern about the status of learning other foreign languages apart from English and fears that English may in fact become too dominant. For example English is increasingly taking on the role of a second national language in many countries such as Sweden, Denmark and Holland where English is the main language of international communication. In a survey conducted in 1989, thirteen countries in the European Union, including Belgium, Spain and Portugal considered foreign language teaching in primary schools to be a national priority. In a growing number of European countries, English is part of the public and family environment, especially through cartoons, television, films, pop music, magazines and newspapers. Thus English is often, but not always, the foreign language of choice. It is perhaps regrettable that this dominance of English pushes other languages into the background, an imbalance which the European Year of Languages has tried to correct.

Why teach a foreign language at primary level?

Europe in the 1960s experienced the first large-scale wave of foreign language learning in primary schools and numerous conferences reported a high level of agreement on language teaching, including UNESCO conferences in 1962 and 1966 (Stern, 1969), and the Council of Europe conferences at Reading (1967). Countries like France began experiments to determine how far primary foreign language learning (FLL) might be successful. A report by Girard (1974) provided a detailed overview of several European FLL projects. This report underlined the need for creating, first of all, the optimal or best conditions for teaching languages. He referred to six important conditions: having appropriately trained teachers, proper timetabling with sufficient timing, appropriate methodology, continuity and liaison with secondary schools, provision of suitable resources and integrated monitoring and evaluation. These conferences and reports highlighted the following issues for introducing early foreign language learning:

- Advantage can be taken of certain aptitudes children have.

- There is no theoretical optimum age to start teaching. The starting age can vary according to country and linguistic situation, although at that time the age of nine was often chosen.

- Early learning of a non-mother tongue language must be integrated into other teaching in the primary school.

- Whatever else may be achieved, the main concern is to prepare the ground so that the most can be made of the teaching which will be received in secondary school.

- The linguistic and pedagogical skills of the teachers are the two most important factors.

One reason for starting to learn a foreign language several years earlier (at age six or nine instead of eleven or twelve) was simply to increase the total number of years spent learning the language. This decision needed to take into account two important considerations: the time factor and the nature of primary methodology. For children it was determined that regular short slots during the week were likely to be more effective than a longer more concentrated slot only once a week. Second, teachers should take account of the methods and the pace of primary school teaching, so that a year of teaching in primary school cannot be equated with a year in secondary school. Another reason most commonly put forward was the fact that young children seem to have a greater facility for understanding and imitating what they hear than secondary school pupils. Imitation is, of course, not the whole picture in language learning, as we shall see in chapter 2, but it seemed a reasonable strategy to try to take advantage of children's language learning skills and aptitudes.

English language learning policies at primary level

Although there is widespread interest and positive developments in teaching English to learners of primary and secondary age, the worldwide scene is often a patchwork of unrelated projects and initiatives. In the European Union, however, teaching English to young learners is part of a wider picture of a policy for foreign language learning where it has been suggested that EU citizens have a personal document called a European Language Portfolio (ELP). This document is intended to act as a guide to people's language learning and to show their competence in different languages and their contacts with other cultures. It is available for all ages, from very young children to adults. The ELP has four aims: to encourage people to learn more languages and to continue learning throughout their lives; to improve their learning and their ability to assess their own competence; to help movement within Europe by documenting language skills in a clear and internationally comparable way and to contribute to a shared cultural understanding within Europe.

Where a policy of teaching English to Young Learners (EYL) is introduced, several conditions need to be met. This is vital both for the teachers involved and for the pupils entrusted to their care. The first condition is that it should be properly planned, ideally taking into account the experiences of other countries which have succeeded. Teachers, teacher educators, curriculum designers, materials writers and assessment specialists must have a clear idea of intended goals and outcomes; ideally they will have been involved through consultation or participation in the process of policy creation. This is especially true where such policies are introduced on an experimental basis, as has often been the case with foreign language teaching in primary schools. Second, governments and private institutions must ensure that adequate resources are provided to ensure optimal conditions so that the 'younger equals better' slogan can be turned into successful reality. This provision includes not only material resources, appropriate coursebooks and other classroom aids, but also appropriately trained teacher educators and teachers. Third, an evaluation of the learning outcomes after a set period is also essential since these are ultimately expected to provide information on the validity of the teaching, and the cost effectiveness of the national spending involved. In France, for example, future plans announced by the Ministry of Education (see Lang, J. 2001) include working towards a clear statement of the outcomes and achievements of learners' foreign language learning.

Aims and objectives

The general aims of early foreign language learning should appear attractive to parents, teachers and administrators and workable for children, while avoiding being over-ambitious and unrealistic. This point was recognized early on in France when early controlled trials in teaching modern languages began in elementary school. The policy document stated that the aim was not the creation of bilingual children but more reasonably, 'to prepare children linguistically, psychologically and culturally for language learning' (BOEN 1989). Generally speaking, foreign language programmes tend to include this wide range of possibilities where, for example, the goals of their programmes are not only learning to use the language but also developing sensitivity to and awareness of foreign languages and cultures. In fact, more than a decade after this report, the aims of primary language learning all over the world can generally be classified under these headings: psychological preparation, linguistic preparation and cultural preparation.

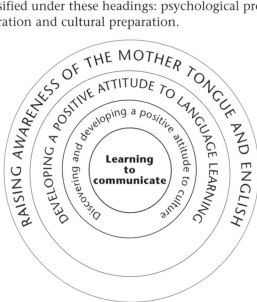

Fig. 1 Objectives of early learning of English

Psychological preparation

The primary concern of foreign language teachers is the creation of as many ways as possible of giving their pupils an appetite to learn. In

Japan, for example, the aims of primary ELT, as stated by the Ministry of Education, include 'to motivate the learner' and 'to learn English for interest and fun'. The Ministry of Education in Indonesia has the objective 'to motivate children to learn English in interesting and fun ways'. In Spain a Curriculum aim of the Reforma is 'recognizing and appraising the communicative value of a foreign language and their own capacity to learn how to use it' (cited in Coyle et al. and Valcarcel (1997). More recently, Kubanek-German (1998:194) has written a survey article of primary ELT in Europe. Here she writes that that 'regional and national guidelines unanimously point out that the children's experience with a foreign language ought to be enjoyable and not put an extra burden on them'. Teachers will be aware of how much parental expectations can be a positive or negative force in L2 learning. Fortunately, in the case of learning English many parents are highly motivated, a feeling which tends to be passed on to their children. However, teachers will have to work hard to nurture feelings of enthusiasm in their pupils. Cajkler and Addelman (2000:1) write that teachers 'should not take it for granted that children will arrive in the classroom with a strong positive attitude to foreign language learning'.

A study of the motivation of young learners in Croatia was carried out by Djigunovic and Vilke (2000). In Croatia L2 learning was introduced in a small-scale project in 1991 with first graders (aged six to seven). The authors' longitudinal study, carried out over eight years, studied these pupils' attitudes in their first year of learning and on three more occasions – after three, six and eight years of study. Using a methodology based on cross-curricular work (using primary subjects) and storytelling, learners in the first grade particularly liked the activities that had a game element. After three years of learning these pupils still liked the L2 and enjoyed their classes, but by this time they enjoyed not only the game-like activities but also the classroom activities which they perceived as learning and not just fun. As their motivation was high, these learners continued enjoying their English lessons. Even after eight years it was found that their motivation had continued to increase.

Kubanek-German (1998:194) also refers to research on the long-term effects of children learning a foreign language. For example, secondary students who had started learning English in the primary school had a slight advantage in reading, writing and listening. In Italy, primary foreign language learners were found to be more aware of the structure of their L1 than others who had not studied a foreign language and had developed greater 'language awareness'. Eight-year-olds showed no anxiety when language learning, whereas eleven-year-olds had developed strategies to cope with language anxiety. Finally, she writes that most studies showed that the courses kindled interest in language learning and in other cultures. If this continues to be the case across most contexts, this will be good news indeed.

Another aspect of psychological preparation is developing awareness of language. Several projects on 'language awareness' were published in the UK in the 1980s for English secondary students learning a foreign language. The aim here was to stimulate children's natural interest and curiosity about language and 'to challenge pupils to ask questions about language' (Hawkins 1984:4). The results of experiments inspired by his work generally showed the usefulness of this approach. More recently, the development of children's 'metacognitive awareness' has been analysed in detail by Ellis (see 1999 and chapter 5). She sees it as an umbrella term which covers four different kinds of awareness: language awareness, cognitive awareness, social awareness and cultural awareness. Developing 'learning awareness' is essentially a way of helping pupils to understand why *and how* they are learning another language. The ideal result is that they become more aware of issues such as information about the kind of materials they will use, the strategies which are likely to help them, and how to build up their confidence. This kind of awareness may include focusing on skills such as noticing, observing, analysing, comparing, deducing, or conceptualizing, all of which are skills which Chomsky (1959) claims are part of children's innate 'Language Acquisition Device', which is triggered as part of first language acquisition. (For more on this refer to chapters 2 and 5.) It is increasingly recognized that awareness of processes of this kind is likely to support the acquisition of the skills and the knowledge needed to communicate in a foreign language. One possible objection to awareness raising is that children do not have the necessary mental maturity to carry out and benefit from such a process of reflection. However, studies show that even young children under school age are more aware than one might expect. Here is an example of a child at two years, six months talking about her first language:

Adult: (pointing to child's foot). *What's that?*
Child: *A footsie*
Adult: (pointing to both feet) *What are these?*
Child: *Two footsies – no two feetsies I mean.*

And a child at three years one month
Child: *Can I have a bit of cheese, please? Cheese, please, that's a rhyme.*   (LINC materials 1991)

Supporters of the 'awareness raising' approach believe that helping pupils to learn to make use, or better use, of their innate abilities of observation and comparison is only one more way for them to learn to communicate in a foreign language. According to Brewster et al. (1992:34), learning to reflect on how the English language functions does not mean taking a course in English grammar. 'All that is implied is a moment of reflection, if the teacher chooses, whenever the opportunity arises, to draw attention to an interesting language feature. Such a course of action will lead to a better understanding of the way the language functions and result in the memorizing of important rules affecting the ability to communicate'. Seen in this light, learning English in primary school is likely to have a much better chance of being integrated into general learning and helping to reinforce learning in other subjects, including the L1 (see chapter 9). At the same time, children will receive an effective preparation for the teaching programmes they will encounter at secondary school.

Linguistic preparation

According to Doyé and Hurrell in a (1997) Council of Europe report, experts favour the goal of developing basic communicative competence in a systematic way in preference to aiming simply for 'language – sensitization' or raising 'language awareness'. In many countries the main language aim for primary ELT is to be able to communicate, or to develop 'communicative competence'. In Spain, for example, they state that the aim is 'not to teach a foreign language but to teach how to use it in communication (Coyle, et al. 1997). The Spanish guidelines continue to give very precise accounts of what children are expected to achieve in all four language skills. For example, young pupils are expected to develop global and specific understanding of simple oral texts related to well-known objects, situations and events. They are also expected to use the foreign language orally to communicate with their teacher and their partners in routine classroom activities and in communicative situations created by the teacher for that purpose. Of course, the kinds of language learning points focused on by teachers or materials will vary enormously according to the pupils' ages and language levels. In the earliest stages, language aims may simply involve getting pupils used to the sounds, rhythm and intonation of English and creating an atmosphere where the child feels able to 'have a go' at speaking a few words in another language with confidence. From the beginning parents and children alike are keen to see evidence of being able to say something in the new language. With the young child this is likely to be singing a simple song, reciting an action rhyme or the ability to say 'My name is ..., I'm X years old', and so on. In line with primary methodology, pupils will probably have the opportunity to learn the English alphabet, memorize simple dialogues, play language games, sing songs and chants, and so on in ways that keep the child interested, motivated and challenged. By con-trast, the guidelines in the European Schools (part of a self-contained educational system consisting of a small number of schools in six mem-ber states of the European Union) are deliberately very broad. This free-dom from rigidly specified aims is intended to 'leave room for personal interpretation and application by the individual schools and teachers in accordance with local needs' (see Housen 1997:42).

Cultural preparation

Another common aim of foreign language learning in many countries is to develop 'intercultural awareness'. In Spain, for example, the govern-ment guidelines include the goal of 'showing a respectful attitude towards other languages, their speakers and their culture' (cited in Valcarcel 1997:230). A common way of maintaining pupils' interest in foreign language learning is to introduce information about the target culture. This is especially effective if this is perceived, rightly or wrong-ly, as something desirable. Teachers of foreign languages in Britain often despair of motivating some of their pupils; many boys in particular are notorious for not being interested in FLL. However, when European football became a topic in one language class, interest miraculously improved! From the first year onwards, pupils can be introduced to real or fictional characters from other cultures and can focus on aspects of their own lives, such as where they live, what they eat, the clothes they wear, hobbies and sports they enjoy, and so on. According to Brewster et al. (1992:50) 'provided it is motivating and not abstract, early FLL in the more relaxed context of primary school has a good chance of encourag-ing children to take an interest and develop a positive attitude towards the foreign country and its people'. Developing cultural awareness is explored in much more detail in chapter 10.

Policy realities

Unfortunately, there is often a mismatch between what policies claim to promote and classroom reality. One study showed that secondary teachers claimed to be using the methodological approach as stated in government policy, but their observed classroom practice showed that they were not. Why does this kind of mismatch between stated aims and actual teaching happen? It may be because a government or insti-tution tries to implement a policy too quickly, so that there is simply not enough time to prepare teacher educators and teachers in appro-priate methods. There may not be enough suitable materials and resources, or teachers may be in the grip of tests and examinations which do not achieve the stated aims, or which even ignore or undermine them.

Policies are not always clear about the end points of the primary phase of learning. What do they consider to be 'successful learning'? Is this the development of children who can talk fairly confidently about everyday needs and topics? Or who can give simple but clear written instructions about how to do something? Children who can retell and rewrite a story? Or who know the rules for countable and uncountable nouns? The area of determining realistic achievements for young learners is in great need of research. Another crucial point policy makers must also think very carefully about is how primary ELT links up with secondary ELT, where accuracy and grammar-based work is a more appropriate part of the programme. This has been the downfall of several attempts at primary ELT, as we shall see in the next section.

From primary school to secondary school

In the past children did not usually learn a foreign language until they went to secondary school. Increasingly, it is likely that children may learn English from the age of nine, six or even younger in either a private or state school or both. In many countries there is very little continuity between primary and secondary schools in all aspects of learning, with the teaching of a foreign language being no exception. Ministries of Education in some countries sponsor programmes for a while, but lose interest and withdraw support when the novelty element has worn off and specialist teachers (perhaps imported) and special in-service training have disappeared. According to Nikolov (2000: 36), this has happened in countries like Italy and Croatia. She writes that 'absolutely no research has been found into how secondary schools build on existing L2 proficiency'. Aside from this problem, there are the now familiar complaints from secondary teachers that primary pupils have not learned anything useful at primary school. In order to build in an element of sustainability, so important for the continuing existence of new projects, it is important that teaching English at primary level is seen as a way of making the secondary teacher's job more challenging and interesting, but not more difficult or frustrating. Early L2 learning is only justified if what is learned serves as a springboard, however modest, for the teaching to come. If secondary teachers are not informed about primary L2 methods and achievements, they may simply view their new pupils as problematic, which of course is very detrimental to primary English. Secondary L2 teachers may feel resentful about having to use a completely different approach, using different materials or providing work at different levels to cater for the range of language levels in their classes.

Where some account has been taken of the necessary continuity of language learning between primary and secondary school it will be recognized that children who have benefited from a properly planned primary programme are better prepared to respond to language teaching in the secondary school. Nothing could be more counter-productive than inaccurate knowledge or language skills which result in the teacher making constant corrections and having to go over what has supposedly already been learned. This is very discouraging for the pupils and can lead to feelings of failure or may replace pupils' initial enthusiasm and motivation with a negative attitude to L2 learning.

Primary teachers need to take every opportunity to make contact with the secondary school English teachers who will be responsible for teaching their pupils when they move on. Specific 'primary/secondary school link' meetings could be organized by the schools' management or by professional language teaching associations. Ideally, secondary school teachers could be invited to observe classes, see displays of children's work or review assessment procedures and results. The promotion of teacher development activities which develop feelings of trust and mutual respect between primary and secondary L2 teachers is very useful. In turn, secondary teachers need to recognize the importance of knowing what is happening in their local primary language classes.

Naturally, there is no question of primary school language methodology modelling the teaching of languages at secondary level. Indeed, some people believe that the first year of secondary schools might well learn something from successful primary schools! A basic concern with providing continuity in children's education means that bridges must be built between the different stages of their language education.

In summary, countries which have introduced foreign language learning at primary level have a core of key questions which they need to address. They include:

- What are the advantages and drawbacks?

- Is there an optimum starting age?

- Who will do the teaching and what kind of training should they receive?

- Who will be the teacher trainers?

- What kinds of methodology can be created which are finely tuned to pupils' ages, abilities and socio-economic group?

- How far is it beneficial to integrate foreign language learning with the primary curriculum more generally?

11

- What are the merits of developing language awareness as well as language competence?

- How can we provide continuity in FLL between primary and secondary schools?

- What kinds of learning outcomes and achievements can we expect?

- What are the best methods for assessing language development in primary pupils?

Those countries that are veterans, or old-timers in this field, especially in the European Union, will probably have answers to many of these questions, but only if research and evaluation continues to be carefully built into projects and initiatives. Novices to this field will still be answering some of these questions as they go along, sometimes being able to learn from others, often not, as learning contexts can be so different. Where conditions appear to be similar, more shared learning between countries would be an excellent move. You will find that the chapters in this book explore many of the necessary issues to begin answering these questions.

Keeping in touch with English language teachers

The ease with which countries are now able to communicate has made communication with other teachers much easier. For example, the British Council has commissioned a worldwide survey of teaching EYL (see website address on page 1). Organizations such as ELTeCS (English Language Teaching Contacts Scheme), also set up by the British Council, have established extensive regional networks for teachers of primary ELT all over the world (see www.britishcouncil.org/english/eltecs). The International Association for Teachers of English as a Foreign Language (IATEFL) also provides an international network for primary foreign language teachers (www.countryschool.com/younglearners.htm). Many useful Council of Europe documents are available from their offices in Strasbourg (www.coe.int).

2 How children learn languages

In this chapter we are going to review briefly some of the latest findings on how children learn both their L1 and L2. We shall consider some of the implications for language teachers to see how far it is true that learning a language younger means learning it better.

Task 1:
Take this quiz about children learning languages (adapted from Lightbown and Spada 1993:xv). Read the questions and make a note of your responses *before* you read the rest of the chapter. Then read the chapter and change your responses if you have changed your point of view. Finally, check the correct answers.

1 How do you think children learn their first language?
   a) by imitating adults
   b) by experimenting and trying out hypotheses about how the language works
   c) both of the above
2 Do children with a high intelligence quotient (IQ) score learn to speak foreign languages quicker and better than others?
   a) IQ is a crucial factor
   b) IQ is not a crucial factor
   c) setting and context are more important
3 How important is high motivation in successful language learning?
   a) not really important
   b) the most important factor
   c) an important factor but not the only one
4 Is it better for pupils to learn a foreign language when they are below the age of puberty?
   a) definitely yes
   b) probably yes
   c) it depends on all sorts of other factors
5 Should teachers use materials with only language structures which have already been taught?
   a) definitely yes, learners must always be supported step-by-step
   b) no, learners must quickly become independent
   c) if new language is contextualized well, learners often welcome a challenge

Answers
1 c) 2 c) 3 c) 4 c) 5 c)

Learning a first language

Recent studies have shown that babies may become familiar with aspects of their future L1 while they are still in the womb! After birth, learning a language starts with a baby producing its first noises and cries. Babies are even able to mirror their parents' use of intonation and stress, for example, by waggling their hands in time to the parents' use of stressed syllables, or cooing with similar intonation patterns to those they have just heard. There are a number of stages through which children pass in the process of acquiring their first language. In the stages below you can find out more about the aspects of the language system they acquire and some of the processes involved.

1 **babbling:** From birth to around eight months babies can hear and produce a wide range of noises and sounds. Some of these sounds will later be phased out as they are not present in the child's L1.

2 **the first 'word':** At about eleven months infants put names (in their own fashion) to the objects and people around them. During the second year, the earlier random vocalizations begin to take on the aspect of genuine communication. Certain sound combinations, such as *mama* and *dada*, tend to be rewarded very positively, even though initially they are produced purely by chance. Through constant exposure to words and by imitating examples heard, the infant learns to associate certain objects with certain sounds.

3 **two words:** Between eighteen months and two years, they enter a genuinely syntactic phase of acquisition by placing two words together (e.g. *there, look, want, more, all, gone*) to create a new meaning e.g. *look Daddy, Mummy gone, there doggy.*

4 **phonological, syntactic and lexical norms:** The third and fourth years are periods of great creativity, when the essential language elements are put in place. The successive grammatical systems which children construct begin to resemble closely the norms of the adults who surround them. Children will have learned all the vowel and consonant sounds of their L1 by school age but some children may have a few problems with individual sounds or consonant clusters. English native speaker children are most likely to have problems with the consonant clusters in thrill, shrill, school, ship or church. Problems with individual sounds are likely to occur with /r/ /s/ or /z/. By the age of five many children will draw on a vocabulary of several thousand words.

5 **syntactic and lexical complexity and richness:** Between six and

twelve, children continue to expand their reading vocabulary and to improve their understanding of words. For example, English-speaking children under eight still respond to *'Tell me your name'* and *'Ask me my name'* in the same way. School-age children who are helped to see the relationship between words and who notice common word structures develop larger vocabularies than those without such training. With regard to grammar, six- to seven-year-olds tend to be confused by certain irrelevant information, complex constructions and the implied meaning of certain words. Chomsky (1969) presented five-year-olds with a blindfolded doll and asked if the doll was 'easy to see' or 'hard to see'. Most of the younger children were misled by the blindfold and responded with 'hard to see'. By nine and ten none of the children were confused by the blindfold. A complex construction like 'John asked Bill what to do' may not be understood until a child is ten or eleven. As children become older they are able to give more abstract and less self-oriented definitions of words. Six- to twelve-year-olds like learning chants, poems, song lyrics and love tongue twisters or jokes. Groups of children often make up secret languages or codes.

6 **conversational skills:** In interactional tasks, young children may not know that they do not understand or that directions they are given are incomplete and unclear. They may simply continue without showing incomprehension or asking questions. Older children are more likely to realize that something is unclear and may try to identify the problem and suggest an alternative. As children get older they are more able to take another person's perspective and are better at using persuasive arguments to get what they want.

In terms of language functions, or what children want to do with language, Wells (1986) found that young children generally pass through five stages before they reach school age. (Although he found that all children passed through these stages, they did this at different ages.) These stages are as follows.

1 First utterances are used to get attention, direct someone's attention to an object or event, get something they want, make requests and simple statements e.g. *Doggy gone.* With such limited resources much meaning is conveyed by intonation.

2 Children begin naming and classifying things, asking questions, using *Where?* or *Wassat* (what's that?). They also begin to talk about locations changing e.g. using *down* or *up*, adjectives e.g. *hot, cold, big, small* and using possessives e.g. *Mummy's bag.*

3 Children then ask many different kinds of questions, often using

intonation with statements e.g. *doggy gone, Mummy?* They express more complex desires using *I want,* refer regularly to events in the past and can talk about on-going actions using *still* or the present continuous e.g. *Daddy doing it, Mummy still in bed.*

4   Children use increasingly complex structures to make a wide range of requests, explain things or ask for explanations, using *Why?.* They have mastered the use of the auxiliary verb *do* to ask questions, followed by *can* and *will.*

5   Children can use the language they need to give information, ask and answer questions of various kinds, make direct and indirect requests, make suggestions and offers, state intentions and ask about those of others, express feelings and attitudes and ask about those of others. They can talk about cause and effect e.g. *if you do that then it will ...* and are aware of things that are habits, repetitive or just beginning.

This list provides useful insights about children's needs and concerns as well as their growing conceptual development. It is interesting to speculate how far these findings have influenced the design of ELT syllabuses for young children.

Different views of L1 and L2 acquisition

We have all observed children acquiring their L1 with ease yet struggling to learn an L2 in the classroom and sometimes even failing. These days it is generally recognized that understanding more about similarities and differences in L1 and L2 acquisition processes can help teachers in the foreign language classroom. Explanations of early L1 and L2 acquisition have changed a great deal in the last fifty years. The most useful and influential views arise from different schools of psychology: behaviourist, nativist (also known as innatist), cognitive – developmental, and social-interactionist.

If we think of language acquisition as a jigsaw, we can consider each of these views as a piece, each providing useful insights, but only a partial explanation. Let us briefly examine their main characteristics.

Behaviourist views

Behaviourism had a strong influence on the *audio-lingual* approach, which can still be seen in some parts of the world. Among other things this approach emphasises repetition in the form of drills, accuracy and the avoidance of errors. It arose from the work of Skinner (1957), who wrote *Verbal Behaviour.* Behaviourists believe that *imitation* and *practice* or *habit formation* are key processes in language development. This view stresses the importance of *positive reinforcement* in L1 and L2 acquisition where correct learning behaviour is rewarded by praise. Nowadays, linguists recognize that although imitation and practice are clearly important parts of language, they do not provide the complete picture. It does not explain children's gift for creativity in language. For example, a child was reported to exclaim 'Thunder!' every time he heard a jet fly overhead. Lightbown and Spada (1993:6) give two neat examples of children learning about the prefixes 'de' and 'un' in English. In the first, David, almost four years old, experiments with the word 'undressed'.

Mother: Get undressed.
David: I'm getting undressed.
I'm getting *on* dressed.
I'm getting on dressed.
I'm getting *off* dressed.

The child is playing with similar sounds and comparing patterns and meanings which he recognizes from other words. In their second example, a father tells his child of six to wait for some bread to be *defrosted*. The child does not want to wait and protests 'But I like it *frossed*'. Both examples show how children are able to understand and apply rules they have worked out in a very logical way, but which then leads them to produce language they have never heard. So we can see that although behaviourism offers a partial explanation for routine aspects of both L1 and L2 language acquisition it cannot explain the acquisition of more complex grammatical structures and lexical relationships.

Nativist views

The nativist, or innatist, view arose originally from seventeenth- and eighteenth-century theories that suggested there were innate and therefore universal features of the human mind. In the 1950s these ideas were revived by Chomsky, who changed forever the way we think about language. In the nativist view, children are pre-programmed to learn a language and are highly sensitive to the linguistic features of their environment. Chomsky (1959) challenged behaviourist views by suggesting an internal or innate Language Acquisition Device, (LAD), now referred to as Universal Grammar (UG), which allows infants to process all the language they hear and to produce their own meaningful utterances. This view inspired a huge range of research studies which revealed the complex ways in which children develop grammatical competence in their L1. This view allowed for the child's creativity as an important part of L1, a factor which has been carried over to L2 learning. Innatists' views were another step in the right direction, although there was not enough consideration of communication with real people in real time. Thus, over time, social-interactionists criticized Chomsky's preoccupation with the structures of language, feeling that other more personal and social aspects of language use were being neglected.

Cognitive-developmental views

According to Whitehead (1990), the cognitive-developmental view emphasised that language development was an aspect of general cognitive growth, claiming that certain thinking skills must first mature in order to create a framework for early language development. This view also stressed children's intentions and meanings and their uses in developing language ability. In terms of L2 learning, the Critical Period Hypothesis (CPH), as proposed by Lenneberg (1967), suggested that there is a specific and limited time for language acquisition. This controversial theory has been put to the test by many other researchers, who have often found that there are many important factors to consider aside from age, such as motivation and learning conditions. In many studies younger children were often found to be less efficient learners of vocabulary and grammar than older learners. For example, a study in Holland with children, adolescents and adults showed that adolescents were by far the best learners, except for pronunciation (see Snow and Hoefnagel-Hohle 1978). Younger learners, on the other hand, did best at pronunciation, story comprehension and storytelling. Because of studies like these, the pure version of CPH is no longer held to be valid, although there is general agreement that early language acquisition has cognitive and linguistic dimensions.

Social-interactionist views

In the late 1970s and 1980s developmental psychologists emphasised the importance of social factors, which leads us on to the current view, 'social-interactionist'. This emphasises the importance of human social interactions, and the role of adult and child relationships in learning. A crucial element in this view is the way language is modified to suit the level of the learner. As a result, many studies were made of the way the chief caregiver, often the mother, talked to the child. Bruner (1983) showed how an innate device, such as Chomsky's LAD, was not able to function without the help given by an adult. They called this kind of help the Language Acquisition Support System or LASS. Bruner said there needed to be a child component, incorporating an innate tendency for active social interaction and language learning (LAD), and a social support component provided by other speakers, especially adults (LASS).

The partner with whom the child interacts provides a structure or framework, which Bruner referred to as 'scaffolding'. The work of Vygotsky in the 1930s (not published in the West until the 1960s) was significant in terms of emphasising the way in which human thinking is dominated by mental processes arising from language. He coined the phrase 'zone of proximal development' (ZPD) to explain the fact that children can do much more with the help of someone more knowledgeable or skilled than themselves than they can do alone. This highlights the importance of social interaction and learning from working with others. Vygotsky then described how the child is able to move away from learning with others to more independent thought and behaviour. The notion of the ZPD has provided us with insights into how teachers can both support and yet challenge learners through the careful design and staging of tasks. The work of both Vygotsky and Bruner has been influential in developing a theory of how children think and learn language and has helped to emphasise the importance of an interactional aspect in learning a foreign language.

It seems that the final picture is very complex. Imitation and practice are important in language learning although children are also immensely creative. No doubt in the future more research will develop other insights and views on the child language acquisition process.

Are the L1 and L2 acquired in the same way?

L1 and L2 learners are different in terms of what they bring to the language learning situation, but similar in their ability to acquire language. What language teachers will really want to know is *How far are the processes involved in learning the L1 similar to those in learning an L2?* Not surprisingly this is still not an easy question to answer as it is such a complex process and depends on many factors, such as the view of language learning you have, the learning context, the learners' motivation, and so on. A behaviourist view, sees the two processes as very similar since practice and imitation are common to both. An innatist view would tend to believe that L1 and L2 learning are both activities which require the child to use past experience to structure new experience. In each case, the learner takes the language they hear and uses it selectively by building on what they already know. Those who have a more cognitive-developmental view believe that there are important differences between the two processes, as the L2 learner is more cognitively developed than the L1 learner. A social-interactionist view would argue that the social context for each tends to be very different in terms of the types and amount of input provided, the types and amount of output produced and more generally the purposes for which language is used. All of these factors affect the extent to which language is contextualized through gestures, intonation, facial expressions, real situations, feelings, intentions or objects. In early L1 acquisition, language is highly contextualized and the learner highly motivated, whereas L2 acquisition can be much more decontextualized, or presented within an artificial context, and where learners may not be highly motivated. Context is all-important as learners have been shown to differ in their ability to cope with contextualized and decontextualized language. The findings reveal that in FLL learners who are good at contextualized tasks, where the learning is supported through visuals, feelings or real situations, are not necessarily good at decontextualized tasks where no such support is provided. However, children who are good at decontextualized tasks in their L1 tend to be good at similar tasks in the L2. A common decontextualized task might be the learning of grammatical rules where there is an emphasis on form but not on creating a meaning or context for its use.

To simplify, we can say that some L1 and L2 acquisition *processes* are very similar, although many of the learning *conditions* are very different. In terms of processes, most learners go though four phases. First they work out rules about how the language works; second, they generalize these across a group of similar instances. Third, they go on to overgeneralize, or use rules where they are not appropriate (e.g. young children learning English go through a phase of saying *goed* and *putted* for past tense instead of *went* and *put*) before finally going on to use language items correctly. With regard to language learning conditions, pupils learning an L2 do not have as much time as L1 learners, they receive far less one-to-one interaction, may not receive such high-quality input, receive input from a much reduced number of sources, and above all, have a very different motivation for learning. This leads us on to a problem we first raised in the introduction to this chapter.

Does younger mean better?

The current, widely held belief that younger learners do learn an L2 better than older learners has given rise to a huge increase in the number of countries which have started teaching English at primary level. Nunan (1999) has argued that, on the whole, this belief has not been conclusively shown to be true. This belief, that 'younger equals better' was originally supported by the CPH as we saw in the cognitive-developmental view. Scovel (1988:2), defined the CPH as 'the notion that language is best learned during the early years of childhood, and that after about the first dozen years of life, everyone faces certain constraints in the ability to pick up a new language'. Classically, the argument goes that after puberty learners seem incapable of acquiring a native-like accent. In 1994, Ellis suggested a modified hypothesis where the critical age for native-speaker-like pronunciation is six years, provided good pronunciation models are available, while for learning grammar the critical age is around puberty and onwards. Some researchers have stated that lower-order processes, such as pronunciation, are learned better when young, while higher-order processes, such as meaning relations are learned better after puberty. According to Lightbown and Spada (1993:50) learners who start later, at ten or twelve, catch up very quickly with those who begin L2 learning when younger. They also add: 'Any school programme should be based on realistic estimates of how long it takes to learn a second language. One or two hours a week – even for seven or eight years – will not produce very advanced second language speakers'.

We can only conclude that an early start is not, in itself, automatically an advantage; an early start is influenced by many learner factors which play a great part in the success of L2 learning. These include levels of motivation and confidence, differences in language aptitude and personality (see chapter 3). These must be taken together with contextual factors, such as the quality of teaching and provision of adequate time for learning. Singleton (1989) concludes that unless a primary ELT policy is supported by high-quality materials, appropriately trained teachers and favourable public attitudes, the experience may be negative and the effects counter-productive. Brewster (2001) reiterates this view in a reminder to educators in East Asia, a context where there has recently been an explosion of activity in primary ELT. This proviso has clear implications for the level of resources governments and institutions need to provide to create effective L2 learning environments for younger learners. The government in South Korea, for example, has decided to fund a CD-Rom-based primary English programme throughout state schools and has ensured they have all the necessary equipment. This is commitment indeed. Currently, the issue of having sufficient numbers of well-trained primary language teachers is particularly crucial in many countries. According to Nikolov (2000), seventy-six per cent of primary teachers in the Czech Republic are unqualified, sixty-four per cent of primary English teachers in Hungary are Russian retrainees, while in Poland there are simply not enough teachers. This is worrying indeed.

Bilingualism and multilingualism

Many children are born of parents with different nationalities or in bilingual or multilingual contexts where there may be an official language, a language used as the medium of instruction in school and another language spoken at home. There is a great temptation to recommend that all children be given a bilingual education since this would seem to capitalize on children's ability to learn languages so easily. In many countries there are bilingual schools where children are taught more or less equally in two languages. Luxembourg, for example, is a country where there is general trilingualism across the nation. In addition to the national Luxembourgian language spoken at home, German is taught from the first year of primary school and French is taught from the beginning of the third year of primary school. These last two languages are the vehicles of primary and secondary teaching. This early trilingualism is complemented at secondary school by English teaching. However, for most schools bilingualism and multilingualism are not and cannot be realistic objectives to aim for, considering the limitations on time, the numbers of pupils, and the conflicting claims of other subjects. It is important to remember that differences in language learning opportunities and exposure to the target language occur not only between countries but even within a country. For example, there is often a rural/urban divide, where children may not have much contact with the target language if they live outside of the main cities. In some countries it may even be difficult to persuade language teachers to work outside of the big cities.

In certain countries such as Denmark, Sweden or Mexico, there are large cities where children may have easy access to English-speaking media – television, films and pop culture – which are denied to children living in the countryside or smaller towns. This means that in urban areas like Oslo or Stockholm children are exposed to a great deal of English and may even come to school having a solid, if unstructured, corpus of English. More importantly, they may come with very positive attitudes to language learning and a higher sense of motivation and interest in learning English than other children who will never meet English speakers or are unlikely to hear English-speaking television radio, films or music. As we know, motivation is one of the most important factors in successful language learning.

Who learns how much of what language under what conditions?

According to Baker (1993) the key question in the development of an L2, or even bilingualism is *Who learns how much of what language under what conditions?* Some of the most important factors in responding to the first part of the question *Who learns?* is influenced by individual learner differences, including age, aptitude and motivation, as we saw in the previous section. For example, studies of the good language learner have shown that successful learners are willing to make mistakes, are good at guessing and making accurate predictions, look for patterns in language and have a lot of confidence (see Lightbown and Spada 1993). The second part *how much of what language?* is governed by factors such as the goals of language learning (as we saw in chapter 1), the curriculum and syllabus and the effects of tests. The goals may focus on the development of communicative competence and positive attitudes to language learning and the target culture. In many contexts primary aged children also develop levels of specific grammatical competence in order to cope with the kinds of tests they have to prepare for. The final part, *under what conditions?* highlights the situation and context under which the L2 is learned. Ellis (1985) suggests that there are three parts to the development of a second language. The first is the **sequence** or general stages through which children move in L2 learning. Ellis suggests that there is a natural and almost unchanging sequence of development: moving from simple vocabulary to basic syntax, then on to the structure of simple sentences, finally moving to more complex sentences. The second part concerns the **order** of language that is acquired, which may differ from child to child and classroom to classroom. The final part is the **rate of development**, the speed of which may vary enormously from learner to learner. Let us look in more detail at the first and last part of this question.

How well children learn an L2 is not simply a matter of what kind of environment they are in, which method or textbook is used, or the type of teacher they have. Kubanek-German (1998) refers to the 'ideal' learner for the communicative approach as an extrovert, talkative, confident, risk-taker. Through research it has been possible to list some of the individual differences that appear to be connected to L2 learning, including the characteristics of 'the good learner'. So far, however, there are no clear-cut results which show exactly how these work, either on their own or in combination with other factors, and their relative importance. Many of these differences affect the speed of L2 acquisition but not the sequence or order. With regard to cognitive style there has been a lot of interest recently in the notion of *multiple intelligences*. This refers to the different kinds of aptitude learners may have which are not usually measured on IQ tests. Eight kinds of intelligence are usually referred to (see chapter 3).

The conditions refer to who is talking to whom, the environment of the interaction, the type of classroom, and the kinds of topics which are discussed. Situational factors and context are particularly important here, as is the type of language input learners receive. The input children receive when they are listening to or reading in the L2 is dependent on many factors: the goals of language learning, the syllabus in use, the teacher's beliefs about learning and language learning, the teacher's language level and teaching style, the size of classes and the type of resources available.

Research has shown that *comprehensible input* is a key factor, which is especially important when dealing with young learners. This means creating contexts where learners can easily understand what is being said because of careful planning concerning the language level, the physical context or the use of supporting visuals. A good way of providing highly contextualized activities can be seen in the use of Total Physical Response (TPR) where children perform physical actions in response to spoken statements (see chapter 4). This has been found to provide high levels of comprehensible input for beginners. Decontextualized pronunciation, grammar or vocabulary drills, on the other hand, provide much lower levels of comprehensibility, especially for young learners. Most coursebooks and syllabuses try to provide carefully controlled language input at an appropriate level of difficulty. Differences in type of input depend on how far the focus is mostly on communicating meaning or on 'covering the grammar' and learning the rules. For example 'real' books (those written for native speaker children and not for FLL), can sometimes be a little more difficult than the carefully controlled language of a textbook. If it is a good story, the children are motivated, and if appropriate visuals are used, it is surprising how much the children will understand as they are focusing on the meaning of the story rather than focusing on its grammar.

A point to note is that listening to comprehensible input does not always encourage *intake*, a term which describes the process of actual learning when new language moves from the short-term to the long-term memory. Only when there has been intake is language actually learned, which means the language has been sifted, processed and organized. The strategies learners use to process language has been a subject of much study (see chapter 9). The need for *comprehensible input* has more recently been complemented by the need for *comprehensible output* or language production.The use of pair work is one of the most important ways of ensuring learners think and produce language independently and draw on the linguistic resources they have been developing.

Task 2

Read this short extract from two children aged nine in their first four months of learning English in the UK (an *immersion* context). They are working on a *What's Wrong?* poster that has lots of funny things that are impossible, such as a car with square wheels. As you read, note down the vocabulary the children have developed and the vocabulary they are lacking in English. Then compare with the description given below.

Child A: *Here is dog. Is clock.*
  Chair is here and dog and radio. And she puts his hand ...
  (laughs).
Child B: *And here ... look, hair is cutted.*
  Her hair is cutted. (laughs)

We can see that the children have learned some simple nouns, verbs and a personal pronoun, the present tense of *be* and *put* and have formed a past tense rule of adding –ed to verbs. They do not use adjectives and are not able to describe where things are or how things are being done. Even though they are not able to say much, the children appear to enjoy the activity and continue using this simple language for some time. This provides a useful snapshot which shows how much the children have learned. It also tells us something about the task, which is probably a little too difficult for learners at this stage because of the range of language which is required to complete it. This language was not modelled or pre-taught in any way. For example, they are not able to say *that's not right; this is wrong* and they do not have sufficient skills yet to explain 'why' using *because*.

Having considered some of the more theoretical aspects of language learning, the question for language teachers is how we can create optimal conditions so that *comprehensible input* becomes *intake*, followed by confident, if not always completely accurate, linguistic *output*. Let us now turn to some of the classroom implications of what we have discovered so far.

Teaching implications

What would happen if we took the view that children learn the L2 in exactly the same way as they learn the L1 and should therefore go through the same stages?

Task 3

In 1969 Stern summarized this view in a set of six statements given below. Read them and decide how far you agree with them. Put a tick by those which you believe in strongly, and a cross by those with which you disagree. Put ID for *it depends* (e.g. on the pupils' age or their language levels).

If L2 learning is like L1 learning then children should learn foreign languages in the following ways.

1 Children should spend all of their time in language classes imitating and practising language in a very controlled or guided way.

2 They should start with separate sounds, then build these into words, then sentences.

3   Children should spend a lot of time just listening without speaking.

4   Only after listening and speaking for some time should pupils add reading and then writing skills.

5   Children should not translate from L1 to L2 and vice versa.

6   It is not appropriate to teach young learners formal grammar.

Your beliefs about how children learn languages will strongly influence how you teach them. You may have ticked several of these statements or you may have frequently responded with ID, or a cross. A behaviourist view of L2 learning is based on all of the above beliefs about teaching methods. The methodology most closely associated with the behaviourist view is the audio-lingual approach. This emphasises repetition and memorization of drills which tend to be decontextualized. Teachers often teach in the same way as they themselves were taught, which may explain why this approach is still so popular. However, it was criticized as far back as 1964 by the cognitive psychologist Ausubel, who warned that decontextualized drills did not have the kind of meaningfulness which could support learners' understanding.

TPR is based on belief 3, where children learn by listening to instructions and performing actions but at first not saying anything. For example, the teacher says *Point to the door and then the window; stand up, turn around three times and then sit down* and pupils carry out the instructions. Later on, pupils will be encouraged to give instructions to other pupils for them to carry out. This approach has been found to be very successful with beginners.

A strict communicative view would hold that translation (belief 5) is not a good thing to be encouraged, although this position is now changing and some use of the L1 can sometimes be justified. Some teachers using the communicative approach would also not explicitly teach formal grammar (belief 6), although they might encourage inductive grammar practice. Here the pupils work from examples of language use and try to work out the grammar for themselves. When teaching very young children and beginners aged four to seven, you may well have agreed with statements 3, 4, 5 and 6. So we can see how much the beliefs of language policy makers, materials writers, syllabus designers or teachers about how languages are learned can have a huge influence on classroom methodology. We shall consider methodology in more detail in chapter 4.

3 How children think and learn

It is interesting that the term *learner-centred*, meaning that children's needs and interests are placed at the centre of planning and teaching, is no longer as commonly used as before. It was often interpreted in the wider EFL world as simply putting fun into learning, whereas what was often necessary was ensuring there was some learning in all the fun! (See Brewster 1995.) In line with current thinking (see Nunan and Lamb 1996, Cameron 2001) we shall use the term *learning-centred* to highlight a greater emphasis on the need to maximize learning and provide both support and challenge in learning. If we want to focus on learning-centred teaching it is vital that we are well-informed about the physical, emotional, conceptual and educational characteristics of children and how theory has shaped our views on how children think and learn. This chapter considers these issues and explores some of the major influences on how teachers think about children's learning and how this may influence their classroom practice.

What is different about teaching children?

If we learn a foreign language as adults, we often have a long-term goal, such as wanting to get a job where bilingual skills are important, or wanting to study further in the country of the target language. These purposes are highly motivating and greatly increase our willingness to spend the long hours it takes to master another language. Young children, on the other hand, are not yet in control of their lives and still have a great deal to learn in their own language, as well as learn another one. At four, eight or twelve, children do not have specific foreign language needs, although some may be under pressure, usually from their parents or the school system, to pass English language examinations.

Young children are different from older learners because children:

- have a lot of physical energy and often need to be physically active
- have a wide range of emotional needs
- are emotionally excitable
- are developing conceptually and are at an early stage of their schooling
- are still developing literacy in their first language
- learn more slowly and forget things quickly
- tend to be self-oriented and preoccupied with their own world
- get bored easily
- are excellent mimics

- can concentrate for a surprisingly long time if they are interested
- can be easily distracted but also very enthusiastic

Of course we must remember that chronological age is not always the same as developmental age. Individual differences in learners, both within and across age bands, is especially marked at primary level. For this reason it is important we do not group all year groups together as if they have the same characteristics and needs. However, for the purposes of this book it will be useful to differentiate generally between three different age bands: 3-6 year olds, 7-9 year olds, 10-12 year olds.

Parental support and interest is a key factor in children's learning (see chapter 19). With good parental support some young children may start school with good concentration and memorization skills, having been introduced to action songs, counting rhymes, bedtime stories, computer games, and so on. They may know the alphabet and how to handle a book, recognize print, use a counting line, and so on. Others will not, and as research shows, such pupils are already at a disadvantage, although some will easily catch up (see more on this in Willes 1983).

Physical and emotional differences

All learners of primary school age have emotional needs, such as developing self-esteem and confidence in learning. Very young learners will still operate in a very egocentric way, where they find it difficult to consider others' needs, tend not to cooperate with others as effectively as older children and can become easily frustrated if their needs are not met. These learners are still developing motor skills, such as holding a pencil, hopping, skipping, balancing and the hand-eye coordination required to colour in drawings neatly, copy simple letters, and so on. They are also more physically restless than older children and require activities which are short, varied and which occasionally allow them to burn off energy. They may be unstable emotionally and have sudden emotional outbursts (for a useful overview see Roth 1998). Very young children need to develop a sense of confidence and self-esteem, to have other children to share and play with, to be involved in learning where they are physically active, have routines that provide a sense of security and a warm, encouraging classroom atmosphere, where they feel they have opportunities to succeed in their learning and receive praise.

Conceptual, educational and linguistic differences

Young children are still developing numeracy and literacy in their first language and up to the age of puberty are still learning to master complex grammatical expression even when speaking or writing their

L1. Three to six-year-olds are capable of symbolic thought, where a picture can be substituted for the real thing, while pupils of seven plus are more capable of realistic and rational thought. The very young need opportunities to choose and decide on actions; to investigate, explore and be curious; be encouraged to question, to work things out; activities which help them to focus and pay attention in order to develop memory and concentration skills; activities which reinforce concepts they may be developing and develop oral skills.

According to the Curriculum Council for Wales (1991:4) 'the aim of educating the under fives is to produce happy, confident, enquiring children, interested in life and enthusiastic about the challenges they encounter'. We may believe that this is not just true for the under-fives but that all children need stimulating experiences to make them enthusiastic about learning. Our views on how best we do this has changed over the years and may differ from country to country. In the next section we shall explore some of the major theoretical strands which have informed our views on children's thinking and learning.

How children think and learn

We saw in chapter 2 how behaviourism heavily influenced our views on how children learn languages. This view was shaped by the way behaviourists thought about children's learning in general, where children were seen as a 'blank slate' who learned by reacting passively to different kinds of stimuli and the positive or negative feedback they received. This view holds that teaching equals learning. This is known as the *transmission* model of learning. By contrast, Piaget presented the child as actively constructing his or her own thinking by acting upon the physical and social environment. All children were seen to go through a series of clearly defined stages of intellectual development. For example, most children between four to eight years are at the *concrete-operational* stage, where all learning develops only where it is heavily contextualized in concrete situations. By eleven, some pupils may move into the stage of formal operations, where they are capable of more abstract thought and can learn in a more decontextualized way. This was widely interpreted as meaning that it is not possible to teach young children some things until they are 'ready'. It is now widely accepted that Piaget underestimated the role of language and the role of adults in helping children to learn while over-estimating the role of play. However, his work triggered enormous interest in exploring how young children think and learn through observing children's behaviour in relation to tasks they were given.

Bruner (1983) investigated why children find school learning so difficult. He discovered that this was because children experienced it as very separate from their real lives. His theory of learning is essentially *constructivist*, a model of learning in which the child is seen as an active agent in his or her own learning, selecting, retaining and transforming information to construct knowledge which is shaped by his or her unique way of seeing and interpreting the world. This, he called *scaffolding*. If we think of building a house we may see some similarities to the ways in which a child learns. In house-building scaffolding is put up to support the building process. This is broken up into stages: first the foundations, then the walls and ceilings (the building blocks), then the systems – plumbing and electrics – which connect everything together. The links and networks between these different stages build up internal strengths so that by the time the scaffolding is removed, the house supports itself. In this way Bruner thought that the child's learning is a process, not merely a product, which can be accelerated or enhanced by breaking learning into stages and providing the building blocks and systems which connect these together. He saw children's learning as moving through three modes of representation, knowing something through doing it, through working with a picture or image of it and through using some symbolic means, such as language. Studies of how very young children consolidate their learning experiences reveal interesting patterns which reflect these three modes.

The work of Vygotsky (1978), is also very important since he emphasised the role of the adult and of language in children's learning. He saw the process of mental development as working on two levels, the present actual level and the future, potential level of development. (See chapter 2.) The difference between the views of Piaget and Vygotsky are that the first believes the child learns through his or her own individual actions and exploration, whereas the second believes that adults/teachers work actively to improve children's level of development. Another major difference between Piaget and Vygotsky is their view of the role of language in learning. Vygotsky held the view that speech precedes thinking, so that very young children find it helpful to speak out loud about what they are doing. From the ages of three to seven children's private speech changes to include conversational speech with others. A major legacy of Vygotsky's work is the importance placed upon developing opportunities to allow young children to talk in order to develop their thinking. His model of learning, *social-constructivist*, sees children as constructing their understandings from the social interaction of their learning contexts, with all its possibilities and limitations. Anning (1991) suggests that children are unique in what they bring to the learning experience but tend to draw on the same kinds of learning strategy. This means that we can think of learners as having individual differences but who learn using similar strategies to other children. The notion of *metacognition,* which is concerned with how children learn to think, plan and remember, has become increasingly important over the last fifteen years. Ellis (see 1999 and chapter 5) and others believe that helping children to gain insights on how they think, plan and remember aids them in developing the confidence to tackle similar and new tasks. The role of the teacher here is to provide a model of the kinds of strategies that are useful (see chapter 5).

We have so far considered some of the most important psychological theories about learning, but many teachers find it difficult to apply these kinds of psychological theory to their actual classroom practice. According to Gipps (1994:26), 'it is now more widely accepted that we need to generate educational theory out of good educational practice'. This can be seen in the way teachers pick out aspects of theories which fit in with their 'common-sense' view, based on classroom experience, of how learning seems to take place. She writes that in the early 1990s most British teachers of young learners (seven years and under) believed the following:

1 Children develop in sequential stages from concrete to abstract levels of thinking. A child must be 'ready' to move on to the next developmental stage and must not be forced to move to a higher level of thinking (e.g. beginning to read or write, recording numbers).

2 Children learn through first-hand (concrete) experiences, particularly through structured play.

3 In social development children move from egocentrism to the ability to empathize with others.

4 Children need to develop competence in their first language to function efficiently as learners.

5 Every child is an individual learning in their own unique way.

This list of beliefs shows very clearly the influence Piaget has had on these teachers. Anning shows how each of the six beliefs given above can be reinterpreted in the light of new thinking about how children learn.

Learning and sequential stages (statement 1)

Early views on developmental stages based on Piaget have led educationalists to underestimate the ability of young children to reason. Teachers tended to focus on what children *could not* do, rather than what they *could* do, which, according to Gipps (1994) has left us with the legacy of low expectations for primary-aged children. This view has been challenged by reconsidering some of the tests used to find out how much children can reason. Donaldson (1978) found that if the reasoning task makes sense to the child, incorporates the child's perspective on life and avoids an adult perspective or context, then the child is often able to reason in a way previously thought impossible. She also challenges the idea that teachers should wait rather passively until children are 'ready' to move from concrete to abstract levels of thinking. Instead, she argues that children can be *taught* how to extend their powers of thinking towards more abstract reasoning. This sort of view accounts for all the more recent interest in *teaching* children thinking skills (e.g. in the UK and Singapore) and in learning how to learn, which for many teachers is an exciting new move. In the British Council Young Learners Centre in Paris, France, pupils are trained to become aware of the learning points of activities so they are able to say what kinds of activities and what kinds of language they are using, rather than simply saying 'I played a game'. This seems to have also helped parents understand the relevance of some of these activities.

Learning, egocentrism and the role of play (statements 2–4)

Within the school context children learn how to become social beings. In many cases this is done by trial and error, but it is useful if adults encourage children to reflect consciously on what they have learned about working in pairs or groups, taking turns in games, and so on. In the foreign language class this would be done with younger children in the L1. In some countries, play, such as games or construction activities, may be an important part of children's learning, especially in the first one to three years of schooling.

Teachers' views on the importance of play depends on a variety of factors, including their views on children's learning, the learning culture of the school and the views of parents and management. For some teachers *play* is seen as providing an important acknowledgement of the importance of imagination and the emotions in promoting intellectual development. Others say that it is important in developing physical and cognitive development, social competence and acts as a kind of 'mental hygiene'. Bruner (1972) writes that it is 'an excellent opportunity to try combinations of behaviour that would not be tried under functional pressure'. Certain kinds of play demonstrate the ways in which children are able to become fully engaged in their activity and sustain their interest for some time. However, there are different kinds of play, each with different purposes, such as letting off physical energy or actively exploring a concept. In fact, studies have found that not all play in schools has a high enough cognitive challenge. In one study, the most challenging kinds of play were found to be those based on music, art and construction, such as building models. What these activities had in common was clear goals and materials that involved *real world feedback;* that is, they show if a given sequence of activities has been successful or not. In some cultures play at school is seen as frivolous and not a major contributor to learning at all. With young children, however, play can be an important aspect of social development. Cognitively challenging play was found to be more likely if children worked in pairs or groups.

The role of the first language (statement 5)

Various studies have shown the importance of discourse, interaction, stories and rhymes in children's linguistic and cognitive development, especially now that children are seen as social beings rather than individual explorers. Wells (1986:44) emphasises the need for adults to interact with children 'about matters that are of concern to the child, such as what he or she is doing, has done or plans to do'. He claims this increases the chances that children and adults focus on the same objects and events and interpret the situation in similar ways. Wells (1986:194) also examines the role of stories in developing children's thinking, writing, 'constructing stories in the mind ... is one of the most fundamental means of making meanings; as such it is an activity that pervades all aspects of learning'. Finally, all cultures have an oral tradition, especially in the form of teaching young children nursery rhymes, action rhymes, skipping rhymes, jokes, traditional tales and songs. These are an important way of attuning the child to the sounds and culture of their L1 and help to provide a sense of security since these oral activities are shared by family members. All of these issues are vital in the development of the child's L2. (For more on this refer to chapters 7, 12 and 14.)

The uniqueness of learners (statement 6)

Much has been made of child-centred teaching, which has had a considerable influence on primary English teaching and materials. Primary ELT coursebooks from the early 1990s, such as *Stepping Stones* and *Big Red Bus* often made reference to pupil- or learner-centered teaching. This term implies that every child is a unique individual who brings a unique set of experiences and understandings to each new learning situation and gradually constructs his or her own view of the world. However, primary education specialists recognize that 'it is possible, and as far as the teacher is concerned, *essential*, to see that there are patterns in the development of learning across children's responses and behaviours' (Anning 1991: 42). She adds that, although it is important to keep insights into the uniqueness of each child and to respect their individuality, it is equally important to recognize their similarities.

Learning styles and multiple intelligences

Although every learner is unique, we have seen how teachers need to be aware of learners' similarities and differences. If, as Anning suggests, teachers focus on similarities in the *patterns in learners' responses and behaviours* then this helps to overcome teachers' feelings of being overwhelmed when faced with a class of thirty or more pupils. Interesting work which can help us in this area was developed from psychology in the 1970s and came to be known as Neuro-Linguistic Programming (NLP). This describes the relationship between the mind and language and how this relationship 'programmes' our behaviour. According to Berman (1998), we take in information in line with our *learning style*. If we have a mainly visual learning style, information is learned mainly through the eye, the auditory learning style is based on a preference for learning linked to hearing, while kinesthetic learning style is based on learning though movement and manipulating things. He writes that in an average class of adults, twenty-nine per cent will be predominantly visual learners, thirty-four per cent auditory and thirty-seven per cent kinesthetic, adding that the understanding of children aged five to seven years old comes through the hands, eyes and ears, so the physical world is dominant at all times. He also writes that most young children have the ability 'to store memories by associating them with their senses and may even have the ability to 'cross-sense'. They may be able to 'hear colour, see sound, taste time and touch smells' (1998:187). This ability tends to be discouraged and fades away as children grow older.

In the typical foreign language classroom it may be impossible to determine every child's learning style, although over time you will probably become aware of individuals' preferences. In addition to the three learning styles suggested by NLP, Gardner (1993) has suggested there are also several kinds of intelligence, not all of which are recognized by school learning. The *Multiple Intelligences Checklist*, as described by Berman, includes eight kinds of intelligence:

1 *Linguistic Intelligence* e.g. a learner with a good vocabulary; a good reader, who learns well from stories and likes doing crosswords

2 *Logical-mathematical Intelligence* e.g. a learner who is good at or likes using computers, is good at problem-solving and likes classifying, sequencing and ranking activities

3 *Spatial Intelligence* e.g. a learner who enjoys drawing, who learns well

from using pictures, charts, maps, diagrams etc.; completing mind or word maps or webs is also enjoyed

4 *Kinesthetic Intelligence* e.g. a learner who learns through manipulating and moving objects and lively activities – action rhymes and games

5 *Musical Intelligence* e.g a learner who learns well through the use of chants, rhymes and songs

6 *Interpersonal Intelligence* e.g. a learner who learns well from pair- or group-work activities such as interviews, games, surveys, etc.

7 *Intrapersonal Intelligence* e.g. a learner who is a good self-evaluator and likes to reflect, as when doing self-assessment exercises, learning diaries, etc.; someone who likes independent learning, such as project work and presentations; someone who likes creative writing

8 *Naturalist Intelligence* e.g. a learner who is good at recognizing patterns in things; someone who notices similarities and differences between things, who is good at classifying and organizing things into groups. This kind of intelligence enriches the other seven intelligences.

Armed with this knowledge, teachers can ensure they provide enough variety in the activities they use so that as much of their pupils' learning potential can be tapped as possible. Older children, perhaps in their last one or two years of primary schooling, may like to do a questionnaire to determine the kinds of intelligence they may have (use the L1; see Berman 1998 for examples).

The younger the learners, the more physical activity they tend to need and the more they need to make use of all their senses. Berman suggests that if children can draw or visualize an image, hum it or move through it first, they may be able to more easily talk or write about it. A language teaching method that works well with beginners and young learners is Total Physical Response (TPR). Invented by Asher in the 1960s, it involves learners in listening to something and then showing their understanding by their actions and responses. Children can also draw a picture while listening to a description, act out a nursery rhyme, follow instructions or make a shape or simple model while they listen to a description of it. This draws on learning by the ear and eye and is good for those with bodily-kinesthetic intelligence. Eight- to ten-year-olds are more able to make decisions about their own learning and have a greater sense of fairness. They are less likely, for example, to laugh at other children's mistakes. By this age learners are able to generalize and classify things so the use of classifying games and activities and the use of grids to sort objects into categories is useful at this stage. Figure 2 below shows the kinds of activities which develop each of the eight intelligences.

Linguistic	Musical
Word games Reading games Writing games Storytelling Show and tell Role-play Using puppets Tongue twisters Crosswords/Anagrams	Songs Action rhymes Chants

Logical-mathematical	Interpersonal
Word puzzles Reading puzzles Writing puzzles Logical problem solving Computer games Number puzzles Classifying Ranking Sequencing/Ordering	Pair work Group work Brainstorming Peer teaching Dialogues Interviews Surveys

Spatial	Intrapersonal
Shape puzzles Mind maps Drawing Visualizations Diagrams Constructing models Maps and coordinates Drawing Learning from videos & CD-ROMs	Learning diaries Reflection Creative writing Project work Personal goal-setting

Bodily-Kinesthetic	Naturalist
TPR Craftwork Dancing Physical activities Action rhymes, songs and games	Patterns Classifying Sorting Nature projects

Fig. 2 Language Activities to Develop the Eight Intelligences

Thinking about pupils' learning

Over the teaching year, whether you are a novice or an experienced teacher, you will gradually notice similarities as well as differences in the ways in which children learn.

Task 1

Look at these teachers' opinions about how their pupils seem to learn most effectively. Think about how far they fit in with your own ideas and mark the statements with T (true) or F (false).

- Children often respond to an initial stimulus such as a set of pictures but need guidance about how to set about doing an activity or task.
- Teachers need to model the skills and language involved in doing a task.
- Children prefer to be given a clear goal when starting on an activity.
- Pupils learn well when they are given meaningful tasks where they can see a purpose to their activities.
- Pupils learn better when there is a relatively relaxed classroom atmosphere where they are not afraid of making mistakes.
- It saves time if pupils and resources are organized so pupils have controlled access to them but are still independent.
- Children need time to absorb all the input they receive so they can later produce related work on their own.

We may call these teachers' statements *common sense* theories, developed over time in relation to the way these teachers were trained and their classroom experience. Think about where your beliefs come from. Are they based on your teaching experience, something you have read, something you heard someone say, a theory, a workshop, common sense or intuition? What is important is that you should know what you believe about children's learning and have some idea where these ideas come from. You will probably find yourself checking your beliefs from time to time to see if they still seem to fit with reality.

Teachers generate their personal theories on children's learning in five main ways: through their own memories of childhood learning, through their teacher training and reading, through reflection while they are in action in the classroom, after being in the classroom or informal discussion with colleagues and, finally, through professional development activities, such as further training or reading. The more experience you gain, the more you will refine your understanding of pupils' learning which may lead you to modify your behaviour. This is a cyclical process which is demonstrated in Fig. 3.

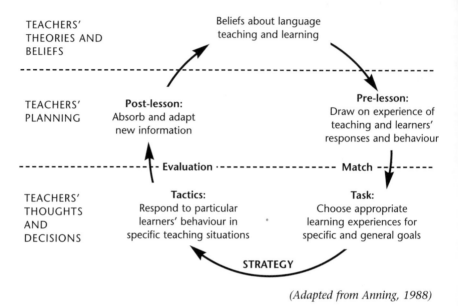

(Adapted from Anning, 1988)

Fig. 3 A cyclical model of teacher thinking and learning

If we return to the notions of learning styles and intelligences, what seems to be implied is that children's learning should be varied so that it takes account of the auditory, visual or kinesthetic style and the eight kinds of intelligence, while Bruner's notion of scaffolding and modes of learning implies that children should be physically involved and perform actions when learning and work with different kinds of visual and symbolic representations of new concepts so they are firmly contextualized. We also know that children of the same age are likely to be at different developmental stages and thus the skill of working with mixed-ability groups is important. These issues will be discussed further in chapters 4 and 16.

TEACHING LEARNING AND LANGUAGE SKILLS

PART 2

4 How to teach English to children

In this chapter we look at useful principles and guidelines for teaching. Then we turn to a discussion of some of the differences in teaching methods and strategies used across a range of contexts.

In her survey review of primary ELT Kubanek-German (1998) wrote that in Europe the question of methodology seems not to be in dispute, since many European countries have been teaching English to young learners for many years and have reached consensus in favour of the communicative approach. It would be interesting to find out how far this is true of other countries. In chapter 1 we saw how other countries, including those in East Asia also have the goal of developing communicative competence, where children are taught to express ideas and feelings in English. Park (2001) suggests there should be a review of the kinds of teaching methods that East Asian countries have found to be effective. Inevitably there will be several differences in the way countries all over the world teach EYL and these differences ought to be respected. However, an important step in making decisions about how you will teach is being informed about the range of possibilities, so that you can compare your methods with others and re-evaluate them. In this way you can make a choice about what you do which seems appropriate to your context, rather than doing something simply because 'it has always been done like this'. Factors which influence classroom methodology include the context within which English is learned and the role it plays within the community, the goals and syllabus for English, beliefs about teaching and learning in general and language teaching and learning in particular. They also arise from the language teacher and her training; the materials, resources and time available; and finally, the amount and type of assessment used. Let us now look more closely at ways in which we can support children in moving from their L1 to L2.

Supporting transfer of language learning skills from the L1 to the L2

The comparison of processes and conditions between L1 and L2 learning shows there are certain principles which teachers need to be aware of and make use of wherever possible. Some of the most important ones are summarized below.

1   Children are excellent observers and have a natural ability to grasp meaning in their L1 from a variety of sources: body language, intonation, gesture, facial expression and the social context as well as language itself. Teachers can help learners draw on this skill in the L2 by ensuring language use is contextualized and has visual support wherever possible.

2   Children learning their L1 often repeat words and phrases to themselves in order to become completely comfortable with their sounds and meaning. Once a child feels he has learned the word, repetition stops. Incorporating repetition, especially with variety, is important but teachers must be guided by the children's reactions to know when enough is enough!

3   In acquiring their L1 children have spent years honing their puzzling-out, hypothesis-testing skills. The use of inductive exercises in the L2, where, for example, they try to work out grammar rules for themselves, mirror precisely what they have been doing in their L1 for years. Teachers simply need to ensure there is enough contextualized, motivating language 'data' for them to work with.

4   Children are skilled at guessing and predicting and teachers can usefully draw on these skills and the other thought processes outlined as part of 'learning to learn'. (See chapter 5.)

5   Children like to talk, even if they don't know much language, often with only two or three words plus key intonation patterns. This is also a useful tactic they can use in L2 development. Learners should be encouraged to do the same, using whatever means to get their meaning across. Although this may lead to over-generalizing of rules, grammatical or lexical inaccuracies such as the coining of new words, teachers should try to provide opportunities for meaningful communication activities wherever possible.

6   Teachers need to create a balance in their classrooms between providing support and providing a challenge. If all language work is over-guided then it becomes too easy, safe or repetitive. Similarly, if all work is challenging, too difficult and threatening, learners become demotivated.

7   When learning their L1 children seem to be good risk-takers and experimenters. Their willingness to 'have a go' should be encouraged and should not be dampened too much by constant correction or an overly strict atmosphere.

These principles are a first step in trying to ensure that we do not underestimate pupils' capabilities and that we focus on a learning-centred language curriculum.

As we have seen in chapter 1, teaching EYL is seen to have psychological, linguistic and cultural advantages for learning languages at secondary school. As we have seen, this can be achieved if teachers create the most effective conditions for learning, because simply having young learners is not in itself enough. How then can we do this? Before we can provide some answers we have to think carefully about the factors listed above which influence the pupils' learning context as they will have an enormous impact on the kinds of methodology a teacher uses. Let us briefly consider some of the most important aspects (see Fig. 4).

Task One

Work with a colleague or on your own. Choose **three** of the aspects from Fig. 4 and discuss or think about the questions. What kind of influence do these aspects have on your teaching? For example, in your professional context it may be hard to develop communicative competence, especially where tests are based on a grammar-based syllabus.

Teaching-centred or learning-centred?

In chapter 3 we introduced the concept of a learning-centred classroom. What does this imply about the role of the teacher? Traditional whole-class teaching, where the teacher is like a conductor, is an important part of language teaching. It is useful for introducing new language, providing whole-class or group language practice, explaining language points or modelling language and procedures for tasks carried out in smaller groups. It can provide inspiration, guidance, structure and purpose to learners. This technique for managing learning, which we shall refer to as *teaching-centred* means the teacher controls the actions in the classroom, does a lot of the talking by explaining, giving directions and asking lots of questions which pupils answer. In some contexts it may be the most common way of managing learning. This may mean the pupils have little chance to do more than repeat what the teacher says and have no opportunities for real interaction. This technique may also mean pupils are expected to be relatively passive, do not spend much time working in pairs or groups and may not be encouraged to reflect on their learning since they feel the teacher is 'in charge' of their learning.

At the other end of the scale, teachers may try to balance these more teaching-centred activities with ones which are more learning-centred or interactional where pupils have a chance to work on tasks in order to engage in organized talk with each other, that is to use language in a less controlled, more creative way. For example, tasks may encourage pupils

The status and role of English	• Do the pupils have much contact with English outside of school?
	• Are they interested in and have access to the culture of English-speaking countries? How far does this affect their motivation?
	• Is English used for learning other subjects such as Art or Nature Studies? Does this affect the pupils' motivation?
The role of the teacher and learner	• Is the classroom mostly teaching-centred or learning-centred?
	• Are the pupils engaged actively in their learning? Do they have some choice in the work they do?
	• Do you sometimes use an activity-based approach?
	• Do your pupils receive training in learning how to learn?
The goals and syllabus for ELT	• How far is pair work and group work considered important in developing speaking?
	• How much grammar practice is there? Are grammar rules explicitly taught?
	• Are listening skills explicitly developed?
	• Which skills are emphasised? Do pupils learn *how* to learn?
The type and variety of materials and resources available	• Do you have a textbook or other materials which you and the pupils enjoy using?
	• How far do you have some choice about the materials or activities you can use in the classroom?
	• Do you have access to supplementary materials, such as song books, books of grammar games, CD-ROMs, etc.?
The amount and type of assessment	• Is assessment nearly always tests? If so, do they take up a lot of time? Do you consider this inevitable, a good thing, or a drain on your energy and time? Do they provide useful information?
	• Does the assessment practice in your school change the way you teach? If so, how far is this useful? How do you feel about this?
	• Are there any forms of on-going assessment? Do they provide useful information?
Class size and ability of the class	• How far do you feel you cope well with your present class size?
	• Do you have strategies for dealing with mixed ability classes?
The amount of time available	• Do you have a very small amount of time daily?
	• Do you have a longer period at least two or three times a week?
	• Is this enough?
	• Which method do you think works best?

Fig. 4 Some aspects of the teaching context

to express opinions, find out information from texts, ask each other questions or make suggestions. Here teachers may base some of their lessons on topics related to the pupils' interests, use pair and group work so the learners have plenty of opportunities to talk or read and write together, and so on. This style also encourages pupils to ask questions or even allow pupils to play the role of teacher (in games, etc.). It may also mean the classroom is organized so the pupils are encouraged to be more independent, for example in choosing their own tasks and having access to the resources they need. In this kind of classroom, learners may also be encouraged to take charge of their own learning through learning to learn activities such as learning logs or self-assessment. The important thing for language teachers is to find an appropriate balance between these two approaches which complies with their expectations and which best promotes effective learning.

Sometimes there may be problems if transmission teaching is the usual style in most lessons but in English lessons pupils are introduced to a more interactional, learning-centred style. For example, if teachers in a traditional school try the communicative approach or task-based approach, both the teacher and the pupils may find this difficult at first. Both will find themselves taking on different roles from usual and there may be problems in the early stages. Teachers may feel threatened if they are no longer so clearly in control and learners may suddenly have freedoms or responsibilities they are not used to. There may be complaints from other teachers who find the classroom next door too noisy or who have the pupils in the next lesson after English and find the pupils take some time to go back to the more traditional role of being more passive and quiet. In this case, discussing your methods with colleagues may be helpful. You might also need to consider introducing pair and group work gradually, where at first it is only a small part of your weekly teaching and is gradually increased to a regular occurrence in your lessons (see chapter 5 for preparing pupils to deal with the methodology you use).

Types of language teaching approach

This section will briefly make reference to six common approaches used in primary schools today. Many teachers draw on aspects of several of these approaches.

Audio-lingual

As we saw in chapter 2, the audio-visual or audio-lingual approaches, popular in the 1950s and based on structuralism and behaviourism, involve the use of repetition of new language, often based on dialogues. It tends to be teaching-centred. Even though this approach is out-dated, modified versions of it can still be seen in several countries. Nowadays it is considered by many to be too restricting with too much emphasis placed on memorization, imitation and exercises involving mechanical and decontextualized repetition. Language practice is carried out with the whole class; it is much less demanding than organizing pair and group work; the language practised is entirely predictable and does not make too many demands on the teacher; and it may be the way the pupils are used to working. It continues to be popular with many teachers since that is how they were taught; it is very manageable; and is especially useful for teachers with fairly low language levels themselves. It encourages children to listen carefully and memorize chunks of language, which are important parts of language learning. However, not enough emphasis is placed on meaning or encouraging children to think for themselves or produce language independently. After the initial novelty factor when using this method you may well find that the children seem rather bored as there is not enough variety to hold young learners' interest and may not encourage a positive attitude to foreign language learning.

Total Physical Response

TPR is very popular with young learners because it develops listening skills, introduces new language in a very visual, contextualized way, involves activity and movement and does not at first put pressure on young learners to speak. In time, some learners may be able to play the part of the teacher and give instructions for children to follow, or describe actions for other children to mime, and so on. Of course, when you use action songs, rhymes and stories, this is a form of TPR.

The communicative approach

The communicative approach, developed in the mid-1970s through the Council of Europe, is based on the social–interactionist theory which emphasises the social nature of language learning and interaction. Recent work in second language acquisition has emphasised the importance of learners producing output to show that intake has taken place. For children this approach means language teachers engage learners in drawing, acting out, listening, talking, reading or writing based on meaningful and contextualized tasks using language which has been carefully prepared for.

Many textbooks based on the communicative approach use a structural syllabus, often organized by linked topics and language functions, for example, Talking about people, Travel, Making plans, as in *Blue Skies*. This approach is often referred to as activity-based and commonly involves the use of three types of activities: problem-solving activities such as identifying, matching, sequencing, prioritizing and classifying; interactive activities, such as making surveys, or carrying out interviews; and creative activities, such as making masks, birthday cards, and so on. All of these aim to develop learners' communicative competence while catering for children's needs and enthusiasms. The embedded thinking and language skills within the activities require the repetition of simple phrases or structures, essential to language learning. However, this approach has been criticized by some for focusing on communication and fluency too much and overlooking grammatical accuracy.

Task-based learning

A response to these criticisms has been Task-based learning (TBL), one of the most recent methodological approaches in ELT. Its name is confusing since it is sometimes used interchangeably with activity-based learning, which we might consider as the weak form of TBL. For example, in Hong Kong secondary ELT teachers have been getting used to a task-based syllabus which identifies the notion of task. It involves: learners in using language for *purposes* which go beyond merely practising the language in order to learn it; a *context* from which the purpose for language emerges; purpose and context stimulating the learners to do something through language; and the purposeful activity leads towards a product (see Littlewood 1993).

In its *strong* form, according to Skehan (1998), TBL is an attempt to improve on the communicative approach by trying to balance accuracy with fluency and by encouraging more authentic output (speaking or writing) from learners. This is done by encouraging learners to make a public presentation of their work, the planning of which gives learners more responsibility and choice for what they present. Public presentations are followed by language analysis activities where the pupils focus on accuracy in language *after* completion of a task (see also Willis 1996). Pupils are made aware of the end point or product (e.g. making a safety poster) right at the beginning, so that the language the teacher introduces and practises is seen to have some point and provides a clear goal. This approach has three phases: pre-task preparation (introduction of new language and procedures to be used), the task itself (children doing the macro task in pairs with a final public summary of their results), and a final phase, language focus (see Fig. 5). The macro-task might involve acting out, recording or writing a story, making a model or board games, writing a quiz, making information booklets with illustrations, collages, surveys, and so on. The idea is to make the point of focusing on particular language clear to the pupils at the outset, so they know why they are learning certain language and more importantly, what they are going to do with it. This helps to overcome pupils being in the dark about why they are learning a particular set of language. In the language focus phase activities which develop language-awareness or involve further language practise are used. Using this approach, teachers encourage their pupils to use the language they have recently learned by providing a framework and support for the macro-task and then allowing the pupils to use the language for their own purposes and meanings. By allowing scope for creativity and personalization the pupils are then more likely to know the kinds of language they actually need. The teacher must encourage pupils to seek specific advice and guidance about this language. A guiding principle in this approach is that pupils are more likely to remember the language they have decided they need, rather than the language the teacher has decided they need. After public performance or display of these macro-tasks the teacher will do some follow-up language work, based on whatever problems and issues have emerged. Some coursebooks based on TBL, such as *Cutting Edge*, are already available for older learners. See also Ellis and Brewster (2002) which applies a modified task-based approach to using storybooks.

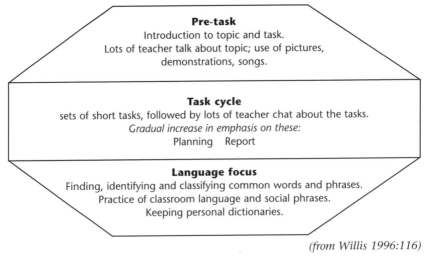

(from Willis 1996:116)

Fig. 5 A framework for task-based learning

Story-based methodology

Storytelling is a universal phenomenon, central to children's social, intellectual and cultural development. In the words of Rosen (1985) stories are 'the commonest possession of humankind – part of the deep structure of the grammar of our world'. Kubanek-German mentions that there is much interest in the use of a story-based methodology. For example, an eight-year longitudinal study of ELT at primary level in Croatia found that it was 'extremely productive' (see Djigunovic and Vilke 2000). Many modern coursebooks are incorporating the use of stories for language development. A story-based methodology such as that produced by Ellis and Brewster (1991 and 2002) provides many examples and is explained in more detail in chapter 14.

Cross-curricular

The cross-curricular approach is linked to the activity-based approach and task-based learning. Here, the development of the L2 is linked to other areas of the curriculum, such as Art, Physical Education, Mathematics or Nature Study. See chapter 9 for details.

Stages in learning

The most common approach in many modern coursebooks and primary schools is the communicative/activity-based approach, although many teachers use a combination of those described above. Classroom procedures for this approach, and others, classically involve the use of three stages which aim to provide the sort of scaffolding which helps children to think and learn with motivation, success and confidence. One model that is commonly used is known as Presentation–Practice–Production (PPP). Another more learning-centred view, as used by the University of Nottingham ITE team, is to call these three stages, Meeting new language, Manipulating it and Making the language your own (MMM). What seems to be common in many classrooms is that the first two stages are very well carried out. However, the final stage is often less effectively used or missed out altogether. Furthermore, opportunities for children to reflect on their learning at the different stages need to be incorporated as described below and in the following chapters.

Meeting new language

The way a teacher presents new language depends on the resources she has access to. These might include the teacher on her own, acting as the main language model or with a native-speaker as a back-up model; the teacher and blackboard, overhead projector or other visuals such as flashcards, puppets, photos, or pictures; or the teacher and a cassette or CD-ROM. At this point the teacher is trying to provide comprehensible input in a lively and interesting way so that pupils use their hearing, sight and knowledge of the world to put the language into context. This means the teacher is responsible firstly for introducing the meaning, form and pronunciation of new language correctly and secondly checking the pupils' comprehension. This stage is characterized by transmission teaching, which is teacher-centred and tightly controlled. Here learners will be corrected but in a gentle, non-threatening way so that they feel relatively unpressured.

Manipulating new language

After an interesting and ideally meaningful presentation the teacher should try as soon as possible to support learners in manipulating the new language in a variety of activities. This stage is also orchestrated by the teacher, at first in a controlled way and then in a more guided way. In this way, the pupils become more and more responsible for remembering the language, but always with some support, such as actions, tapes, charts, pictures, and so on. In the controlled manipulation stage, which is usually repetition of some kind, the teacher will be quite strict about correcting the pupils' language, as she is focusing on accuracy. This includes accurate pronunciation and word order, as well as choosing the right words and their correct forms. Moving from controlled to more guided manipulation, the teacher will focus more on communication where the pupils select the language they want to use from the range of new language they have encountered. At this point the class is likely to be divided into teams, groups or pairs.

Making the language your own

In this stage, the pupils are likely to use pair or group work for activities with a clear purpose so they need to communicate. Here the pupils are using the language they have practised in a much freer, less controlled way, but are preoccupied with getting their meanings across and understanding others' meaning. For example, a class of six-year-olds in Taiwan were presented with an action song about opening and closing their hands. After presentation and practice the children were asked to adapt the song in some way. Even though their language was very limited the children quickly came up with ideas for opening and closing some part of their body. Volunteers eagerly went to the front of the class and sang the song while substituting opening and closing their hands with eyes, mouths and even pinching their nostrils open and closed! This kind of personalization is very motivating. Here too much correction by the teacher would be very demotivating and inappropriate since the pupils had clearly grasped the meaning very well and were willing to 'have a go'. The teacher can always recycle the language the next day, reinforcing aspects of accuracy, such as pronunciation or word order. At this point the pupils' language may contain some errors which the teacher should note and evaluate. If the errors seem to be generalized across most of the class, she will have to recycle these language points. If the errors are more individual the teacher can either gently correct the pupil or decide not to interfere and wait to see how far these errors are self-corrected over time. While monitoring groups or pairs it might be useful to have a notebook handy so you can remember the kinds of problems the children had. Alternatively, the mistakes the children are making can be written on a piece of paper and given to them while they work so that you do not interrupt their flow of thinking too much. Train the pupils so that they know what to do when this happens. Remember that it is unrealistic to expect children to use the new language perfectly at this stage. This stage is important for developing pupils' interactional skills, listening and speaking, as well as literacy skills, reading and writing. In this way, communicative competence also refers to developing the ability to communicate meaning in simple writing as well as speech. Finally, children should be encouraged to review what they have done and learned and be given plenty of opportunities to recycle language through a variety of activities. This is discussed in more detail in the following chapters in Parts 2 and 3.

Task design

In task design it is useful to distinguish between tasks and activities, which are frequently used as if they were interchangeable. Tasks need to be supported by a previous focus on language forms, skills and strategies developed through activities. Activities prepare pupils for the language and thinking demands of a task by providing different kinds of support.

Activities

Activities, like traditional exercises, focus on the guided teaching and learning of specific items of language, skills or knowledge. They have language practice as their main aim and include such things as becoming more familiar with new vocabulary, grammar and language functions or practising skills such as listening for detail using charts. Activities focus on form and meaning to some extent but are not in themselves purposeful or meaningful; they rehearse a particular set of sub-skills, language items or task procedures; they usually consist of a cognitively simple set of operations and have reduced learner control. They are used as a means of preparing pupils for more independent work on tasks. Activities are often done in pairs or individually and might include: listening for specific sounds and words to notice new sounds and words; pronunciation practice e.g. matching the word stress by using large and

small cards; practising new vocabulary using flashcards; sequencing letters, words, sentences to practise spelling, vocabulary, discourse patterns;
labelling a picture or diagram to practise new vocabulary; matching parts
of a sentence and gap-filling/cloze exercises to practise new grammar.
Activities often form the main part of coursebooks and accomanying
workbooks. They can be done in class or as homework. (See Fig. 6.)

Tasks

Tasks, like the final language outcomes, emerge after pupils have studied
a particular set of language and help to provide a context to ensure that
learning has taken place. We have already seen the way that tasks
require a context and a meaningful purpose which requires pupils to do
something with language, often resulting in a polished product for a real
audience (not necessarily just the teacher but other pupils, another class,
parents, etc.). Tasks encourage pupils to personalize language, pursue
their interests and use language in an independent and hopefully creative way. Tasks can be done individually, in pairs or in groups.
Examples include the following:

- drawing/writing/performing a new version of a story which has been
  used in class

- writing and performing a simple play

- making and playing a board game

- planning and creating objects such as models, masks, etc.

- devising a survey, carrying it out and presenting the results in some
  form (spoken or written)

- creative speaking or writing such as posters, stories, radio programmes, class magazines, poetry, letters or recordings to imaginary
  characters in a story

- investigating a topic such as Bears and presenting the information

This information is summarized in Fig. 7.

When planning to use a final task it is important to do it as if you
were one of the learners. In this way you can check that you have prepared your learners sufficiently or have provided them with strategies
for finding out from you or elsewhere. Activities should isolate the necessary key language and contain repeated vocabulary and structures at
the learners' level so that there is comprehensible input. The teacher
must also check that the small steps which lead up to the final task are
prepared for so that the pupils feel confident with each step. If the tasks

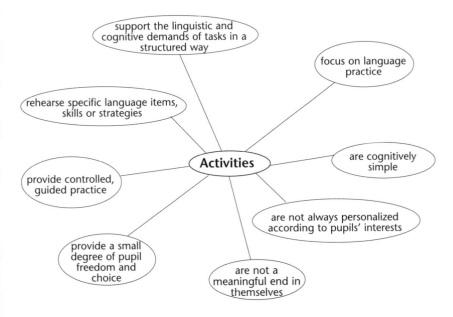

Fig. 6 Characteristics of activities

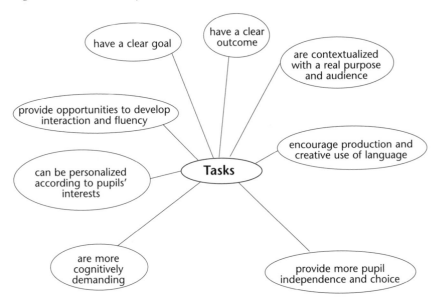

Fig. 7 Characteristics of tasks

are carefully staged so that procedures or language is recycled then there is a clear sense of progression, which helps to provide the right level of support and challenge. Tasks may also need to be differentiated so that they are suitable for children with mixed or different levels and abilities. This can be done by altering the kind of input, the amount of visual support, the kinds of thinking involved in doing the task and the kinds of output or product which it demands. We look at this in more detail in chapter 16.

Meeting pupils' needs

We shall end this chapter with a series of questions to guide us in the management of the teaching and learning context. See whether you would like to add any questions, delete some or adapt some. Then reflect on the kinds of responses you would give and their reasons or origins.

Is there a comfortable and relatively stress-free environment in your classroom? Do you think this is important in language learning? Is English often being used purposefully, for real communication and learning? Is the English language you use comprehensible to the children? Do you have a clear idea of the language learning objectives in your classes? Do these meet the needs of your pupils? Are children given enough opportunities to actually use the language which has been modelled for them? Are the children given opportunities to use language with different audiences – each other, with other adults where relevant, with other classes? Is there a reasonable balance between cooperative and competitive learning activities? What kind of balance do you think there should be? Are children encouraged and given opportunities to work with peers in problem-solving and collaborative learning situations? Does the classroom organization and use of resources give the pupils adequate support in their learning tasks? Are your expectations of what the children can do realistic and sufficiently high? Are the needs of pupils' different ability types and learning styles acknowledged and catered for sufficiently? Does the assessment of pupils take account of pupils' strengths and weaknesses, ability types and learning styles? How far does it reflect the kind of language learning you wish to encourage?

5 Learning to learn

This chapter aims to clarify the terminology of learning to learn by providing an overview of what is meant by this term. It goes on to examine some common anxieties teachers express about the implementation of learning to learn in classroom contexts, and then considers the benefits of learning to learn for both pupils and teachers. Practical solutions and techniques for implementing learning to learn are then provided by proposing a general methodology and specific techniques.

Definitions of learning to learn

Learning to learn – also referred to as 'learner training' by EFL/ESL teachers – is a term which encompasses a wide variety of activities designed to develop metacognitive awareness and learning strategies. It is primarily concerned with the processes of learning and aims to focus pupils' attention on how they learn, in addition to what they learn. It takes into account that different learners have different ways of learning and different preferences regarding activities and learning materials. It therefore aims to gradually lead pupils to a conscious development of their own learning strategies and awareness of how they learn, so they can become more effective and independent learners.

The development of metacognitive awareness

Metacognition is a term first coined in the 1970s and there has been much debate over a suitable definition. Brown (quoted in Nisbet and Shucksmith 1986:30) defines it as 'knowing about knowing'. This includes the knowledge and self-awareness a learner has of their own learning process, and may be the key to effective learning.

Research has shown (Nisbet and Shucksmith 1986:42) that even quite young children possess a considerable degree of metacognitive knowledge which they are rarely given credit for, and this can be developed. Classroom practice also shows that children are capable of understanding information about classroom procedures and benefit from being given this information. Given the opportunity and asked the right questions, children can be helped to express themselves in a purposeful and meaningful way about their learning experiences. The teacher, as a catalyst in this process, has a crucial role to play.

In a young learners context, it could be argued that metacognitive awareness is a term which incorporates the following strands: language awareness, cognitive awareness, social awareness and cultural awareness. All of these overlap to some extent.

Language awareness: The aim here is to stimulate childrens' interest and curiosity about language 'to challenge pupils to ask questions about language' (Hawkins 1984:4) in order to develop understanding of and knowledge about language in general, including the foreign language, the L1 and, if appropriate and depending on the context, other languages. This would involve using metalanguage (in the L1 or target language) to describe and analyse language, to make comparisons between the L1 and L2, and to discover rules about the language.

Social awareness: This area of language learning can be related to Vygotsky's (1978) socio-cultural theory of learning: that higher cognitive functions are internalized from social interaction. This will involve children in collaborative activities which, in many contexts, may involve a new understanding of how to behave in class; to establish a working consensus which will contribute towards building respect; and to learn to interact and cooperate in activities and to develop positive attitudes to sharing and working together in class.

Cognitive awareness: The main aim here is to help children understand why and how they are learning a foreign language at school, and that in addition to linguistic outcomes, it also offers important personal, cognitive, cultural, affective and social gains. It involves explaining to children how they are going to learn a foreign language in class, the type of materials they are going to use and the activities they are going to do, as well as getting them to think about how they learn.

Cultural awareness: Girard's (Brewster et al. 1992:33) definition of this important area 'to develop understanding and openess towards others' involves children in activities which enable them to discover similarities and differences between themselves and other people and to see these in a positive light. It aims to develop tolerance and positive attitudes to the foreign language culture and people and draw children away from a mono-cultural perspective.

The development of these different strands of metacognition is essential to the development of the whole child, and to their realization of their own ability to learn and to the role they play in the learning process.

The development of learning strategies

It is generally agreed that it is useful to recognize the existence of two major groups of learning strategies. Metacognitive are those which are more generalized and used to regulate learning. Cognitive are those which are more task specific and involve actually manipulating the subject to be learned, in this case, doing things with language. Research has shown that the combination of metacognitive and cognitive strategy training is particularly effective in helping learners learn how to learn, and to be able to transfer strategies to other tasks and subject areas. 'Students without metacognitive approaches are essentially learners without direction and ability to review their progress, accomplishments and future learning directions.' (O'Malley et al. 1985:24). They applied this scheme to language learning and added a further category which they called socioaffective, strategies which are used by learners to involve themselves in social and group activities in order to expose them to language input. This three part typology is useful in that it is relatively simple to apply and to extend, especially in the young learners' classroom. A further group, communication strategies, allows pupils to maintain communication in English and negotiate meaning and are described in chapter 6. Many strategies used for learning English can also be applied to other subject areas. Some of the related strategies to each category are also described below.

Metacognitive strategies

These encourage children to think about and to reflect on aspects of the learning process as described below.

Planning learning

It is generally the teacher who takes the main responsibility for planning learning. However, by being well-organized and explicit the teacher can model how planning can take place and inculcate good planning for the future. As children's confidence and knowledge develop, they can gradually take on more responsibility for planning certain aspects of their learning.

Hypothesising

Pupils can, for example, be encouraged to work out the rules of grammar for themselves by looking at examples of the foreign language and working out why, for example, *a* or *an* is used in front of certain nouns. Children can also hypothesise about meaning in a story.

Comparing

Pupils can be encouraged to analyse and compare differences and similarities between English and their L1. This can arouse their curiosity about language and develop language awareness. They can also compare different aspects of daily life from their own country with that of the target culture to become aware of cultural variety.

Self-questioning
Pupils can be taught how to ask themselves questions about their learning in order to reflect on the content and processes.

Self-assessment
Pupils can complete self-assessment sheets in order to reflect on the content of learning, upon how they learn as well as to reflect on their own performance throughout a lesson and their contribution to the class. This in turn will help them monitor their progress and maintain motivation, and highlight strong and weak points.

Self-correction
Where possible, provide opportunities for pupils to check their own work either individually or in pairs. This helps them take on responsibility for their own learning and work out where and why they may have made a mistake.

Reviewing
Pupils can be taught to review systematically in order to aid long-term retention and to identify what they know and do not know.

Selecting activities
It is useful from time to time to give pupils a selection of different activities to choose from. This allows pupils to choose activities according to their own interests and needs, decide for themselves what to do, and plan their own work.

Cognitive strategies
These include, for example, memorizing, sorting, classifying, matching, predicting, using a class library or dictionary. They involve pupils in doing things with the language and their learning materials and relate to specific activities in specific skills areas such as listening or reading. In some skills it is often the nature of the task which will determine the type of strategy to use, i.e. listening for specific information for a picture dictation or reading in chunks when skimming a text. With other skills areas, however, such as vocabulary development or speaking, there appears to be more variety in terms of individually successful strategies and personal choice. For example, some pupils may prefer to memorize words by associating them with a picture, others may prefer to repeat them aloud several times. (See chapter 6 for vocabulary learning strategies.) Figure 8 lists common activities found in materials for young learners and the skills and strategies they develop. It also shows how many activities require pupils to use and develop a combination or cluster of strategies.

Activity/task	Skills focus	Strategy
Listen and sequence	Listening	Listening for specific information Sequencing
Picture dictation	Listening and drawing	Listening for specific information Transferring spoken information into pictorial form to show understanding.
Bingo	Listening Reading pictures or words	Matching words to words or pictures to pictures
Sorting	Developing vocabulary	Classifying words into meaningful groups
Handicrafts (eg. make a snowflake)	Listening Speaking	Listening for specific information and following instructions Observing
Action rhyme	Speaking	Practising pronunciation and rhythm Memorizing vocabulary through actions and coordination
Sequencing a rhyme	Reading and writing	Using rhyming words as clues to meaning Sequencing, eliminating, making links
Working out a secret code	Reading and writing	Observing Problem solving by transferring letters from a code into words and sentences Making links
Remember and write	Reading, speaking, listening and writing	Memorizing
Listening to a story	Listening	Listening for general meaning Using visual and audio clues as aids to meaning Predicting, making links
Pair work: information gap	Speaking and listening Writing	Memorizing Transferring language Working independently
Writing a shopping list	Writing and developing vocabulary	Memorizing Developing personalized lists
Making sentences from a model	Reading and writing	Observing a model Generating written patterns
Matching captions to pictures	Reading and writing	Observing Using visual clues as aids to meaning Matching

Fig. 8 Activity types and related cognitive strategies

Classifying

When pupils classify items into different groups, this reinforces a basic concept and can be a useful memory aid when learning vocabulary.

Using visual and audio clues as aids to meaning

We make use of a variety of clues to help work out meaning in our L1, for example, tone of voice, facial expressions, gestures, visual support, and so on. This is usually done at a subconscious level. When deciphering meaning in the L2, pupils will need to use these clues to a greater extent. It is therefore important that they first become aware of what they are and are prompted to use them.

Predicting

Pupils can be encouraged to use a variety of clues from the context to guess possible content. When encouraging anticipation, it is important that the teacher accepts all appropriate suggestions even if they do not correspond exactly with what is said or happens. The main aim here is to encourage pupils to anticipate the general meaning, for example, what could happen or what could be said next and then to check whether their expectations match the reality of what they actually hear or read. This involves pupils actively and personally in the learning process and can develop self-confidence.

Risk-taking

It is important that pupils build up enough confidence so they are willing to take risks and try something out in the L2. This will equip them for occasions when they do not have a teacher with them, another pupil to ask, or a dictionary, and so on. The teacher can encourage risk-taking by inviting pupils to guess the meaning of words; to attempt to pronounce a new word; to hypothesise; to discuss a learning strategy, and so on.

Organizing work

Work related to the English lesson can be organized and stored in different ways: in an exercise book or a folder and labelled and dated; as personal vocabulary sets, made by cutting out pictures, colouring and labelling; as personal picture dictionaries; as rhyme or song books, and so on. Pupils can also collect pictures and make collages of specific language, for example, food packets, clothes labels and shop signs. This actively involves pupils in the learning process and personalizes their efforts.

Socioaffective strategies

These are developed by children collaborating and cooperating in language-learning activities. Opportunities for developing these are usually set up through pair or group work activities, project work, interviews and surveys, etc. Working with each other in pairs or groups provides pupils with the opportunity for taking on responsibility for their own learning by working independently of the teacher for part of a lesson. It can also involve them in planning and directing their own work.

Teachers' anxieties about learning to learn

Despite the growing interest in and acknowledgement among the EFL teaching profession of the importance and benefits of developing learning to learn with children, many teachers are still reluctant to encourage pupils to reflect on their learning experiences.

Task 1

Think about any anxieties you may have and, if possible, discuss these with a colleague. Then compare yours to those below. Do you share any of them? Do you have any others?

At a seminar in Paris in 2001, teachers listed their main concerns as follows. They felt dubious about implementing an approach they themselves had not experienced and also felt pressurized by constraints of the syllabus and limited time. They felt there was a lack of guidelines in published materials and were unsure how to integrate learning to learn into their lessons. Some were worried about having to use the child's L1 to develop this aspect of their learning and whether or not it improved childrens' linguistic performance. Many also believed that childen are too young for this aspect of learning and not capable of expressing their opinions or views about how they learn, or of understanding explanations about what they are going to do and why. We shall consider solutions and techniques for overcoming some of these anxieties, but first let us consider the benefits of learning to learn for both pupils and teachers.

The benefits of learning to learn

What's in it for the pupils?

Although there have been few empirical studies to evaluate the effects of learning to learn in terms of linguistic performance, most teachers have observed increased motivation and a more questioning, active and personal involvement in their learners as valuable and justifiable outcomes. We can assume that 'the more informed (and aware) children/learners are about language and language learning the more effective they will be at managing their own learning' (Ellis and Sinclair, 1989:2).

Early L2 learning also aims to prepare pupils for the more formal and exam-orientated courses in secondary school. Learning to learn provides them with the basic learning tools for this as well as learning skills for life. Here are some comments (translated from L1) from children who have had a learning to learn component integrated into their English lessons:

> *The lessons are very interesting and they have taught me a lot of things that I didn't know about myself and English. (Wilfried, aged 10)*

> *We can speak in English, we are freer and we make progress together, trying to understand each other. (Aurélie, aged 10)*

> *I feel as though I have learned English for myself. (Abderakim, aged 9)*

What's in it for the teachers?

If pupils are more motivated and more involved in their learning, it follows that teaching and learning will be a more enjoyable experience for both yourself and your pupils, and will facilitate lesson planning and classroom management. Learning to learn also recognizes individual differences in children's learning in that they may use a variety of learning strategies at different times depending on a range of variables, such as the nature of the learning task, their learning style, their mood, and motivation levels. This will help teachers deal with diversity and differentiation within their class. Here is a comment from a teacher in Turkey who has integrated learning to learn into English classes:

> *They participate more, they ask more questions at the right time and to move on to the next stage in the course of an activity. They feel confident and happy.*

Another benefit for teachers who implement learning to learn is that in order to do this, they have to be clear about the general aims of a lesson and the aims of each activity within that lesson. They have to think carefully about how they are going to inform their pupils of these aims so they make sense to them. This kind of reflection means that teachers need to continuously question their own teaching and beliefs which will help them become more aware of their own professional growth (see chapter 20).

Practical solutions and techniques

A Methodology for learning to learn: The Plan-Do-Review Model

It is possible to introduce a methodology for developing learning to learn which does not interfere with the syllabus and can be applied to existing classroom contexts with little disruption. Such a methodology would consist of three stages, corresponding to the typical structure of most lessons. Applied to the skills areas, for example, listening to a story, these stages are usually referred to as pre-, while- and post-listening. These stages provide a framework in which teachers can incorporate opportunities for children to plan, do and review (Fig. 9) through reflection, experimentation and further reflection thereby combining metacognitive and cognitive strategy training and representing the on-going cyclical nature of learning as follows:

- Children think about what they already know and what they need to do to plan and prepare for an activity.

- Children experiment, that is, they do the activity or task.

- Children engage in further reflection to review and assess what has been done.

Chapter 17 discusses lesson planning in further detail and proposes a plan which applies the plan-do-review model to the overall lesson structure as well as to activity cycles within the lesson. This enables teachers to provide systematic learner training in an explicit way.

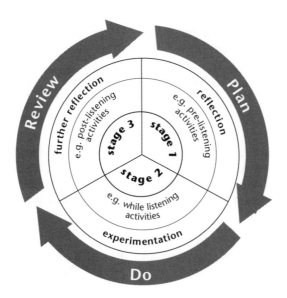

(adapted from HIGH/SCOPE. www.highscope.com)
Fig. 9 A framework for implementing learning to learn.
The Plan-Do-Review model.

Techniques for developing metacognitive strategies

Providing methodological preparation

Methdological preparation as defined by Dickinson and Carver (1980:2) includes helping learners understand and use metalanguage – language for describing language, language learning and learning strategies. This involves stating and informing children of the aims of a lesson, giving clear signposting throughout lessons and informing them of the value and purpose of classroom activities. This is important as the method-ological approaches to teaching English may contrast to the way other subjects are taught at primary school. Children may not understand the teacher's reasons for using activities such as songs, games, pair work, sto-ries, role-plays, etc. regarding them as an opportunity to relax and have some fun rather than ways of learning English.

The way you provide methodological preparation for children will depend on their conceptual level and the approach used for teaching their L1 in school. For example, if the L1 is taught in a way that requires children to analyse language and learn the metalanguage to describe language, the teacher can capitalize on this knowledge. Regarding chil-dren's conceptual level, it is important to know what concepts they have grasped in their L1 before these are introduced in the foreign language. One way of making these concepts clear and meaningful to children is to describe them in functional terms, for example, talking about where things are, talking about what we like or don't like, etc. Teachers need to think carefully about the language they will use in class with their pupils. It needs to be clear and precise, related to a direct learning expe-rience and accessible to pupils. It may initially need to be given in the L1 but, little by little, pupils will acquire this metalanguage in English.

Task 2
Think about how you will explain the aims of your next lesson to your pupils and how you could explain the purpose of the following activi-ties: a song, working in pairs, watching a video extract, listening to a story, playing a game. Willis (1981) and Slattery and Willis (2001) pro-vide useful examples of classroom language.

Encouraging active reflection

Getting children to think about and discuss their learning is a vital aspect of developing the child's self-awareness. This can be done in the following ways:

Asking questions that probe: What are the right questions to ask to encour-age active reflection? They need to be extremely clear and directly relat-ed to a learning experience. Unless the questions are well-formulated and concrete, in language that is clear and accessible to the children, they will not understand and will not be able to reply in a way that helps them, or their teacher, become aware of their learning processes. A good question then must be probing and an invitation to think so that it makes children justify their responses, it must focus their attention and encourage observation, invite inquiry and stimulate because it is open-ended. It should be productive and seek a response and generate more questions (see Fisher 1990:76).

Running teacher-led review sessions: Children constantly need to recycle what they have learned so they don't forget, and to perceive progress, maintain motivation and aid memorization. The need for this should not be underestimated and opportunities for recapping, revising and reviewing need to be built into lessons on a systematic basis so it becomes a classroom routine. This can be at the beginning of a lesson to revise work covered in the previous lesson: *What did we do last lesson?*, throughout a lesson after each activity cycle: *What did you learn? What did the activity get you do?* and at the end of a lesson to provide a general summing up of work covered: *What did we do today? What did you learn today?* This will help pupils understand what they have been learning and why, it helps pupils perceive progress and helps them understand what they do and don't know so they can identify what to revise. Working in this way does require a little extra time but this can easily be found if the teacher is prepared to take a few minutes away from the content of the lesson to focus on the process. It does, however, need to be set up and managed carefully so children perceive it as their 'special time' when what they say matters. The teacher will need to take on a guiding questioning role in order to focus children on the different stages of a lesson.

Initially, in response to a question like *What did we do today?* children will reply very literally, and will want to talk about all the activities in a general way. The extracts below have been translated from the L1.

Words spoken in *English* are in *italics*.

Task 3

Read and compare extracts 1 and 2. What does the teacher do to develop children's greater metacognitive awareness?

Extract 1: five- to seven- year-olds working on a story entitled *How the Kangaroos Got their Tails* for a ten-hour story-based class. This extract is from the final review session.

T   What have we done this week?
P1   We cut out some masks.
P2   We made a book.
T   Why did we make a book?

P3   To write the story of the kangaroos and their tails.

T   So we spoke mainly about the kangaroos, *kangaroos.*

P4   We worked on the spiders.

T   on the spiders, because ...

P5   we made some nice spiders

T   Yes, some nice spiders *nice spiders, not yukky spiders. OK*

P6   We worked on the computers.

T   *OK our book, our book,* our book. The book I read to you on the first day.

T   *How the kangeroos ...*

T+Ps   *got their tails. Good and there's a ...*

Ps   *big kangaroo and a small kangaroo.* (Teacher continues to elicit story mainly in English).

T   *So we talked about our book and that* helped us study some vocabulary: colours ....

Extract 2: Nine- to eleven-year-olds. End of class review session, a two hour class during the school year, (based on *The Snowman*).

T   What did we do today?

P1   We played some games.

T   OK, we played some games, but which games?

P2   We drew a snowman.

T   You drew a snowman.

P3   We continued the story

T   Wait. We're going to speak about the game and then we'll come back to the story. OK the game, let's speak about the game. Why did we play the game? What language did you learn?

P4   To learn the parts of the body.

T   *Good. The body. Can you tell me which parts of the body?*

Ps   *Head, body, eyes, mouth, nose, neck, arms, legs.*

T   *What about the clothes?*

P5   *Necklace*

T   *Necklace, yes, but the snowman's not wearing a necklace. What's the snowman wearing around his neck?*

P5   *a scarf.*

T   *a scarf, good. And a ...*

Ps   *a hat, and buttons*

T   *and buttons, good. So we played the game ...* We played the game to learn the parts of the body and some clothes but also to play together, and each person had to take a turn. Very good.

Extract 1 shows how pupils reply to the initial question very literally, they want to talk about all the activities they had done. The teacher makes several attempts to focus the pupils' attention on the story and finally gets them to retell it. She is also introducing limited metalanguage. Finally, she summarizes and recaps. In extract 2, pupils again want to say all the things they have done but the teacher shows greater control, quickly intervening and directing the review session by nominating the point for discussion and focusing the pupils' attention on the game. She reassures P3 that she will discuss the story after. She elicits from the pupils what they learned from the game and finally summarizes and informs pupils of the social, collaborative aspect of the game. She is modelling for the pupils the types of questions they can ask themselves as they become ready and able to take on responsibility for their own learning.

Completing written self-assessment and activity evaluation: Self-assessment is an important way of encouraging pupils to take on more responsibility for their own learning. Some course materials now include end of unit self-assessement or diary activities but these sometimes involve children in little more than mechanical acts of drawing or sticking a smiley face if they liked a unit or an unsmiley face if they didn't, with no consideration of the reasons why. The emphasis here is on 'learning something rather than on learning to learn' (Wenden 1987:160). Children can be confused by self-assessment if its purpose is not clearly explained, because they may feel there should be a 'right' answer and they expect to be marked for such work. In reply to questions like *What did you enjoy most/least?* pupils are likely to reply, for example, 'the song'. This tells us little so the teacher needs to probe further in order to lead children to a greater understanding of themselves as learners.

Self-assessment sheets can either follow a general format for use at the end of each lesson or unit of a coursebook, or a specific format related to a particular learning opportunity such as a special event or after a mid-year test (Fig. 10). Even children as young as five can be asked to assess their work. The coursebook *Pebbles* suggests children keep an *About Me* book in which they record and review their work at the end of each unit. Children can also be asked at the end of a lesson, a story or the school year what they liked about their learning and express this in pictorial form. For older children, questionnaires allow time for silent reflection and individual responses but the teacher must take into account, when evaluating responses, the child's ability to express their views in a written form. If the child is not yet able to produce the necessary language in written form, the teacher may have to help the individual child to put his thoughts into writing. A teacher-led question/answer session obviously allows more spontaneity and flexibility as the teacher can pursue an unanticipated point that may arise, and pupils also benefit from listening to their peers.

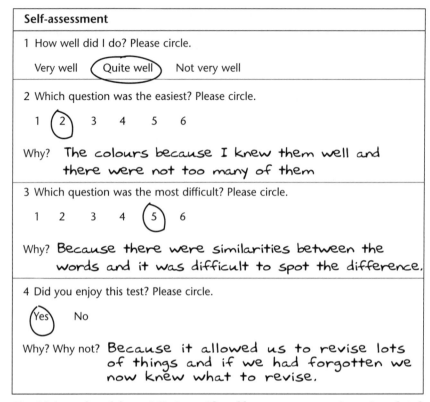

Self-assessment
1 How well did I do? Please circle. Very well   (Quite well)   Not very well
2 Which question was the easiest? Please circle. 1 (2) 3 4 5 6 Why? The colours because I knew them well and there were not too many of them
3 Which question was the most difficult? Please circle. 1 2 3 4 (5) 6 Why? Because there were similarities between the words and it was difficult to spot the difference.
4 Did you enjoy this test? Please circle. (Yes)   No Why? Why not? Because it allowed us to revise lots of things and if we had forgotten we now knew what to revise.

Fig. 10 (translated from L1) *A specific self-assessment questionnaire related to a mid-year test.*

Comments:
Question 1 invites pupils to give their own evaluation of their performance. Question 2/3 invites pupils to think about which questions were the easiest/most difficult and to say why. The replies indicate an awareness of manageability regarding quantity and an awareness of similarities which made words difficult to differentiate. Finally question 4 indicates an awareness of the importance of revision as it helps pupils identify what they do and don't know and what they need to revise.

Discussing in groups/peer questioning: As children become older and more familiar with such techniques, the teacher-led session could be transformed into a group discussion led by individual pupils. The initial teacher-led session will have provided opportunities for questions to be modelled that pupils can subsequently ask each other. Alternatively, the teacher could give the group a list of standard questions to structure the discussion.

Explaining an activity: Explaining how to play a game or how to do an activity to other pupils is extremely motivating for children. Thinking about the procedures and or rules involved and the different stages of an activity will involve them in a great deal of reflection, as well as provide language practice, either spoken or written.

Reflecting silently/self-questioning: Once pupils have participated in some or all of the above techniques, they will have gained a certain amount of practical experience of how to think about their own learning and evaluate their performance. You can ask children to reflect silently on what they have done, how they did it and how well they did. You may, however, like to write a set of questions (or have these on a poster that you can produce at the end of each lesson).

> *What did I learn today?*
> *What activities did I do today?*
> *What did the activities get me to do?*
> *Did I find them useful? Why? Why not?*
> *What did I find the easiest/the most difficult today? Why?*
> *How well did I do today? Why?*
> *What do I need to revise?*

These questions could also form the basis of a whole-class review session or a written self-assessment. The benefit however of having a whole-class review session is that pupils listen to each other and at the same time become aware of the fact that different children learn different things and have different preferences about content and learning.

Techniques for developing cognitive strategies

Children get lots of implicit practice in the classroom in experimenting with different cognitive strategies but most classroom situations and materials rarely inform children explicitly about why they are using certain strategies or get them to reflect on how they are learning. When developing cognitive strategies, then, teachers need to add the missing metacognitive dimension and demonstrate strategies with transfer in mind. This will help pupils to see how certain strategies can be used with other tasks or different subjects. For example, a self-testing strategy using two-sided cards can be used for practising English vocabulary, times tables or countries and their capitals. In fact, virtually any class activity may be used for learning to learn. All that is necessary is to focus attention upon the learning process aspect of an experience, which always exists side by side with the content. In this way, the implicit becomes explicit.

Here are some of the techniques that can be used for developing and helping children become aware of cognitive strategies.

Discussion and activity evaluation: Using the technique of discussion the teacher uses questioning strategies to elicit and draw out of the children how they did an activity which leads them to a conscious statement of the main strategy they used. It is a kind of analysis or post-mortem of the event where the teacher wants to concentrate the children's attention on one particular task and related cognitive strategies.

Modelling: This technique can involve a combination of demonstration, verbalization (think-aloud techniques) of the processes involved in doing a task and questioning. Modelling involves the transfer of control from demonstrator to pupils through a sort of transition in which language is the most important factor. As Vygotsky (1978) points out, if a child is going to control and direct his own thinking, then he or she must become conscious of it. Below the teacher is introducing the strategy of self-testing using two-sided cards. After that she encourages the children to think how the strategy could be transferred to other activities or subject areas. The teacher does not tell the children what to do, instead she gets them to work it out for themselves through supported and guided questioning. The children have learned the vocabulary for pets and part of an activity was to write the animal words on one side of small cards, approximately 6 x 3 cms, and to draw a picture on the other.

T: OK, class let's check the animals. Put your cards on the table with the pictures face up, like this. I'll call out an animal and you hold up your card. Dog! (Teacher looks for her card and holds it up). OK everyone. Ready? Listen carefully. Cat! Good! (She continues checking).

T: Now how can we remember the words after the lesson?

Ps: We can revise at home.

T: Yes, good. How can we do that Paul?

Ps: (Silence and general shuffling.)

T: OK, look everyone. I can use my cards. Look, I'm putting the picture side face up. Now let me think. Bird. (Teacher looks for the card and holds it up). Do you think I am right? How can I check?

Ps: You can look at the word on the other side.

T: Yes, good. Let's all try it together and then by ourselves. Mouse! (Everyone holds up the picture). OK now check. Are you right? Good.

T: Now by yourselves. Think of an animal. Say it to yourself. Find the card. Are you right? Check! Turn over the card.

Explaining, prompting and practising: Explaining a strategy involves naming the strategy, telling why to use it and how to use it. Children get lots of implicit practice through different activities or task types by using a variety of strategies (see Fig. 8). At some point in the process, children must understand the significance of what they are doing and why. Children can learn different strategies but they rarely use them spontaneously. The teacher will use some or a variety of the above techniques thereby providing a great deal of support in the initial stages by prompting and reminding children of the strategy and when to use it. Gradually, with practice, the teacher will adjust the level of support and as children develop awareness of the strategy and begin to show they can use it independently, she will phase out support.

Evaluating: We have already seen a few examples of evaluating performance through review sessions and discussion, and completing self-assessment charts or diaries. Another technique that can be used is to write guidelines for other pupils on strategies used.

Expanding: This involves the transfer of strategies to new tasks or content as we saw above with the self-testing strategy.

Techniques for developing socioaffective strategies

In chapter 17 a lesson is described as a type of organized social event in which children will be involved in cooperating and interacting together in language learning activities. Here are some techniques for developing socioaffective strategies:

- Drawing up a class contract at the beginning of the school year between yourself and your class. This will establish ground rules that you can refer back to when necessary.

- Develop interpersonal intelligence through pair or group work. This necessitates the sharing of information and collaboration in order to complete an activity or task. It requires a degree of autonomy and responsibility to work independently of the teacher.

- Peer help/correction/support encourages group support and friendship. Pupils should be allowed to help each other or to ask each other for help.

- Appointing a class monitor(s) so that everyone has a turn for being responsible for ensuring that the classroom is tidy, ensuring that the noise level is kept low, distributing equipment and materials and making sure that as far as possible, English is spoken as much as possible.

- Project work is ideal for pupils working together in small groups who research a topic and put together their findings in some form or another such as a display, a book, a presentation.

- Pupils can be encouraged to practise English as much as possible outside the classroom with their peers, their parents or native speakers. They can even be encouraged to have imaginary conversations with themselves in English or with puppets they may have made in class.

- Teaching formulaic language equips pupils with the language necessary for dealing with a situation where they don't have the necessary English but they can nevertheless participate with dignity and confidence and keep the flow and pace of the lesson going, e,g, *I'm sorry I don't know. Can you ask me again, please? Can you repeat please.*

- Use materials that develop cultural awareness and citizenship education. Many storybooks, for example, address issues of tolerance, feelings, friendship, equality, etc. (see Ellis and Brewster 2002).

- Being fair, providing positive reinforcement and explaining correction techniques. The teacher needs to provide children with successful learning experiences. If the teacher constantly corrects a child this could bring about a sense of failure, a lack of response, and dependency upon the teacher.

Evaluating learning to learn

A great deal of research needs to be carried out in order to investigate the rate at which a learner learns how to learn. As seen above, teachers also want evidence that this can be developed in order to be convinced of its value. One possible way of providing this evidence, is to record review sessions, as this enables linguistic data from classes to be collected and analysed in order to identify the techniques and language functions used by teachers. This can provide linguistic evidence of developing awareness as the extent to which children are able to respond to questions will provide clues to their levels of awareness. A framework for evaluating metacognitive awareness derived by Sinclair (1999:104) arose from research with adult learners of English in Singapore using three levels or stages of metacognitive awareness. This has been adapted by Ellis (2000:87) to make it suitable for younger learners in order to categorize examples of their responses to teacher-led review sessions. The three levels or stages of awareness refer to an initial stage where pupils are largely unaware, as evidenced by little understanding of the purpose of activities and little or no use of metalanguage, to a transition stage where pupils are becoming aware and demonstrate some understanding and rationale of what they are doing and the use of some metalanguage. In stage 3 children would demonstrate a competent use of metalanguage.

The linguistic evidence in Fig. 11 appears to support our observations that children generally know how to cope with learning tasks but that this knowledge is intuitive and unreflective. Systematic reviewing has provided evidence that pupils do gradually begin to use appropriate metalanguage to reveal an informed and conscious knowledge which they can apply to new tasks. The framework also highlights the changing nature of the teacher's intervention, so that the less aware pupils are, the more teacher intervention and guidance is required, moving from very direct questioning and summarizing to more eliciting. The framework provides a useful starting point for monitoring and evaluating pupils' growing awareness of their learning.

As can be seen, the teacher has a crucial role to play in implementing learning to learn and needs to expand their role (Wenden 1985:982) as described throughout this chapter.

Level of meta-cognitive awareness	Pupil language characterized by	Examples of of pupil language	Teacher guidance and intervention	Examples of teacher language
Level 1 Largely unaware	Description with little or no understanding/rationale	We cut out some masks. We played some games. We drew a snowman.	Directing and focusing pupils' attention	OK class, let's check the animals.
	Little or no use of metalanguage	A colour. Parts of the kitchen.	Nominating topic	Wait. We're going to speak about the game and then we'll come back to the story.
	Few or no questions		Asking probing questions	What did the activity get you to do?
			Seeking responses	How can I check?
			Initiating most exchanges	What did you have to do so you could draw? What did you have to listen to?
			Controlling turn taking	Wait! We played bingo. Why?
			Repeating	Yes, good a colour Good. Concentrate and ...?
			Giving information/explaining	So we know the size. Now we can make another guess or prediction in the same way about Friday.
			Introducing metalanguage	Listen to what? The keywords, the noun

Level of meta-cognitive awareness	Pupil language characterized by	Examples of of pupil language	Teacher guidance and intervention	Examples of teacher language
			Praising/evaluating Summarizing	You have to listen to specific words, the nouns and adjectives, before you can complete your picture. Good. Well done. So we played a game to learn … So to do a picture dictation you have to … So what did you have to listen to?
Level 2 Becoming aware (transition stage)	Description with some understanding/rationale Questions Beginning to use metalanguage	We can use our cards to test ourselves at home. Concentrate. We had to reconstruct the text. The nouns and the adjectives.	All of the above but more: Eliciting Prompting Modelling	Could you use this in any other lessons? Look, I'm putting the picture side face up. Now let me think. Bird. Do you think I am right? How can I check?

Fig. 11 Evaluating linguistic evidence of developing metacognitive awareness in children.

Level of meta-cognitive awareness	Pupil language characterized by	Examples of of pupil language	Teacher guidance and intervention	Examples of teacher language
Level 2 (contd)		*Memory and writing.* *To remember and spell.*	Using more metalanguage Summarizing	We did the chant to help you memorize the vocabulary, for the rhythm and the pronunciation.
Level 3 Largely aware	Confident and competent use of metalanguage Lots of questions			

Fig. 11 Evaluating linguistic evidence of developing metacognitive awareness in children (Contd).

6 From sounds to words to structures

This chapter looks at the scope of pronunciation work and the kinds of techniques and activities you can use to raise pupils' awareness of good pronunciation. This is followed by how children learn vocabulary and how to teach it. Finally, we look at the learning and teaching of grammar.

The scope of pronunciation

Teachers need to consider carefully the fact that pronunciation is not just about individual sounds, which are only one aspect. The range of pronunciation features in the speaking of English at primary level includes: individual sounds and consonant clusters (English has many); syllables and stress; weakly stressed and strongly stressed syllables in words e.g. compound nouns, verbs, adjectives, long words; how stress works in phrases and sentences; how stress is used to contrast things; how stress is used in sentences to change their meaning; how the sounds in some words are joined up and link together in phrases and sentences; how intonation is used to refer to old information; how intonation is used to refer to new information; and how intonation is used in question tags e.g. isn't it, can't he?

Individual sounds

There will always be differences in pronunciation between the pupils' L1 and English. There may be some consonant sounds which are not present in the L1 but which occur in English, or vice versa. Or the two languages may have the same consonants but they occur in a different place in the word, or there may be consonant groups or clusters which occur in English but not in the L1. Some differences can lead to problems and some may be more difficult to master than others. The pronunciation of vowels is more likely to cause problems; the teacher needs to demonstrate the way in which the face looks when sounds are made, for example, how open or closed the mouth is, how rounded or spread out the lips are. Try, wherever possible, to demonstrate the word on its own first of all, but move quickly to putting it in a sentence so that pronunciation practice is more meaningful. It may be necessary to spend a little time making the children aware of the differences in sounds, /ɪ/ and /iː/ for example, using the technique of developing *sound awareness*. Children may find it difficult to tell the difference between two sounds if they cannot, first of all, hear that the sounds are actually different. The teacher can use listening exercises and games to help the pupils focus on the sounds they find difficult. With these the children learn to hear differences between sounds by playing games where they say if two sounds are the same or different, or by picking out the difference between a series of words with two different initial sounds (e.g tin and thin) or spotting the 'odd sound out' in a series (e.g. fill, feel, fit). Children can practise puffing out air with initial /h/ as in /hen/ and feeling the air on their hand in front of their mouths. 'Puffing out' also takes place in English with initial /p/, /k/ and /t/ as in *pop, cat* and *time.*

Sounds in connected speech

It is important that pronunciation teaching does not concentrate entirely on the production of individual sounds. Practising how sounds blend together in informal speech is equally important. One of the pronunciation features present in English is 'linking' where certain sounds are run on together to avoid a jerky, staccato effect. This happens most commonly where a word ending in a consonant or a vowel is followed by a word beginning with a vowel. Four examples can be seen in the following action rhyme:

Chop, chop, choppity-chop.
Cut off the bottom,
And cut off the top
What there is left we will
Put in the pot:
Chop, chop, choppity-chop.

Here we see how words ending in a consonant sound (not spelling) link up with the next word if this begins with a vowel sound e.g. *cut off, there is*. Linking the words in this way helps to keep the smooth flow of English. This rhyme is also useful for practising the consonant /tʃ/ and the short vowels /ɒ/ /ʌ/and /ɪ/. You will need to draw the children's attention to examples of linking so that they notice it when they say rhymes. A very useful overview of the pronunciation problems of speakers with different language backgrounds can be found in the back of Kenworthy (1987) which refers to problems with English sounds for speakers of Arabic, Chinese, French, German, Greek, Italian, Japanese, Spanish and Turkish.

Stress and rhythm

English is a 'stress-timed' language, which means that stressed beats occur at roughly equal intervals of time, regardless of how many syllables there are between each beat. A useful way of demonstrating this is to ask the children to clap to the strong beats, while adding more and more syllables between the claps (strong beats are in capital letters):

ONE TWO THREE FOUR
ONE and TWO and THREE and FOUR
ONE and a TWO and a THREE and a FOUR
ONE and then a TWO and then a THREE and then a FOUR

Songs, rhymes and jazz chants are an excellent illustration of the way in which stress and rhythm work in English. Again, the children can be asked to clap the rhythm to help them pick out the main stress in each line. Words which tend to be stressed are important 'content' words which give the main part of a message. These words include nouns, verbs, adjectives, and adverbs. When a word is stressed, three things tend to happen: the stressed word sounds slightly louder than the others, the vowel in the stressed word is clearly pronounced; and so tends to sound longer.

Try to notice this with the examples above. The words which are not strongly stressed are usually said rather quickly or lazily to fit them in. This means that they may sound blurred as the vowel sounds in them are not pronounced as clearly. In fact, these vowels often change to an easily pronounced vowel, such as /ə/; /ɪ/ and /ʊ/. Words which are not strongly stressed are referred to as 'weak forms'. These occur most commonly with grammatical words in a sentence, such as the articles, auxiliaries of verbs or modals, and pronouns or prepositions, when they are not a very important part of the message. Weak forms in the rhyme above are *the, and, we,* which are pronounced /ðə/; /ən/, /wɪ/.

Songs and rhymes will be particularly useful for the teacher in developing the pupils' awareness of how English sounds (see chapter 12).

Intonation

Some of the most important functions of intonation in English are to help emphasise the most strongly stressed word in a sentence; to show the grammatical function of what is being said, for example, whether something is a statement or question, and to show feelings and emotions.

The most usual intonation pattern in English uses a *falling tone*

to make a short statement: *My name's Carlos*;

questions with wh-words: *Where's my bag?*;

commands: *Stick it on here*;

and exclamations to show surprise, anger or give a warning: *Be careful!*

77

The *rising tone* is used

to make requests: *Can we open it?*;

to make questions from statements: *He's too tired?*;

in Yes/No questions:*Would you like a lift?*;

and in clauses or phrases that come before the main clause in the sentence:

What there is left we will put in the pot.

More recently the use of the rising tone, even for statements has become more frequent in American, Australian and British English, especially with the younger generations.

Techniques and activities

Usually pronunciation teaching forms an integral part of the presentation of new words and sentence patterns and subsequent practise activities. Exercises using *minimal pairs* have been very popular in the past (these are words that have one sound difference between them like *pig* and *peg*). However, you will find that for young children long stretches of decontextualized practice like this is boring and demotivating. They are useful for raising awareness of sounds or for remedial work, but need to be converted into more game-like activities to provide interest and avoid meaningless repetition (see Hancock 1995 for useful ideas which can be adapted for younger children). Teachers should use the correct word stress for two or three syllable words like eigh<u>teen</u> (oO) and <u>e</u>lephant (Ooo). Children should be able to hear the stress on these syllables, and can visualize them if you use symbols such as large or small circles or squares to show the stress. Beware of only presenting new words on their own. They need to be placed in a sentence as soon as possible to achieve their proper rhythm and stress. For example, if you have been teaching prepositions, it is difficult not to emphasise them once you put them into a sentence. Normally they have weak stress unless you are contrasting them with a different meaning. For instance, you may find yourself saying *I'm going to put it ON the table*. What this actually means is *I'm putting it on the table instead of under it, in it, over it* etc. (contrastive stress). In other words, this is a good example of *classroomese*, artificial language, heard only in the foreign language classroom. Many practice activities using discourse level activities such as surveys (see Fig. 16) or dialogues involving repetition, create 'hidden' opportunities for pronunciation practice but are contextualized and more meaningful. Let us take a look at some traditional games but which have a pronunciation twist: *Snap, Dominoes, Happy Families* and *Bingo* (see Fig. 12).

Game	Purpose	Procedure and materials
Stress Snap Stress Dominoes	To practise recognizing the word stress within 2 syllable words	Use Snap or Dominoes cards which have 2 syllable words and patterns Oo (like tiger) or oO (as in eighteen). Pupils have to match up sections which have the same stress pattern.
Sound Bingo	To practise recognizing similarities and differences between sounds/discriminating sounds	Use Bingo cards which have minimal pairs on them, using either pictures or words. Students have to cover words which are the same or which have the same vowel or consonant sound.(Start with only two or three sounds at first.)
Happy Sound Families	To practise recognizing similarities and differences between sounds/discriminating sounds	Use cards which have words grouped into four different vowel or consonant sound sets e.g. found, house, mouth, sound; chop, cheese, church, catch. Mix them up, deal them out and players try to find families by asking each other for words e.g. Have you got a word with /tʃ/ in it?
Phonics Song from Paul (1996:16)	To practise saying sounds and distinguishing between them	Cards with double letter sounds on one side and pictures of the associated things or animals from a song on the other. After practising the song on cassette spread out double flashcards on the table or floor. The children take turns to choose which sounds or pictures to substitute into the song by touching the cards as they sing
Tiddleywinks from Paul (1996:16)	To practise saying sounds and distinguishing between them. To practise writing and spelling	Enlarged Tiddleywinks board and coloured counters. Each child or team has 2 or more counters and takes turns to use one counter to flick the other one on the board (the 'flicker' should be larger than the other). When most of the counter lands on a square the pupil writes this letter or double letter sound on a piece of paper. She collects as many sounds as possible and then uses these to write words. Each child gets a point for each word; winners gain the most points.

Fig. 12 Some traditional games for practising pronunciation

Pronunciation goals

Pronunciation skills are developed over a long period of time, although, as we have seen, young learners may have some advantages in this area. We need to emphasise that children's pronunciation will only be as good as the models they hear and their main model may only be the teacher. We must recognize that it is unrealistic to expect that most primary language teachers will speak with native-speaker-like pronunciation. If this is so, it has huge implications for teachers since they still need to achieve a reasonable level of *intelligibility*. Intelligibility is an important concept in pronunciation teaching since its main goal is to ensure that speech is 'good enough' to be understood by a native speaker, even though there may be signs of a foreign accent. Many language teachers will have a foreign accent, but certain features are harder to understand than others. Long hesitations between words, putting equal stress on every syllable or the wrong syllable, or using the wrong intonation are sometimes more likely to interfere with intelligibility than using the wrong vowel or consonant sounds. For example, French people find it difficult to pronounce the /ð/ sound in *mother* and so say something like *mozzer* (first syllable stressed). In context this word is usually quite intelligible. However, it is much harder to understand this word if /ð/ is pronounced correctly but the word stress is put on the second syllable instead of the first (moTHER).

This brings us to another question, what kind of accent or pronunciation would teachers and pupils like to have? In many countries, an American accent is the most popular. In many coursebooks the correction of pronunciation errors is not over-emphasised because of the availability of good speaking models on cassettes or CD-ROMs that accompany the materials. Most coursebooks provide plenty of opportunities to practise pronunciation through repetition, pair work, songs and rhymes and pronunciation activities and games. If the coursebook does not have audio materials then the teacher has to work much harder to provide good models of spoken English. If you need to work on your own pronunciation, chapter 20 provides some suggestions.

Learning English vocabulary

In this section we will consider how children learn vocabulary, how much vocabulary young learners are expected to learn, what vocabulary to teach and how to teach it. Finally, we will consider vocabulary learning strategies.

How children learn the meaning of words

When teaching vocabulary in a foreign language we need to bear in mind that children are still building up their L1 vocabulary and are still in the process of acquiring and organizing concepts. This makes the learning of vocabulary in a foreign language a complex matter. Furthermore, it is a continuous process that can carry on throughout their lives. Children are faced with three different but related vocabulary learning tasks which Aitchison (1987: 87) calls labelling, packaging, and network-building. In the labelling task, children must discover that sequences of sound can be used as names for things. For example, a *ball* or a *biscuit*. In the packaging task, children must find out which things can be packaged together under one label. Cameron (1994:31) points out that children learn basic level meanings before their superordinates or subordinates and she gives the example of *chair* and *dog* which will be learned before *furniture* or *rocking chair* and *animal* or *Dalmation*. In the network-building task children must work out how words relate to one another.

Knowing a word

Vocabulary learning involves many different types of knowledge. Table 1 adapted from Ellis and Sinclair (1989:64) and Cameron (2001:77) has taken the different strands of metacognition as defined in chapter 5.

It can be seen that the types of knowledge may not all be equally important for 'knowing' a word. For example, we can assume that in the early stages of learning less importance will be paid to aspects of form, such as spelling, grammatical description and the grammatical changes that can be made to a word. More attention is likely to be paid to how a word is pronounced, its meaning and its use. Importance will also depend on whether or not the word is required for active or receptive use and the usefulness of the word for future use.

Vocabulary size, selection and learnability

Let us now move on to the thorny issue of how many words to teach. A realistic target for children learning a foreign language might be around 500 words a year but this will depend on many different factors such as the learning conditions, time available and learnability of a word. With regard to learnability, here are seven factors adapted from White (1988:50) that are useful to take into account:

1 **Demonstrability**: Is it easy to convey the meaning of the word? For example, concrete basic level meanings like *car* are easier to convey than an abstract noun like *transport*.

2 **Similarity to L1**: Is there any similarity between the foreign word to the L1?

Metacognitive awareness	involves	example
Language – receptive awareness	Understanding a word when it is spoken and or written	
Cognitive – awareness of effective memorizing and recall strategies	Remembering it and recalling it when it is needed	
Language – conceptual awareness	Using it with the correct meaning	Not calling a *table* a *chair*
Language – grammatical awareness	Using it in a grammatically correct way	*She dances very well* (not *She dances very good*)
Language – phonological awareness	Pronouncing it correctly i.e. so other people can understand	
Language – collocational awareness	Knowing which other words it can be used with	*A fast bike* not *a quick bike*
Language – orthographic awareness	Spelling it correctly	*Medal* (not **medle*)
Language/social – pragmatic awareness (style and register)	Using it in the right situation	*Wiggle your bum* (Ellis 1997) The use of *bum* is acceptable in this context of a playground clapping rhyme but not when speaking to a teacher.
Language/cultural/social – connotational awareness	Knowing if it has positive or negative associations	*Smarty* has negative connotations of someone who is clever but conceited. *Clever* has positive connotations.
Language – metalinguistic awareness	Knowing how to describe a word	*Medal* is a noun *Fast* is an adjective

Table 1 Knowing a word

3 **Brevity**: Is it a short or long word? The assumption is that long words are more difficult to learn than short ones. *Plane* should be easier to learn than *aeroplane.*

4 **Regularity of form**: Is it a word that has regularity of form, e.g., a new noun with a regular plural *apple/apples* will be easier to learn than a new noun with an irregular plural *foot/feet.*

5 **Learning load**: Is part of a word already known? For example, a child may know *bed* and *room* but not *bedroom.* The assumption is that if one or more components are already known separately, the effort required to learn the new word will be lower.

6 **Opportunism**: Is the word relevant to the child's immediate situation? This may include, for example, vocabulary related to the classroom environment.

7 **Centres of interest**: Are the words likely to be of relevance of and interest to children?

The final factor, centres of interest, is also emphasised by Ur (1985:287) in her survey review of courses for younger learners for 'their contribution to authenticity of expression, or "fun" value'. Most courses for young learners will include basic vocabulary essential for communication as well as child-centred words. These words will be the ones your pupils will want to learn and find the easiest to learn and remember, but may not immediately be on the tip of your tongue!

Task 2

Write five words in English related to the following topics: Witches, Dinosaurs, Toys, Castles, Chocolate. Now predict and write down five words that you think an eight- or nine-year-old would write for each of the topics and compare your words with those written by a variety of children in Fig. 13. The aim of the task is to compare your predictions with those of children. You may also like to ask a child you know to do the same task. What are the similarities and differences? (See below for further comments on this task.)

Agreement about a realistic target varies widely as Rixon (1999:58) has shown in an analysis of seven internationally available coursebooks. She made an inventory of 889 separate vocabulary items present in one or more of the seven books. The range of total vocabulary items for individual books went from 181 to 459. One hundred and thirteen words appeared in five or more books, but only twenty-nine were found in all seven. This, indeed, shows a very low area of common consent. Ur (1985:282) mentions three useful criteria for selection and ordering of language items: frequency, usefulness, simplicity, and other lexical items for authenticity and fun. In terms of frequency, however, if we take the first 200 words from the Cobuild Corpus (Carter and McCarthy 1988:149) we can see that they are mainly function words, articles, prepositions, pronouns etc., for example, *the, of, and, to, a, in, I, he, for, your, on,* etc. with only six content words listed in the first 150, the first *people* coming in at number 72. Function words, although used very frequently, are a much smaller set than content words and are used mainly to carry grammatical meaning. Content words are nouns, verbs, adjectives, etc., and carry lexical meaning even out of context. Generally speaking, children will pick up function words through continued exposure and use in different contexts. Content words, however, can be taught in carefully planned ways and can be linked into networks of meaning. We would expect, therefore, a syllabus for young learners to have a higher proportion of content words. Regarding usefulness, she defines this as 'useful vocabulary items covering a wide field of daily experience'. She also found in the books she reviewed that the number of vocabulary items varied greatly from 200 to 300. The

	Witches	Dinosaurs	Toys	Castles	Chocolate
Ben, 6 years, French/English					
1	monsters	big one	car	kings	caramel
2	scarecrow		tree house	queens	ice-cream
3	Frankenstein			princes	jelly
4	broom			princesses	
5				horses	
Ruby, 8 years, English/French					
1	wizard	big	play	kingdom	good
2	Snow White	carnivorous	fun	museum	brown
3	nasty	scary	happy	soldier	white
4	magic power	don't exist any more	some people have got a lot	princess	black
5	owl	explorers/ bones	some people haven't got a lot	prince	paper
Raphael, 9 years, French					
1	ugly	there are none left	play	big	good
2	different	giant	puppet	king	brown
3	broom	dangerous	paint	old	black
4	not real	eat grass	computer		white
5					squares
Eliott, 10 years, French					
1	horrible	pre-history	Toy Story	knight	delicious
2	magic	Tyrannosaurus	Buzz	horse	sweet
3	spell		Woody	war	ice-cream
4	magic wand		Play Station	kill	sweets
5	toad		Nintendo	king	square
Ana, 10 years, Spanish					
1	big nose	big animals	teddy bear	towers	delicious
2	wart	reptiles	little eyes	small town	rectangle
3	broom	big nose	soft	many people	pieces
4	hat	little eyes	bow	battlement	creamy
5	dress	two little hands	two hands, two feet	wood/stone	brown
Gyung Gyu, 11 years, Korean					
1	strange	big	funny	old	sweet
2	scary	scary eyes	cool!	beautiful	black
3	old	cruel	exciting	nice	small
4	bad	A long time ago	making toys	a long time ago	makes me fat
5.	Harry Potter		cute	big	expensive

Fig. 13 Vocabulary associations of children

84

selection of vocabulary was largely erratic with an excess of too many relatively rare words and too many essential ones left out leaving children with large gaps in their knowledge of basic lexis, or limited to too simple language which comes out as bland and uninteresting. She asks why coursebook writers do not work from a checklist of essential items such as that suggested in *The Threshold Level* (van Ek 1980). The problem is that *The Threshold Level* was not written with children in mind and, although the Cobuild Corpus contains a number of texts taken from children's literature, there is no recent large-scale study of children's language that could inform course writers. As Rixon (1999:64) writes ' A modern corpus of children's language at the 'right' age is something to look forward to'.

The conclusion we can draw from Ur's review and Rixon's study is that vocabulary seems to be mainly selected randomly by course writers. They may be relying too much on adult intuition or copying previous syllabuses, and selecting vocabulary on the basis of what they **think** children use or will want to use. As the task above may have revealed, (even though the topics are adult-selected!) an adult's choice of vocabulary may differ significantly from a child's choice of vocabulary. The examples in Fig. 13 also highlight the variety of associations they make. It was also significant that some children found it hard to think of five words related to some of the topics whereas others were difficult to stop! This may have been that some of the topics were more abstract and distant from the child's reality although Dinosaurs was a particularly popular topic among all age groups in a recent survey (see Fig. 14) among ninety bilingual children at the British Council's Young Learners Centre in Paris. The aim of this survey was to find out what topics children wanted to study and revealed that many of the topics selected by teachers as potentially interesting were not rated so interesting by the pupils! See Fig. 14 for the results of this survey. It can be seen that all age groups wanted to study some topics so it is at this point that the teacher needs to intervene. Teachers need to consider the potential of each topic in terms of the language that can be generated, the skills and strategies that can be developed through related activities, and how these best match the conceptual level of the pupils. In this way, informed choices can be made about the most appropriate topic for the different age groups although the initial choice of topics has been child-led. (See chapter 9 for further details.)

The vocabulary teaching and learning process

Children will go through five main stages guided by their teacher in their efforts to learn new words and attach these to words they already know.

Age	Teacher's choices of topics	Pupil's choices of topics
5–6 year-olds	Family Toys Animals	Animals (wild) Money Pirates Dinosaurs Food and diet Teddies (pupil's added topic)
6–7 year-olds	Bears Animals (wild) Food	Food and diet Toys Animals (pets) Pirates
7–8 year olds	Pirates Castles Homes	Toys Dinosaurs Sports and games Pirates Castles
8–9 years-olds	Chocolate Dinosaurs Space	Animals (pets) Chocolate Toys Animals (wild) Dinosaurs Sports and games Egypt
9–10 year-olds	Transport Money Sports and games Inventors	Dinosaurs Space Animals Chocolate Inventors Pirates
10–11 year-olds	Egypt Native Americans Wild life and conservation Explorers	Animals (wild) Animals (pets) Chocolate Dinosaurs Sports and games Egypt

Fig. 14 Topic choices

Stage 1: Understanding and learning the meaning of new words

When introducing vocabulary it should ideally be presented in a context which is familiar to the child. Visual support is also very important to help convey meaning and to help pupils memorize new vocabulary. As words are often remembered in groups which have something in common it is helpful to introduce them in

- Lexical sets:e.g. shops, fruit, rooms in a house
- Rhyming sets:e.g. *bat, rat, hat, mat*
- Colour sets:e.g. things that are green: *a pea, a leaf, an apple*
- Grammatical sets:e.g. adjectives, verbs, prepositions, nouns. This will

also help children recognize patterns in words such as *–or, -er, -ist,* for jobs, *-ly* for adverbs, etc.

- Partners, or collocations,:e.g. *play the piano, ride a bike,* (verb + noun) or *easy class, loud noise* (adjective + noun)
- Opposites or male and female:e.g. *hot/cold, boy/girl*

Grouping words together in this way can help pupils associate new words with words they already know and aid retention and recall.

Teachers often ask how many new words it is possible to introduce per lesson. Unfortunately, there is no definite answer as this will depend on the learnability factors listed above, as well as the linguistic and conceptual level of your pupils and how rich and memorable the context is in which the words are presented. It is probably wise, however, not to overload your pupils by introducing too many new words at any one time, and to spend time more valuably on consolidating words they know and how these can be used with other words. It should also be remembered that some children cannot rely solely on a word being presented orally. Depending on the age of your pupils, some may like to see the written form of the word in order to aid retention. However, do not write the word on the board until you have practised its pronunciation first.

Some techniques to introduce new vocabulary and convey meaning are by demonstration:

- *Using objects* or things brought to the classroom because introducing a new word by showing the real object often helps pupils to memorize the word through visualization.

- *Using drawings* on the blackboard or on flashcards. The latter can be used again if they are made with card and covered in plastic.

- *Using illustrations, pictures, photos, flashcards* found in the language learning materials you are using or by making your own visual aids, using pictures from magazines, and so on.

- *Using actions, mime, expressions and gestures* e.g. adjectives: *sad, happy;* verbs: *swimming, running, jumping,* etc.

- *Pointing, touching, tasting, feeling, smelling* whenever possible, getting pupils to use their senses, to help memorize words and understand their meanings.

- *Using technology* see *WordBird* in chapter 15.

Other techniques are verbal:

- *Explaining:* Giving an analytical definition: *a present is something you give to someone on a special occasion like a birthday*

- *Defining the context: The winner of the swimming competition gets a medal*

- *Eliciting:* Once a context is established, you can elicit vocabulary items from pupils *What does the winner of a swimming competition or a marathon get?* You may need to do this in the L1 and pupils may give the word in the L1 but it shows they are thinking in the appropriate semantic area. This technique is far more motivating and memorable than giving pupils a list of words to learn.

- *Describing: It's made of metal and looks like a coin* (a medal). Using opposites: *It's the opposite of black* (white). This technique allows pupils to associate words with a concept they already understand in their L1 and often pupils will learn two words instead of one.

- *Translating:* If none of the above techniques work, then translate. This technique saves a lot of time.

Stage 2: Attending to form

This can involve, depending on the age and level of your pupils, all or some of the following:

- Listening and repeating
- Listening for specific phonological information (consonant and vowel sounds, number of syllables, stress pattern)
- Looking at/observing the written form (shape, first and last letters, letter clusters, spelling)
- Noticing grammatical information: (*an apple:* a countable noun, needs an article, in this case *an* because the word begins with a vowel)
- Copying and organizing

You can follow this procedure:

Convey the meaning of the word in one of the ways above. If a child knows the word, ask them to say it aloud. If it is correct, use this as your model. If not, say the word aloud yourself. Ask the class to repeat. Check pronunciation. Say it again and again if necessary. Ask individual pupils to repeat the word and then the whole class again. You may then want to write the word on the board for pupils to look at and possibly copy down and organize in their exercise or vocabulary books.

Stage 3: Vocabulary practising, memorizing and checking activities

This involves children in activities requiring them to do things with the words in order to make strong memory connections by learning words in groups, as shown below.

- Classifying/sorting: Pupils sort words into categories. For example, hot and cold things, sweet or salty foods, red things, farm animals, African animals, and so on.

- Giving instructions: The teacher gives an instruction, focusing on specific vocabulary. For example, *Show me a red square; Go to the door; Show me a table; Touch the green book; Point to the window,* and so on.

- Picture dictation: Pupils draw what you say. It can be simply *Draw a circle; Draw a green square* or *He's wearing blue jeans, a red jumper and black boots.*

- What's missing?: Ask pupils to look at the pictures carefully then tell them to close their eyes. Remove an item from the board. Pupils open their eyes and tell you what is missing. You could ask the rest of the class, *Is he/she right?* The game can also be played as a team game.

- Kim's game: Played the same way as above but objects are used and displayed on a tray or a table.

- Wordsearches: Children enjoy searching for English spelling patterns and if the words are all of one category it can reinforce categorization skills.

- Sequencing: Jumble up pictures on the board. The teacher or a pupil gives instructions: *Put the chocolate cake first,* and so on.

- Labelling: Pupils label a picture in order to practise different nouns from lexical sets.

Stage 4: Consolidating, recycling, extending, organizing, recording and personalizing vocabulary

Children often seem to learn new words relatively quickly but in order for these words to enter their long term memory they need to practise regularly, consolidate and recycle words in different contexts. What can pupils do with words as they learn them? Many ask to write them down as this aids retention. Here are some techniques you can propose, which will allow pupils to build up their own personalized vocabulary systems. (See also Philpot 2000 which provides some excellent suggestions on making word records.)

- *Vocabulary books*
  Encourage pupils to create their own vocabulary books. Discuss ways of organizing these, for example, alphabetically (words or words + pictures and drawings), by topic or situation, by grammatical groups (nouns, adjectives, verbs, etc.), colour sets and story features (setting, characters, the events, etc.).

- *Collages*
  Pupils collect pictures around a particular theme and stick these on to a large sheet of paper which can be used to decorate the classroom and can be added to on an on-going basis.

- *Word networks/webs/trees*
  Encourage pupils to build up their own word networks taking as their starting point a topic for example, Transport, and then writing down words they associate with this.

- *Clines or steps* degrees of temperature: *hot, warm, cold, freezing;* sizes of animals from big to small or vice versa: *elephant, gorilla, mouse*

- *Word stars*
  Pupils arrange words which rhyme on a star diagram which will help them recognize letter-sound relations.

For many of the techniques above, recommend that pupils use a ring folder so that they can add new pages as and when necessary. In this way, pupils will see their collections of words grow and they can modify and cross reference as they discover new connections between words. Encourage pupils to write words neatly and, if they wish, to write the word in their language too. Have a special time for pupils to show and talk about their vocabulary books or display them in the classroom. Also encourage pupils to use dictionaries and, if possible, make a class dictionary. There are a number of attractive dictionaries available for children: Ashworth and Clark (1993), Vale (1996), Wright, (1985) which also include vocabulary activities. The *Oxford Elementary Learner's Dictionary of English* is useful to introduce children to a monolingual dictionary.

- *Word boxes, banks, envelopes, bags*
  Pupils can make their own sets of vocabulary cards and store them in boxes, envelopes or bags in groups such as those suggested above. They can also add to their collections on an on-going basis and monitor their vocabulary learning. Discuss what information the children are going to include on their cards. This may simply be the word and a picture or a translation. Pupils may like to include other information. such as word class (noun, adjective, verb, etc), a short sentence giving an example of how the word is used, information about the way the word is pronounced, where and when they learned the word, etc. Vocabulary cards are ideal for self-testing.

- *Mobiles*
  Combine a craft activity with a vocabulary learning activity, making

it a very tactile and visually rewarding experience. Mobiles are ideal for helping children group words in lexical sets.

Stage 5: Developing strategies for vocabulary learning

Children need to become aware of and develop strategies for vocabulary learning so they can understand and memorize words more effectively, discover patterns with words, and know how to make informed guesses about the meaning of partially understood or unknown words. This in turn will help them become more actively involved in their vocabulary learning and more independent. The strategies in Fig.15 are organized under the three main strategy types, metacognitive, cognitive and socioaffective as described in chapter 5. Communication strategies have been grouped under socioaffective as most of these are of a collaborative nature. (see Riley 1985:108). Schmitt (1997:206) makes a further useful distinction between discovery strategies, what people do to find out the meaning of new words, and consolidation strategies, what people do to learn and remember words.

Children are usually very good at guessing or inferring meaning from context in L1 and often transfer these strategies spontaneously to the L2. It is useful to consider what knowledge contributes to contextual inferencing so we can support children's learning and help them become aware of and use the following clues.

Linguistic knowledge

- Grammatical clues: prior knowledge of the language, links and similarities to L1

- Textual clues: punctuation, use of capitals, speech marks

Extra-linguistic/world knowledge

- Visual clues: illustrations, mime, gestures, expressions

- Audio clues: sound effects, onomatopoeic words, word and sentence stress, pace, volume, pauses, disguised voices

- World knowledge: prior knowledge of the situation, the topic, the culture   *(Adapted from Nagy 1997:76)*

We can see that in the earlier stages of foreign language learning children will make greater use of extra-linguistic/world knowledge than linguistic knowledge, and that storybooks and the technique of storytelling provide an extremely useful resource for developing contextual inferencing.

	Metacognitive	Cognitive	Socioaffective
DISCOVERY	• Becoming aware of a variety of clues to help guess and predict meaning	• Using a variety of clues to help guess and predict meaning • Using a dictionary to find out or clarify meaning • Researching/looking for words on food packets, shops, clothes, etc.	• Asking a teacher, classmate or parent for meaning or clarification of meaning • Requesting help/asking how to say a word • Defining or describing to get the interlocutor to provide an unknown word or solve a communication problem: *It's a type of ... It's like a ... It's got ...* • Using vague mention words to get the interlocutor to guess and provide the unknown word: *It's a thing for ... It's something you ...*
CONSOLIDATION	• Planning and organizing a vocabulary record keeping system in order to monitor vocabulary learning • Deciding and planning to do self-testing • Deciding to look for patterns in words • Reflecting on learning and reviewing regularly • Thinking about preferred ways of learning words	• Keeping a vocabulary record keeping system and linking new words to known words • Self-testing • Looking for patterns in words and for words commonly used together • Finding/drawing a picture to illustrate a word or creating a visual image • Collecting things • Using a dictionary to check meaning/spelling • Sorting words into meaningful groups • Classifying words into hierarchies • Repeating words silently/aloud several times • Repeating words aloud with accompanying actions, gestures or expressions • Copying/writing a word several times and then recording in personal system • Matching words to pictures • Trying to use new words • Labelling pictures, objects in the classroom/at home • Looking for recently learned words in storybooks, the internet, the neighbourhood, at home, etc., and noticing how they are used	• Practising words with a classmate or in a group • Teaching a word to a member of the family or peer • Peer testing • Making and playing word games with friends • Singing a song or saying a rhyme to practise vocabulary

Fig. 15 Vocabulary learning strategies

Learning English Grammar

Approaches to the teaching of grammar have over the last fifty years almost gone round in a full circle from grammar-translation methods to the communicative approach and a return to approaches which focus on form. In line with this development, publishers have brought out a number of attractive grammar activity books for children (see Seidl 1992, Philpot 1994, Bourke, 1996, 1999, Vale 1998) which present grammar through topics and meaningful contexts and provide activities which offer both controlled practice and creative language use. See also Ur (1988) which contains a wide variety of activities suitable for children or easily adaptable.

What grammar to teach?

Before looking at ways we can teach grammar, it is useful to consider what grammar to teach. Lewis (1986:9-12) breaks down grammar into three accessible and manageable categories:

- Facts: these are non-generative and cannot be applied generally, for example, the plural of *foot* is *feet* and not *foots*. Once pupils are aware of this category, they can be encouraged to simply accept the facts for what they are and learn them.

- Patterns: This category can be dealt with fruitfully in the classroom by helping children look for patterns. Once a pattern has been noted, children can generate new language. For example, *My favourite (colour/desert) is (blue/ice-cream)* etc. This can be confidence-boosting and motivating.

- Choices: The use of certain grammatical structures is a matter of personal choice, for example, *I've played tennis since I was eight* or *I've been playing tennis since I was eight.* Pupils will need a lot of time and exposure to language before they develop a deep understanding of the relationship between grammar and meaning and its subtle distinctions. This category of grammar will concern our pupils in more formal learning of English at secondary school.

We can see that the most useful contribution we can make to our pupils grammar learning is by helping them to work on the first two categories.

Teaching grammar

Although formal teaching of grammar is not usually a major objective in the young learners classroom, teachers can most usefully contribute to children's understanding of grammar by using form-focusing techniques in meaningful and interesting contexts in which pupils are involved actively. Without the acquisition of basic sentence patterns and attention to the form of language, problems with basic structures and, consequently accuracy, will continue, and children will be unable to participate in activities which focus on purposeful communication.

Sequencing grammar learning activities

Appropriate language use requires a knowledge of both the form and the functions of a language. Children should therefore be provided with opportunities from an early stage to use grammatical structures for real communicative purposes. This will make language learning much more meaningful and motivating.

Batstone (1994:51) proposes three useful stages:

- Noticing new language input which involves focusing the pupil's attention on the language forms so they notice and become aware of the structure and meaning

- Structuring knowledge of the language system which involves pupils in manipulating forms and meaning in controlled practice

- Proceduralizing, involving learners in fluent language use and communication where they formulate their own meanings in contexts over which they have considerable control

These stages combine a focus on accuracy and fluency and incorporate opportunities for reflection, experimentation and further reflection in accordance with the MMM stages presented in chapter 4 and the Plan-Do-Review model in chapter 5.

These procedures can be used for teaching most structures. Fig. 16 is an interview activity to practise the question and answer *Do you like ...? Yes, I do/No, I don't* derived from the story *The Very Hungry Caterpillar.* Food vocabulary introduced through the story is revised and the teacher introduces the question *Do you like sausages?* and elicits replies modelling questions and answers as necessary. She gets individual pupils and the whole class to repeat. Using flash cards of the food items, she then invites individual pupils to ask other pupils the questions. This provides a controlled opportunity for practice. When she is confident that her pupils can ask and answer the question, she demonstrates the interview activity and distributes worksheets (Fig. 16). She monitors and assists as necessary. Finally, pupils collate the information they have collected on

their worksheets in the form of a bar graph which offers a concrete outcome that they can display in the classroom.

It can be seen that pupils move from a situation which is carefully
directed by the teacher to one where they are working independently
and using English for a genuine purpose. See the typology of speaking
activities in chapter 7 for further ideas.

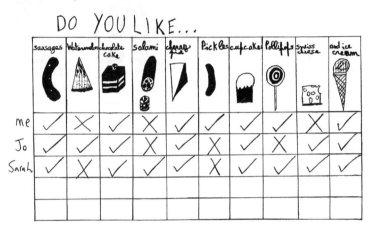

Fig. 16 An interview activity and example of a pupil-produced worksheet

Discovery grammar activities

A discovery grammar activity turns grammar into a problem-solving
activity where pupils consolidate knowledge of a structure that has been
introduced or establish the structure for themselves without an explanation from the teacher. Pupils analyse data and through guided questioning by the teacher establish the rules and patterns of the language
for themselves. For children who may have learned their L1 in an explicit and analytical way, they could be asked to compare English to their
own language and spot similarities and differences. Here is an example
which focuses on word order and the context is taken from the story *Meg
and Mog*. The adjectives of colour and size (*black, big, long, tall*) and the
nouns (*shoes, stockings, cloak, hat*) have been introduced through the
story. Pupils listen and sequence the pictures in the correct order.

*She put on her black stockings, her big black shoes, her long black cloak
and her tall black hat.*

Children are now asked the following questions to encourage them to
reflect on word order in English and to make comparisons with their own
language. Depending on the level of your pupils this may be done in
their L1. Which words are adjectives? Which words are nouns? Where do

Fig. 17 Meg and Mog *by Helen Nicoll and Jan Pieńkowski*

adjectives go in English? Where do adjectives for colour go? Where do adjectives for size go? Where do they go in your language?

To provide further practice, the following words are written on cards and stuck on the board. Individual pupils come to the board and make a phrase by putting the words in the correct order. For example, *Her long, black cloak.*

This activity shows how pupils are helped to work out rules for themselves through discovery learning. The model descriptions provide the basis for discussion, comparison and hypothesis. The pupils are then provided with further examples to experiment with and to test out their 'rule'. This problem-solving approach helps pupils to develop their thinking capacity and curiosity about language and build up their confidence.

Classroom related language

Finally, don't forget all the natural, spontaneous occasions that arise through classroom talk which provide ideal opportunities for children to notice patterns. You may like to write some of these in speech bubbles and display them around the classroom. See chapter 7.

Developing strategies for grammar learning

1. *About Me* books/Language Files
   Even from a quite young age children can be encouraged to develop their strategies for grammar learning. In *Pebbles 1 & 2 Teacher's Books* children are invited to personalize their learning by making their own *About Me* books or My Language File in which they review and

record the main language items of each unit and use the structures they have practised.

2 Self/peer-testing: pupils can test themselves on irregular forms such as plurals, past tenses, etc.

3 Pupils can mark changes in form with coloured pens, for example, the third person 's'.

4 Pupils can look for patterns and create their own My Pattern Book of English Grammar.

5 Pupils can compare grammar structures in English and in their language. What is the same(different)?

6 Encourage pupils to learn from their mistakes by keeping a list of their errors and writing out a self-corrected version for each one.

7 Listening and speaking

Developing Interactional Skills

In this chapter we shall demonstrate techniques for developing pupils' communicative competence so they can talk about personal things or about specific information *with someone else*. As we have seen, simply providing pupils with opportunities to learn new words and repeat them will not develop communicative competence.

Learning to listen in English

The initial stages

If someone is giving you a message or opinion, then of course you have to be able to understand it in order to respond. Listening to a foreign language is hard work, especially for young children. In the early stages, the pupils may spend much of their time listening to the teacher while playing simple games, singing songs, saying rhymes or listening to stories and simple instructions, as in TPR. The teacher will have to decide how much of the general 'classroom language' such as instructions, questions or praise will be in the pupils' L1 and how much in English. It is likely, of course, that the amount of English you use for these purposes will increase as time goes on, but it is useful to get the pupils used to simple routines and the English that goes with them.

It is important to remember that listening is not a passive activity. Always asking children to simply 'listen and remember' may make them feel anxious, places a great strain on their memory and tends not to develop listening skills. The teacher will be able to support children's understanding more effectively if she directs her pupils' attention to specific points that have to be listened for. She can do this by using activities that actively support learners' understanding and guide their attention to specific parts of the spoken text. This might include the use of visual materials, for example, pictures to match or sequence, or perhaps written support such as the completion of charts, as we saw in chapter 6. *All* of these techniques and procedures are what we mean when we talk about scaffolding. Let us turn to more specific guidelines which will be useful when planning how to develop pupils' listening skills.

1 Give the children confidence
We should not expect pupils to always understand every word and they should know this. Your advance planning will give you a clear idea of

what you expect the children to be able to do. For example, do you want them to get a general idea of a story, known as the 'gist', the first time they hear it? Will you expect them to pick out key words but not all the detail? It may only be on the second or third hearing that the pupils will be able to recall the exact sequence of events in a story. Your gestures, tone of voice and visual aids will help children feel confident about what is important to concentrate on.

2 Explain why the children have to listen

Make sure the learners are clear about *why* they are listening, what the main point or purpose of the activity is. This means spelling out which part of the message they need to focus on and what they are going to do. This helps to build up learners' confidence and reduce anxiety.

Different kinds of listening purposes are described below.

- *To physically settle pupils*: to calm them when they are too boisterous. There will often be some form of mental engagement.

- *To stir pupils*: to stimulate or allow them to physically 'let off steam' if they seem bored or tired (see chapter 16).

- *To improve the general listening attitude:* listen for enjoyment, improve concentration span, or develop the memory.

- *To develop aspects of language*: listening to improve pronunciation, stress, rhythm and intonation, as well as familiarity with new words and structures. Listening to learn songs and rhymes provides pronunciation practice, while listening to stories may provide practice in tenses or vocabulary connected with the topic.

- *To reinforce conceptual development:* some spoken texts, such as stories, can act as useful revision for reinforcing concepts such as numbers, size, or cause and effect, which will have been covered in other areas of the school curriculum.

- *To interact with others:* activities which encourage children to work with others require the learners to negotiate meaning by listening and asking questions, checking meaning, agreeing, and so on.

- *To provide support for literacy:* older children can be encouraged to make connections between spoken and written English by picking out written words or statements which are part of a spoken message.

3 Help children develop specific strategies for listening

An important strategy that the teacher should teach is 'intelligent guess-work'. Pupils are used to drawing on their background knowledge to work out something they are not sure of. Teachers need to be aware of this so that they can ensure they provide support and raise pupils' awareness about the benefits of doing this. Some important listening strategies include:

- *Predicting.* Before learners listen to something it is useful to encourage them to guess what they think they will be listening to. Use pictures to encourage them to guess the topic, the language or some of the details. While they are in the middle of listening, stop to ask them what they think might come next. In both cases this encourages learners to check whether their expectation matches the reality of what they hear, which helps to keep motivation high. It also allows key words and ideas to be introduced which will help to give learners a feeling of success and confidence.

- *Working out the meaning from context.* Although the teacher might like to act out or even translate new words before the children listen to something, she also needs to encourage them to use pictures, their general knowledge or the message itself to work out the meaning of unfamiliar words. (See chapter 6 for more on this.)

- *Recognizing discourse patterns and markers.* Words such as *first, then, finally,* or *but, and, so* give important signals about what is coming next in a spoken text. Sequence markers are especially important in stories and instructions.

4 Set a specific listening task

It is useful to think of listening in three stages: what pupils do *in preparation for* listening (pre-listening activities); *while* they listen so they remain active (while-listening activities) and *after* they have listened (post-listening activities), e.g. produce a drawing, make a tape, answer questions, and so on. For example, if you ask learners to listen to a simple description and then label a plan of a bedroom, useful pre-listening work might focus on key nouns, adjectives or prepositions to show where things are. The point of pre-listening activities is to do some of the following: personalize a context, provide motivation and interest, build up a picture of useful background knowledge and introduce useful words, structures and concepts.

In order to make listening an active, learning-focused process, teachers need to develop a repertoire of different pre-, while- and post- activity types which 'fit' different types of language. When listening to a series of actions in a narrative, for example, a listening task which asks the children to rearrange a series of pictures, or put numbers by pictures describing different actions, supports the child's understanding very well. If learners are asked to listen to a long stretch of English without visual support and are asked to simply recall the facts, they are in reality being 'tested' rather than 'taught'. There is a huge variety of while-listening activities which put into place all the ideas we have discussed so far about the learning-centred classroom. Table 2 shows you some examples, their purpose and the kinds of materials that are required. All of the activities contain a learning to learn element. The activities are graded according to level of difficulty although this depends on the kind of message, such as its length, topic, linguistic complexity and the number of ideas contained within it. You might like to go through the list and see how many of these are relevant to your pupils' needs and interests and which ones you regularly use.

5 Organize listening

The development of listening skills does not have to rely on the availability of a cassette or pre-recorded material. Most listening is in fact based on teacher talk. However, if you do have a cassette of published listening materials, this is useful to provide a good model of spoken English. It may be useful to introduce variety by setting up a 'listening corner' in one part of the classroom for one or two groups to use at a time while the rest of the class does something else. This can be created by screening off a corner, with a cupboard or screens, to provide a quiet area for children to listen in pairs or groups. A cassette recorder is needed for this purpose, ideally accompanied by a set of materials such as pictures, a book, or sentence strips for learners to use as they listen. The activities can be made 'self-correcting', so that the children can find out quickly whether a listen and sequence activity, for example, has been completed accurately.

Learning to speak in English

This section will consider pupils' expectations when they come to the English classroom, the initial stages of their learning and the organization of speaking activities. Also, a typology of activities to develop speaking is proposed.

Expectations

Most children equate learning an L2 with learning to speak it and, because most come to the foreign language classroom with a good mastery of their L1 and learning it seemed to be relatively easy and effortless, they expect it to be the same with the foreign language. They want immediate results and even after their first lesson, will want to show other children in the school or members of their family that they can speak some English. If children are to maintain initial motivation, they

Activity type	Purpose	Materials
1 Listen and repeat Examples of this are found in games such as Chinese Whispers where one child whispers a message to another who then passes on the message to another child and so on. The last child repeats what they have heard and the class compares this message with the original. Other listen and repeat games ask the learners to repeat something only if it is true.	• Listening for details to improve memory and concentration • Listening with enjoyment to improve listening attitude • Listening to physically 'settle' or calm pupils	Short, spoken messages such as instructions, or statements containing no more than ten words
2 Listen and discriminate The learners' attention is often focused on pronunciation features such as listening for words which rhyme, or selecting phrases which have the same rhythmic pattern. This is especially useful when using songs and rhymes or stories which have rhyming sequences. Use Find the Pair or Odd-Man-Out type activities.	• Listening for detail to discriminate between sounds and rhythmic patterns • Providing ear-training to improve pronunciation • Listening to physically 'settle' or calm pupils • Listening to encourage mental activity and problem-solving	Sets of three or four words which contain a matching pair Songs and rhymes Rhyming stories
3 Listen and perform actions/follow instructions This kind of activity (TPR) is used with instructions (Being a Robot), action songs, rhymes, or games such as Blind Man's Buff or What's the Time Mr. Wolf? Asking learners to trace a route on a plan or map is quite difficult and should not be used if the children find this difficult in their mother tongue.	• Listening for enjoyment • Listening to improve memory and concentration span • Listening to the use of prepositional phrases, e.g. *on the left-right*; or discourse markers, e.g. *first, then, next*; and action verbs, e.g. *put, fold, turn* • Listening to 'stir' pupils, make them more lively, relieve boredom etc.	Action songs and rhymes Plans or maps Instructions for games, e.g. origami (paper-folding)
4 Listen and draw/colour Picture dictation is often used to help children focus on key nouns and on adjectives used to describe their colour, size, shape, and so on. The whole picture can be drawn, or a picture which has missing items can be added to as children listen.	• Listening to develop concentration on specific items e.g. specific verbs/actions • Listening to consolidate understanding of concepts and new vocabulary, e.g. round, square, large, small, blue, yellow • Listening to physically 'settle' or calm pupils	Short, spoken descriptions which can be accomplished by drawings which pupils finish or colour in

Activity type	Purpose	Materials
5 Listen and predict This kind of activity has already been referred to and is particularly useful in drawing on pupils' previous learning.	• Listening to increase motivation and concentration • Listening to activate schemata or previous knowledge • Finding out which words or concepts pupils already know • Listening to encourage mental activity and problem-solving	Question and answer sessions based on, e.g. general knowlede, pictures or the cover of a book or story Predict content or key words from a picture Draw a word or mind maps about a topic Complete a quiz to draw attention to what pupils already know
6 Listen and guess This kind of listening is often based on the description of something whose identity the children have to guess.	• Listening for detail to pick out key vocabulary used to describe, e.g. parts of an animal's body • Listening to encourage mental activity and problem-solving	Short, spoken descriptions which can be accompanied by a selection of items for pupils to eliminate
7 Listen and label This activity is used with drawings, maps or diagrams where the learners are asked to listen to a description of an animal, person, or place in order to label key parts.	• Listening to develop reading and writing skills or to develop concepts • Listening to physically settle pupils • Listening to encourage mental activity and problem-solving	Written labels provided for pupils or written words on the blackboard for pupils to copy
8 Listen and match This usually involves matching pictures to spoken words and is common in games such as Bingo. Older children can be involved in activities which ask them to match pictures or written statements to other written texts, such as speech bubbles taken from dialogues or stories.	• Listening to consolidate new vocabulary and structures • Listening to encourage mental activity and problem-solving • Listening to settle pupils	Bingo cards Worksheets on which children draw a line to connect a picture with the correct words or written labels or speech bubbles to match with pictures

Table 2 While-listening activities

Activity type	Purpose	Materials
9 Listen and sequence As described earlier, this activity is usually based on pictures or written phrases which are rearranged into the correct order while listening to a story or set of instructions.	• Listening to improve memory and concentration span • Listening to consolidate new vocabulary and structures • Listening to physically settle pupils • Listening to encourage mental activity and problem-solving	Pictures or written statements Worksheets with boxes in which children number the order of details listened to
10 Listen and classify This activity is also usually based on pictures. The children listen carefully to descriptions, for example, different animals, which they then have to sort into different sets. This should be accompanied by some kind to key visual, e.g. a table, matrix, Venn diagram etc. (see chapter 9).	• Listening to improve concentration span and to consolidate new vocabulary and structures • Listening to physically settle pupils • Listening to encourage mental activity and problem-solving	Pictures Worksheets using written words on the blackboard which pupils copy into the appropriate column of a chart while listening Key visuals, e.g. a tickchart, Venn diagram, matrix or grid
11 Listen and transfer information This involves an exchange of information in pairs or groups. The pupils might be asked to carry out a survey or questionnaire where they each ask each other questions and listen carefully for the answer, e.g. favourite sports, birthdays etc. The responses are recorded on a key visual to help the children remember details and to consolidate their understanding.	• Listening to improve interactional skills • Listening to encourage mental activity and problem-solving • Listening to develop key study skills, i.e. using and interpreting charts, simple 'date handling'	Worksheets to carry out surveys and questionnaires with columns for pupils to complete. For example: **About us** |	you	your partner
Colour of eyes		
Shoe size		
Best skill			

Table 2 While-listening activities (Contd)

need to be given opportunities to speak English as soon and as much as possible, so as to be made to feel that they are making progress and fulfilling their expectations, thus avoiding disappointment.

The initial stages

It is important that children leave their first few lessons with some English to 'take away'. It is therefore useful to begin an English programme by teaching children vocabulary for basic concepts, such as numbers, colours, and so on, which can provide the basis for subsequent activities. First lessons often focus on teaching simple greetings and introductions. Pupils could also be given English names, although they should be allowed to keep their own name if they wish. Teaching pupils a few rhymes and songs at the beginning of their course will also give them the impression that they are learning to speak English quickly.

Many language programmes begin with a lesson to help pupils understand why they are learning English, which may include eliciting names of famous people who speak English and countries where English is spoken. You can ask them to think of any English words they know, such as *hamburger, tennis, football, jeans, hotel,* etc. Attention can be focused on how these words are pronounced in comparison with their own language, providing a useful introduction to the features of English pronunciation. The aim is to heighten children's awareness of language and to build up their confidence.

Formulaic language

In the early stages of learning, not much spontaneous speech can be expected from pupils. Much of the English they will learn to produce in the initial stages will be formulaic language, language that is produced as whole chunks rather than being put together word by word. It often consists of routines or patterns which children memorize and which enable them to communicate with a minimum of linguistic competence. As this type of language is repeated regularly, children learn it quickly and have the impression that they can speak a lot. Such language consists of:

- simple greetings: *Hello! How are you? / I'm fine, thank you. And you?*

- social English: *Did you have a nice weekend? / Have a nice weekend!*

- routines: *What's the date? What's the weather like today?*

- classroom language: *Listen. Repeat. Sit down. Work in pairs. Good.*

- asking permission: *Can I/May I go to the toilet? Can I clean the board? Can I wash my hands? Can I look at a book?*

- communication strategies: *Can you say that again, please? How do you say ... in English, please? What does ... mean, please? I don't understand. Can I have a ... please?*

By hearing this language over and over, children learn to use it. These phrases could also be written out in speech bubbles and stuck around the classroom.

A typology of speaking activities

The speaking activities shown in Table 3 progress from those which provide tightly controlled practice to those which provide freer communicative language use. See chapter 6 on learning English grammar for a suggested procedure for presenting new structures.

Organizing speaking activities

Some of the speaking activities described in Table 3 require pupils to work together in pairs or groups or to move around. Consideration will need to be given on how to arrange the classroom in order for these activities to be carried out smoothly. Chapter 16 describes this in more detail.

Pupils may also like to record themselves from time to time and listen to their recordings afterwards. For example, activities such as retelling a story could be recorded and played to pupils in other classes. Most pupils find this activity very motivating and it can help them become aware of the structures and vocabulary they are using and of certain aspects of English pronunciation. Ideally, a quiet area or corner in the classroom is needed for the recording to take place. This could be integrated into the 'listening corner' (see page 101).

The gap between children speaking L1 and L2 is a large one but with practice pupils will gradually build up their confidence and spoken language. They need a wide variety of activities, different patterns of interaction and opportunities to maximize talk in the classroom in order to sustain speaking. The teacher needs to develop a repertoire of activities providing a balance between control and creativity, repetition and real use and provide varied models of spoken English.

Activity type	Purpose	Materials
1 Look, listen and repeat The teacher shows a picture, says the word and pupils repeat: *Look! An elephant. Repeat!* When the teacher is satisfied with her pupils' pronunciation, she can move on to another word. Once several new items have been introduced, the teacher can check by showing a picture and asking, What's this? and pupils reply *An elephant*.	• To introduce new vocabulary or structures • To focus on form and pronunciation • The same technique, using a word card instead of a picture card will provide basic reading practice	Picture cards e.g. animals, food, colours, actions, clothes Word cards as above
2 Listen and participate Examples of this are found in storytelling sessions or when rhymes or poems are recited in class. Pupils are encouraged to participate by repeating key vocabulary and phrases.	• To involve pupils actively when listening to stories or rhymes • To provide a meaningful and familiar context in which to repeat language items	Storybooks, rhymes, riddles, poems
3 Reading aloud Some games, like phonetic Bingo or Snap, require pupils to read words or sentences aloud.	• To practise pronunciation and sound/letter combinations	Bingo boards and cover cards Snap cards
4 Memory games Games like 'I went to market and bought ...' and Chinese Whispers require children to repeat a certain structure or word.	• To develop memory skills • To practise pronunciation • To provide hidden pattern practice • To improve concentration and listening skills	Short spoken messages or lists of items
5 Dramatization A story or situation can often be acted out, thereby involving pupils in a variety of different related activities such as memorizing lines, making costumes and props, making posters and invitations. Short dialogues can also be created around a situation and acted out with puppets	• To provide a memorable occasion for practising spoken English • To develop confidence • To develop memory skills • To provide integrated skills practice • Develop social skills of interaction and turn-taking	Storybooks Scripts (optional) Various materials for related activities Puppets

Table 3 A Typology of speaking activities

107

Activity type	Purpose	Materials
6 Rhymes, action rhymes, songs, chants, tongue twisters These are learned as chunks of language and involve pupils in imitating and miming. Some rhymes and songs offer ready-made dialogues. Rhymes or songs with actions also provide exercise and encourage body control.	• To develop memory skills • To provide pronunciation practice • To consolidate or introduce new language	Rhymes, songs, chants
7 Retelling a story This activity involves pupils in retelling a simplified version of a story. Children can often be helped in this activity with picture prompts, or by matching speech bubbles with pictures.	• To check if pupils have understood the main events in a story • To provide pronunciation practice, as well as some storytelling techniques, such as disguising the voice, alternating pace and so on	Storybooks Captions written on cards or in speech bubbles, picture prompts
8 Using flash cards Flash cards are often used to prepare pupils for freer activities such as pair work or questionnaires and surveys. The teacher gives a flash card to a pupil to prompt him/her to ask a particular question. The teacher can then ask the class. *Is it a cat? Is that right?*	• To provide controlled practice where pupils are focusing on producing the correct grammatical form and pronunciation	Flash cards e.g. fruit, objects, clothes
9 Guessing games These types of games usually involve pupils in asking questions or describing something or someone. For example, pupils draw a picture of an animal or think of an animal they would like to have as a pet, without showing the class. The class must guess what it is: *Is it a cat?* and so on. Pupils can also describe someone in the class without saying his or her name: *She's got long hair. She's wearing a red pullover,* and so on, and the other pupils must listen and guess.	• To provide a realistic context for practising the pronunciation of specific structures	None

Activity type	Purpose	Materials
10 Information gap These activities are usually carried out in pairs or groups and often involve pupils in asking and answering questions. The aim is to find out what this is in order to complete, for example, a worksheet.	• To give pupils a chance to work independently of the teacher • To practise fluency • To use the language for real communication • Develop social skills of interaction and turn taking	Worksheets for pupils A and B
11 Questionnaires and surveys Pupils interview other classmates about, for example, their abilities, their likes and dislikes, and record the information on a chart.	As above, and • To practise listening skills • To use the information collected for a specific purpose	Worksheets for pupils to complete. See Fig. 16.
12 Dialogues and role-play Role-play provides an opportunity for language that has been presented in one context to be used in another. For example, pupils could act out a shopping dialogue, making use of the 'shop corner'.	• To provide fluency practice • To extend language use • Develop social skills of interaction and turn-taking	Pupils may be given role cards, for example, Pupil A — *You want to buy some biscuits* — **customer** Pupil B — *You haven't got any biscuits* — **shop assistant**

Table 3 A Typology of speaking activities (Contd)

8 Reading and writing

Learning to read in the L1 and L2

One view of learning to read, held by educationalists such as Cummins (1979), is that the development of reading skills in a foreign language is greatly assisted if pupils have developed strong reading skills in their first language. In this view, the positive relationship between the two is a result of children being able to transfer L1 reading skills to the L2 (see Carlo and Royer 1999). There is not enough research to show conclusively whether this is true or how the transfer mechanism works, although it appears to make intuitive sense to many teachers.

In some contexts it has been decided to encourage speaking first and leave reading until later, especially if the pupils are still not fully literate in their L1. Teachers of very young children may not use a coursebook at all, or may use coursebooks such as *First Steps*, which rely on pictures alone. In other contexts, where they start learning English later, children may be quickly introduced to coursebooks in their first English class and be expected to begin reading and writing in English as soon as possible.

What do children already know about reading?

When children learn to read successfully in their L1, they develop different forms of awareness and knowledge. *Awareness and knowledge about print*: the realization that print represents speech, and is written in a certain direction. The challenge for children, of course, is to find out *how* print represents sounds. *Graphophonic knowledge:* how certain sounds occur together. Phonological awareness refers to an awareness of syllables, *onsets* and *rimes* (rime is not the same as rhyme). Onset refers to the consonants or consonant clusters preceding the vowel in a syllable; *rime* refers to the vowel and any consonants following the vowel within the syllable. Thus in the word BAT /b/ is the onset and /at/ is the rime. The use of songs, rhymes and rhyming stories help to build up this knowledge. *Lexical knowledge:* that certain words are very common, collocate or go together (e.g. at the seaside). Teaching sight reading of high frequency words develops this ability. *Syntactic knowledge:* helps children to 'chunk' phrases and to predict what might come next in a sentence or story. *Semantic knowledge:* knowledge of the world and experience of life and culture helps pupils to have expectations about literacy events. It seems highly likely that if a child has developed all of these kinds of awarenesses in one language they will soon realize that they apply to the new language also, but in different ways. This process will be enhanced if teachers engage the pupils in activities that help them to make these links.

Learning to read in English: the initial stages

It is important not to place too many reading demands on younger learners who are still learning to read in their L1. Developing good levels of literacy in the L1 and good oral skills in the L2 are the most important objectives.

Which teaching methods are in use?

In many countries general agreement about the most effective way of teaching reading means using a *balanced* approach with several methods. This includes *phonics,* working out sound/letter correspondences to develop 'word attack' skills. This approach aims to consolidate children's phonemic, phonological and morphological awareness. It highlights the recognition of individual sounds and sound blends or combinations so that the words can be 'sounded out'. However, meaning is not always highlighted, so sounds and words may sometimes be presented in sound sets but little other contextualization.

Most teachers use a balance of activities that focus on sounds, letters and words but also activities that promote word recognition associated with meaning, for example the *Look and Say* and *Language Experience* methods. Look and Say is based on encouraging sight recognition of the most common words, such as *the, he, she, is, are,* so that part of reading becomes automatic. In a recent article Dlugosz (2000) recommends the Look and Say method and also describes its use with some Polish children where they listen to texts many times until they become familiar with words and their graphic representations. Language Experience is used with young children and tries to make print meaningful by encouraging personal events to become part of a simple text. If something interesting happens in the school or classroom the teacher can scribe a sentence, ensure the pupils understand it and then show the pupils how the written word corresponds to the spoken word. The foreign language teacher will need to consider the difference between 'sounding out' and 'reading with understanding' in her English class.

Coping with English orthography

Once children are introduced to the written word in English they will quickly discover that English spelling does not always help them in their reading. Even English native-speaker children are reckoned to be a few months behind Italian- or Spanish-speaking children in their reading because of the difficulties of the English writing system. Children in many countries will have a working knowledge of the Roman alphabet, although children from countries with a different alphabet, such as India, the Middle East or East Asia, will need to spend more time learning to form letters or to orientate their handwriting from left to right.

Developing print awareness

Decorate the classroom with *functional print,* such as alphabet friezes, flashcards, posters, words of songs, or signs, using published material or materials you make yourself. You can make labels for equipment such as card, scissors and glue. Provide displays with information or questions written in English that can link to classroom routines. Other examples include *environmental print,* examples of written English available in the local environment, e.g. T-shirts, food labels or advertisements.

Supporting reading in the initial stages

It is important to introduce reading after the pupils have some basic knowledge of the spoken language so that it quickly becomes meaning-based and not simply decoding. Nevertheless, reading in English in the early stages will combine 'meaningful' reading in sentences supplemented by independent reading at the letter and word level. This stage is important for those pupils who are not used to the Roman alphabet.

Generally the teacher should support pupils' association of letters, words and pictures through songs, visual aids, games, and so on. Simple games such as *Dominoes, Snap* or *Bingo* and puzzles like word searches help learners to become familiar with typical letter combinations to form words. At first pupils will be introduced to pictures only, then pictures and words together as flashcards. Once the pupils are more confident they will be able to cope without so much visual support, but it will still remain an important support for many years. When designing flashcards, words with similar sounds can be written in the same colour, for example, *bed, head, guess* or words in a lexical set e.g. *table, chair, lamp.*

Ensure that the child experiences reading as purposeful and enjoyable rather than simply a meaningless, repetitive activity. Pupils enjoy listening to simple dialogues and stories which are well illustrated and have an interesting story line. In the very early stages pupils can simply listen as the plot unfolds and the illustrations are shared with them. This is especially easy if the teacher is able to obtain any *Big Books,* which are very large versions of popular stories and rhymes. Teachers may be interested in producing their own big books using versions of stories they think are useful.

Reading to learn: the later stages

As pupils become more confident in reading their own language, they use reading to learn. After an initial introduction to English learning, pupils will be expected to cope with the independent reading required of a coursebook. Pupils are often introduced to and learn new vocabulary or grammar through reading short texts in the form of dialogues, descriptions, instructions or short stories, often lavishly illustrated to support the pupils' understanding. They may be learning how to learn through their reading. Much of the advice given in the section on teaching listening also applies to teaching reading.

Reading strategies

When children are listening to spoken messages they are trying to understand and interpret information in a similar way to when they are trying to understand and interpret written messages. This means they will often use similar strategies. Research has shown that actively encouraging learners to use comprehension strategies helps them understand both spoken and written passages more effectively (see Wallace 1992). If learners know, for example, that they are listening to or reading something to get a general picture, they will listen or read in a slightly different way than if they are expected to listen or read in detail for specific parts of a message. A learning-centred approach to reading uses activities in a three-stage model: pre-, while- and post-reading. Activities using visuals such as charts provide an intermediate stage in reading development and also provide a framework to support children's listening and speaking skills. Reading practice may also be derived from listening work or may lead to writing. In this way, reading becomes integrated with other language skills.

Reading activities

Traditionally, pupils are asked to complete gap-filling activities or comprehension questions after reading a text. Since all teachers know how these work we shall focus here on other activities which provide variety in the classroom and cater for different learning styles and intelligences. Reading to learn activities which are meaning-focused are often referred to as DARTS (directed activities related to texts). These focus on the processes and outcomes of reading. DARTS include *reconstruction activities* and *analysis activities*.

Reconstruction activities

Here the text has been modified by the teacher in some way so that the pupils can match parts of sentences or 'speech bubbles' to characters, fill in gaps in sentences or texts (words, phrases or titles), sequence parts of a sentence or text (a dialogue, story, life cycle of an animal, set of instructions, a diary, etc.), predict the next parts of a sentence or text after reading a section at a time, complete tables, flow charts, matrices and other key visuals or graphic organizers, and complete pictures or diagrams with colours, labels or missing parts.

Analysis activities

Pupils hunt for specific information to organize it in some way. This is more difficult and at primary level the pupils can underline specific parts of a text, perhaps in different colours, to show different things. They may underline any *shape* words in blue and any *size* words in red (cover the text in plastic and use wipeable pens), label parts of a text using labels provided by the teacher (e.g. with recipes use labels like *what we are going to make; what we are going to need*) and create their own questions from a text for other pupils to answer.

Reading awareness activities

It is also helpful to reinforce the idea that reading is used for a variety of purposes. Language awareness activities can be encouraged by asking pupils to notice similarities and differences between alphabets (the absence of accents for French speakers or tildes for Spanish speakers) or by counting how often letters occur in words (the letter 'e' is the most common letter in English). Older pupils can be introduced to the notion of genre, or text type, where pupils are introduced to the names of different types of text, such as *greetings card, menu, comic, brochure, manual, advertisement.* They are then asked to label different types of text with these names (this is a good use of a collection of authentic texts that are often too difficult for children to actually read). The pupils can compare specific text types, such as comics or menus, with examples in both their L1 and L2. You can then provide them with prompts such as *They both have... The first one has X... but the second one has Y...*and a selection of words, such as *address, greeting, pictures, ending,* and so on. Make sure you try and have a wide range of text types around the classroom which are described or labelled in English.

Reading activities for both stages

All the listening activities described in Table 2 can also be adapted for reading activities. Table 4 describes some of these reading activities which range from the simple to the more complex and explains whether

Activity type	Purpose	Materials
1 Sequencing letters, parts of words, whole words or sentences and sequencing them to make words, phrases or sentences. The pupils read and sequence items	• Learning to read: building up letter and word recognition, morphemic and syntactic awareness • Reading to learn: checking understanding at sentence level • Reading to physically 'settle' or calm pupils • Reading to encourage mental activity and problem-solving	Flashcards or worksheets with letters, prefixes, words. Moveable cards are good for a kinesthetic learning style
2 Matching or mapping pictures and words or two halves of a sentence so that they make sense. The pupils read and match the parts so that they make sense. The extracts can be on tape also to reinforce listening skills	• Learning to read: developing syntactic awareness • Reading to learn: developing concepts of, e.g. cause and effect/problem and solution if these are the examples provided • Reading to physically 'settle' or calm pupils • Reading to encourage mental activity and problem-solving	Pictures and short texts, e.g. speech bubbles. Cards or worksheets with cut up sentence parts Moveable visuals and written cards are good for a kinesthetic learning style
3 Speaking using written prompt cards or language in a graphic organizer. The pupils read the cue cards, tickchart, flow chart, etc. to remind themselves of words and sentence patterns and practise using them	• Learning to read: developing syntactic awareness • Reading to learn: understanding how markers like *but*, or *first, then next* organize discourse • Reading to 'stir' pupils • Reading to encourage mental activity and problem-solving	Flashcards with words and/or pictures Graphic organizer such as a tickchart or flow chart to say, e.g. *I can swim but Maria can't.* or *First we wash the fruit, then we peel it, next we cut it,* etc.
4 Completing details/taking notes in a graphic organizer. The pupils read a text, e.g. simple description, set of instructions or a story and transfer information to a chart with clear headings	• Learning to read: developing syntactic awareness. • Reading to learn: practising study skills when using graphic organizers • Reading to physically 'settle' or calm pupils • Reading to encourage mental activity and problem-solving	Graphic organizers, some with partial notes to provide support through example, others can be left blank to provide differentiated activities

Table 4 Activities to develop reading skills at primary level

Activity type	Purpose	Materials
5 Reading and using a graphic organizer to make statements or ask questions. The pupils refer to a flow chart, a life-cycle chart, etc. to practise describing something or asking questions	• Learning to read: developing syntactic awareness • Reading to learn: practising study skills when using graphic organizers • Reading to physically 'settle' or calm pupils • Reading to encourage mental activity and problem-solving	Graphic organizers, examples of statements or questions as a model
6 Classifying words to make lists or sets of various kinds. The pupils read lists of words which belong to 4 different sets and sort them into groups under headings. Classifying mixed up detail from 2 stories. The pupils read sentences from 2 stories which have been jumbled up. They write them out separately	• Learning to read: practising understanding the meanings of words and sense relations (inclusion). • Reading to learn: practising comprehension; using simple discourse markers to understand texts • Reading to physically 'settle' or calm pupils • Reading to encourage mental activity and problem-solving	Lists of words. Categories or story 1, story 2, etc.
7 Checking written statements. The pupils read sentences or short texts which have deliberate mistakes in them to do with language, the ideas, the layout, the organization, and so on. The pupils correct mistakes. Good for faster pupils	• Reading to learn: consolidating spelling, comprehension • Reading to physically 'settle' or calm pupils • Reading to encourage mental activity and problem-solving	Sentences or texts with deliberate mistakes
8 Understanding genre or text types. The pupils learn words for different kinds of text, e.g. manual, TV guide, menu, brochure and match text type to their label and purpose, e.g. this is a kind of sign it gives us a warning	• Reading to learn: to develop awareness of text types, their layout, purpose, etc. • Reading to encourage mental activity and problem-solving	Different examples of text type + 2 sets of card, one with the text type name on, the other with the purpose which pupils match

Table 4 Activities to develop reading skills at primary level (Cont'd)

the activities focus on *learning to read* or *reading to learn*. The learning to read activities include developing phonemic skills or sight recognition of key vocabulary, while those based on reading to learn are often integrated with other skills – speaking, listening or writing. The reading to learn activities emphasise reading for meaning and may also develop concepts, study skills, thinking skills, such as problem-solving and a greater awareness of texts and discourse. Some activities can be carried out at simple and more difficult levels. This range of activities provides useful alternatives for checking reading comprehension and provides variety, thus helping to maintain the pupils' interest in reading.

Organizing reading activities

Some of the activities described in Table 4 can be used with the whole class, while others can be done individually, in pairs or in groups. When using group work any supplementary reading activities should be clearly labelled and/or colour-coded to show their level of difficulty so that the children can organize themselves and work independently. More details about classroom management and resources can be found in chapter 16 and Part 3. More details about using stories and setting up a book corner to promote reading skills can be found in chapter 14 and in Ellis and Brewster (2002).

Learning to write in the L1 and L2

The kinds of writing activities pupils do tend to fall into two sets in the same way that they do for reading: *learning to write,* where pupils are involved mostly in tightly guided copying which focus on 'surface' features, such as handwriting, spelling, punctuation and using the correct words and grammar. In *writing to learn,* there may be less tightly controlled writing activities, moving to much freer or even creative writing where there are higher cognitive demands and a greater focus on meaning and personal expression as well as form.

The demands of activities and tasks for productive skills (speaking and writing) can be divided chiefly into two. The first is connected with *choosing the right language* while the second is concerned with *thinking* and *having ideas,* such as remembering, choosing, selecting, ordering, prioritizing and interpreting visual clues using a picture or graphic organizer. The language demands of a writing task depends on which category it falls under. In learning to write, the focus on form and 'surface' features means that writing activities tend to focus on word or sentence level writing only. Pencil control and hand-eye coordination can still be a difficulty for young children, as will forming letters of the

Roman alphabet for those not used to it. As soon as the activity becomes writing to learn the number of demands shoots up. They now include choosing the right vocabulary, grammar, sentence patterns, spelling and layout, having ideas and joining them, thinking of writing as communication and focusing on the message and the reader.

It is important to understand what native-speaker children can do in terms of writing at different stages so that teachers do not make unrealistic demands on children writing in a foreign language. Kroll and Wells (1983) (cited in Tann 1991:189) have identified stages through which English native-speaker children appear to progress, both in terms of their writing skills and their attitudes to writing. The *preparatory stage* is when the child acquires the basic mechanisms of handwriting and spelling, which become automatic for most children by the age of seven. This is preceded in most pre-school children by drawings and scribbling, which are not always as random as might first appear. From the age of around seven years and older, children reach the *consolidation stage,* where writing is still personal, colloquial, situational and context-bound (as in news time, writing captions for drawings, stories). Children are willing to rub out or alter letter shapes or spellings, but are rarely willing to revise or edit their work. Between seven and nine years of age many native-speaker children are becoming fluent story writers; Graves (cited in Tann 1991) suggests that by the age of nine children are more aware of the notion of *audience.* This means they develop much greater awareness of the fact that the success of writing depends on its communicative effectiveness with others, rather than writing being simply for oneself. Personal writing is still important at this stage, however. The *differentiation stage* at around nine or ten years of age shows evidence of writing structures becoming more distinct. The structure of a story, for example, becomes more shaped and organized and sentence structure becomes more formal and less colloquial. Children are more aware of a range of text types and the different purposes and audiences for these. The STRIMS project (Malmberg 1997), a longitudinal study of pupils' language development carried out in Sweden found that there were large individual differences in pupils' writing ability which appeared to be closely linked to their writing performance in their L1. Not surprisingly, pupils who struggle with writing in their L1 do not excel in writing a foreign language.

When should children learn to write in the foreign language?

Children learning English may not write very much in the first year or two. In Korea, for example, Lee (2001:23) writes that the seventh revision of the primary ELT curriculum 'deliberately and distortingly prohibits written English from being taught at the beginning stage'. He clearly disagrees with this view but official policy holds that since Korean teachers do not normally use English as a medium of instruction the introduction of written English from the first year would encourage teachers to teach English 'mainly by explanation in Korean'. In Austria, where writing used to be 'banned' in the early stages, some pupils were found to be inventing their own writing systems in order to capture a visual form of what they were learning. This is because writing is a good memory aid. In some contexts, such as Taiwan, pupils are expected to focus on writing in the foreign language class very quickly, sometimes even at the kindergarten stage (pre-school). Perhaps this is because written products easily provide a visible sign of effort to pupils, teachers and parents, even if the work does not provide evidence of real learning. Teachers need, therefore, to be especially sensitive to the different demands and purposes of written tasks they impose on their pupils and to be aware of a variety of ways of supporting their writing.

The initial stages

In the early stages of learning to write in an L2 young pupils may still be consolidating their concept of print. Copying at this level provides opportunities to practise handwriting, learn and consolidate their understanding of new vocabulary, develop an awareness of and confidence in English spelling and practise a range of simple sentence patterns they have learned to use in speaking. An important principle at all levels is that children should not be asked to write something that they cannot *say* in English. Pupils in the second year may move on to practise writing sentences and very simple, short texts. Much of this writing provides specific language practice, as in selecting and spelling words correctly, using the correct word order, using grammatical structures accurately and linking sentences together with simple conjunctions. Writing practice also helps gradually to widen and consolidate the range of vocabulary, grammatical structures and sentence patterns they can produce. It is helpful to provide plenty of practice in the meaning and spelling of basic words so their use is familiar and gradually becomes more automatic. Children enjoy personal writing, so it is a good idea to personalize writing tasks, where possible. The more pressing need is to ensure writing is contextualized and, where possible, sometimes relates to a real-life situation, as when pupils write up the results of a survey they have carried out with classmates. Older pupils will become more aware of writing for an audience and so displaying children's work and having them produce written work for others to read and respond to is a good idea.

English spelling

English spelling is illogical and difficult and is not easy for young children to learn. According to Palmer (1991), there are four main ways in which children learn the spelling of words: visual, auditory, linguistic and kinesthetic. From our reading of how children think and learn in chapter 3 this will come as no surprise. With *visual style*, learners respond to the shapes of words and the patterns of letter strings within them and have a feeling whether something 'looks right'. With *auditory style* it is better for learners to sound the word out as they can recognize the relationship between sounds and letters or groups of letters. With *kinesthetic style* spelling is a graphic-motor skill and the writer lets the hand remember the kind of movements and shapes made when producing words. *The linguistic style* is one some children might draw on as they grow older and develop skills in seeing relationships between words based on grammar, meaning, and so on. However, it is important to remember that a multi-sensory approach is probably best for all young learners. See Palmer (1991) for a list of 100 most basic spelling vocabulary.

There are many useful spelling games you can play with younger learners. Here are two examples.

Hide and seek encourages children to look at groups of words and to use the 'look, say, cover, write, check' approach.

Materials: Flashcards with selected words related to topics, units from coursebooks, etc.

Method: Choose one child to stick six (or more) of the words on the blackboard. The class close their eyes while one card is removed. The pupils then try to write down the missing word. After practice with the whole class, this can be played in groups of two to five. More than one card can be removed when the pupils are familiar with the game.

Noughts and crosses aims to practise personal spelling lists using the 'look, say, cover, write, check' approach.

Materials: A traditional noughts and crosses board divided into nine squares. Noughts and crosses cards to cover the squares. A set of flashcards.

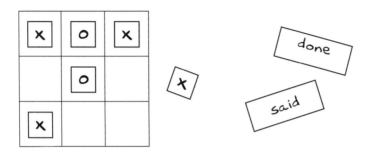

Method: Each player should have a set of cards showing some words which she finds difficult. This is given to the other player. The first player chooses a spelling word from the list, shows it to their partner and lays it face down on the table. The second player then tries to write down the spelling. If it is correct, she can cover one square on the noughts and crosses board. The game continues until one player has three cards lined up horizontally, vertically or diagonally on the board.

The 'look, say, cover, write, check' technique that you can teach your pupils for self-testing their spelling is as follows:

1 Look and notice the letter shapes and number of letters, think about the word and make a mental picture. Make this picture big then small, in different colours. If the word is right you can draw a real picture of the word.
2 Say the word and then the letters out loud. Listen carefully.
3 Write the word in the air with one finger several times, making it large and small.
4 Cover the word and try to write it correctly on paper, syllable by syllable.
5 Make sure you have a letter for each of the most important sounds.
6 See if it 'looks right'. If not change it.
7 Now check to see if the spelling is correct; if not, repeat stages 1–6.

Guidelines for a supportive writing classroom

- Reinforce the connection between writing and speaking English and reading and writing in English. Use a range of activities such as rhymes and stories, big books to show your enjoyment of reading and writing, and instill enthusiasm for reading and writing in the pupils.

- Try to develop an awareness of environmental print.

- Make sure your own classroom has many examples of English writing, functional print.

- Develop the concept of English letters with letter cards, magnetic or plasticine letters and alphabet games.

- Have special 'letter days' where children bring in things which begin in English with a particular letter. Label and display them.

- Count the words in a line of print or clap for each word spoken to develop a concept of word.

- Reinforce the concept of words and letters with alphabet songs, jingles and games.

- Create a Post Office with pupil made stamps, letters, envelopes and a post box. Have a Shop Corner with lots of written labels, such as Shop Open/Closed; board prices, shopping lists, play money.

- Help pupils build lists of high frequency words from their reading and writing using personal picture dictionaries.

- Compile a class news book where you write news very simply with the help of the class. This is then illustrated by the pupils (e.g. in a rota).

- Organize resources so that there are *word bank* cards placed around the room which pupils can refer to. The cards show a word and a picture, where possible, and are helpful for checking spellings and word meanings. They may be organized according to units in the coursebook, topics, spelling patterns, a story, and so on. Word cards can also be organized as *sentence makers* so that they make up whole sentences which the pupils piece together. Cards can also include simple punctuation such as full stops, question marks and exclamation marks, as shown below (taken from *Spot's Birthday Party*).

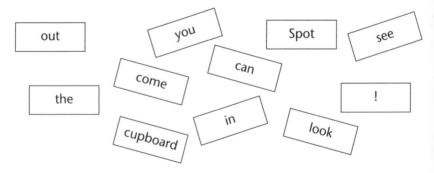

This kind of activity needs modelling, which you can do by having very large word cards which the pupils hold up in front of the class as you discuss the word order.

Writing in the later stages

After two years of English, many pupils will have mastered some of the more basic skills in writing and should be encouraged to produce writing for a specific context and audience which goes beyond the practice stage. Guided copying at sentence level and above can be supported through the use of support frameworks and graphic organizers such as pictures, written models, tickcharts, flow charts, grids, and so on (see chapter 9). These give learners support in producing written work within clearly defined constraints. For example, the use of a Venn diagram to classify information can provide a simple sentence pattern such as 'My guinea pig eats lettuce and my cat drinks milk but my tortoise eats lettuce and drinks milk too'.

Which diagram is correct?

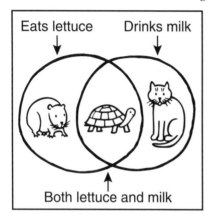
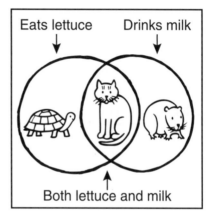

This sentence pattern, using the simple present tense and *but* to compare two pieces of information, can be used with a tickchart also. The next stage can be practice with more complex Venn diagrams, ending with the pupils creating their own diagrams for other pupils to create sentences. Pupils can also produce some of the activities outlined earlier, such as word search or gap-filling, for other pupils to complete.

If the children are asked to write riddles, for example, they must be able to produce their ideas in spoken English before they are asked to write sentences. They should also have a written version available for them to refer to. More creative writing activities, which encourage the children to compose their own sentences or texts, provide useful and motivating practice in planning, organizing ideas and understanding the conventions of discourse. As children grow in confidence some might like to become more involved in choosing text types for themselves. In planning the

123

vocabulary they want to use, they can do word maps for example, where they map out some of the key ideas and vocabulary for writing a description or even a poem (after being presented with a model and having access to word banks or a dictionary). Figure 18 is one for the word *tiger*.

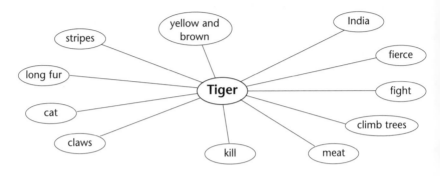

Fig. 18 A word map for tiger.

Charts with notes can also be used to provide support in organizing writing and can reduce some of the cognitive load of writing texts, as seen below.

Thinking questions	Language I need
What does this animal look like?	A tiger is …
	It has …
Where does it live?	It lives in …
What does it eat?	It eats …
How does it move?	It walks and runs … It can also …
What does it like doing?	It likes to …
	It likes climbing …
Anything else?	

This structure and set of sentence patterns can be recycled for describing different animals.

Even with older children, writing tasks should always be prepared for by specific activities, including the technique of modelling, which provides for the rehearsal of key vocabulary and structures. If writing is always strictly controlled, with children usually completing rather impersonal and mechanical exercises such as gap-filling, they will tend to lose interest in writing. It would be rather boring for all writing to remain at the practice level, although it is unrealistic to imagine that one can encourage creativity without specific practice at word or sentence level. *Dictogloss* is a creative way of using gap-filling and dictation that has been adapted for use with bilingual pupils of ten- and eleven-year-olds in the UK by Jupp and Harvey (1996) from an original idea of Wajnryb (1991). The basic procedure is:

1 Prepare pupils with a range of pre-listening activities to listen to a story to introduce the topic and key words. Give the pupils a list of the key words.

2 Read the story once, not too fast. After the first hearing the key words list is read through and pupils find the words. Pupils listen to the text a second time and while they listen they tick off the words from the list. Afterwards pupils complete gap-filling activities.

3 Pupils re-tell the story orally in pairs, using the completed gap-filling text and pictures.

4 Pupils now re-tell the story in writing working in pairs or individually, trying to reconstruct the text together. They do not try to reproduce the text exactly but recreate the main meanings with grammatical accuracy and well organized ideas.

5 Display finished versions and discuss the stories produced.

6 A variation is that pupils try to create a different ending.

7 This task involves listening for detail, predicting words, matching spoken to written words, working out what is missing from sentences by using memory, clues from visuals and the context and constructing coherent sentences. It also involves discussion and drafting and revising a text. It provides a good example of the way in which writing can be integrated with other skills and how pupils can produce writing collaboratively.

Guided activities at sentence level and above for older pupils may include putting words in the correct order, matching sentence halves and copying, gap-filling using visuals or words, writing captions for pictures, writing speech bubbles or dialogues, creating sentences from a tickchart, and sequencing sentences. Such activities provide practice in handwriting, spelling, identifying lexical sets, learning or reinforcing meaning, grammar patterns, organization of ideas and integrating writing with other skills.

It is useful to bear in mind that writing to communicate is also an important aspect of the writing process, thus it becomes increasingly important for teachers to create opportunities for older children to do this. Once some pupils have been studying English for three or four years they will be ready to produce a wider range of text types or longer pieces of work, provided they have support. This kind of activity develops skills in producing different kinds of text, for example, posters, advertisements, poems, plays, letters, menus, stories, factual accounts, instructions for making things, and so on. Here an awareness of text types, or genres, and their conventions is important. These might include features to do with layout, style and language used or how ideas are organized.

To develop a greater awareness of different text types, the children should ideally have collected, discussed, and read a variety of text types, perhaps in both the L1 and in English. Although the language in some of these texts is a little difficult, they are all adaptable and provide a humorous introduction to reading and writing text types. In fact, this kind of activity does not necessarily need to be kept until the last stage of learning; children can write very simple texts such as birthday cards at a much earlier stage. Producing different text types needs to be guided, but after modelling and rehearsal can also provide opportunities for pupils to express their own meanings and be more creative.

Personal writing includes such forms as diaries, shopping lists, reminders and recipes. Social writing may involve thank you letters, invitations, congratulations, text messages or instructions. Examples of public writing are letters to other classes, forms, posters, menus or class magazines. Creative writing can include shape poetry, riddles, stories, plays, songs or designing food packets. And study writing can include personal dictionaries and self-assessment.

When supporting writing tasks with older children it is important to keep the same basic principles in terms of preparing pupils through talk. The teacher should also be aware of the language demands and thinking demands. The language demands can be broken down into key language functions, such as identifying, describing and comparing people, places and things, writing instructions, describing a simple process or cause and effect, sequencing events or classifying. The language functions can then be analysed into key words, not just nouns but also verbs, adjectives and adverbs, and key sentence patterns. For older pupils the structure of the different text types can be represented by visuals or graphic organizers, so that, for example, a story has a flow chart of main events or a chart showing characters and events. Figure 19 represents the story *Princess Smartypants*:

The story	Action 1	Action 2 etc.
Who?	Princess Smartypants	
Where?	In the King and Queen's castle	
When?	It is time for her to marry a prince	
Action?	She tries to find a husband	
What's wrong?	She does not want to marry	
What happened next?	She asks a prince to do a very difficult task	
What happened in the end?	The prince cannot do the task	
And so?	She does not marry him!	

Fig. 19 Flow chart

With older pupils it is useful to provide variety and not ask them simply to write compositions or stories. Figure 20 below outlines some activities and their purposes.

Less guided/freer activities	Purposes
Write a range of text types based on a model e.g. a description, a postcard, menu, shopping list, greetings card, play, poem, riddle, joke, interview, a news article	To practise handwriting and spelling
	To reinforce understanding of word meanings, practise using new vocabulary and grammar patterns
Use a graphic e.g. a grid to describe characters, or a story chart or map to produce a new story, a cycle chart to describe the life cycle of an animal or alien	To practise word order within sentences
	To practise interpreting visual information
Re-tell a story with a different ending	To practise having and organizing ideas
Write a letter to a character in a story	To practise different types of layout
Write up a survey, investigation or mini-project.	
Correct mistakes in a written text	

Fig. 20 Activities and their purposes

Although many of the activities in this chapter have been described under separate headings, it can be seen how they usually link with other skills. For example, a reading activity can be based on listening to a story, which in turn may lead to re-writing the ending. This integration of skills is important, especially as the pupils make progress and become more confident in using English.

Responding to writing

The way in which teachers respond to or mark writing will depend on the kind of writing focus the writing activity practises and the age and language level of the pupils. Where the focus is on *surface features* such as handwriting or spelling or on *language forms*, such as new vocabulary and sentence patterns, and the activity is based on very tightly controlled copying, you are more likely to insist upon accuracy. Pupils may receive grades, gold stars, marks out of ten, and so on. The main point is to develop a sense of what each child is capable of, so that you build up a picture of when a child has tried very hard or has been rather sloppy. You can then recognize both accuracy and effort.

Where pupils are struggling to incorporate their own words or meanings into sentences or texts which are not so tightly controlled, the teacher may be more inclined to comment on the content and the child's willingness to 'have a go' at writing. In this case you might want to write short comments such as *Very interesting/exciting/funny. I enjoyed your story; I liked your ending; Can you tell me why...? Can you think of some other ...? What do you think ...? Well done. You have tried hard.* (See chapter 18 for more on stickers and stamps to show progress.)

9 English across the curriculum

In this chapter we will consider the reasons for creating links between language learning and the primary curriculum. We then turn to starting points and techniques for this approach and ways of creating a supportive, cross-curricular classroom.

Why make cross-curricular links?

Linguists, such as Widdowson (1978) and van Lier (1996), have suggested that teaching EFL in the school sector is very effective if it is linked to school subjects and topics since it is not only time-efficient but in terms of school-aged pupils is more authentic than simply learning English for social purposes. This approach has become more popular at primary level since the 1990s and has been described in the earlier works of Holderness (1991), Halliwell (1992), Brewster (1999) and others. In Spain the Reforma guidelines for the new curriculum state that 'foreign languages can be instrumental in developing an interdisciplinary/globalizing approach, e.g. through project work based on the environment. Pupils can use the L2 to express knowledge they have acquired from other areas of the curriculum. Drama, Music, and Art and Craft are obvious areas that can be linked with foreign language study'.

Many countries are now interested in this approach and some have been trying it out for some time, including Austria, the Basque country, Finland and Portugal. Interest in using a range of topics, both general ones and those more related to school subjects, is stimulated by some of the characteristics they seem to have in common. They draw upon pupils' everyday experience, thus allowing for links to be made between home and school and encouraging pupils to bring general or school knowledge to their language work. If they are based on the children's interests, they are motivating and engaging. They meet the children's educational needs by reinforcing concepts, content and learning skills which are useful in other curriculum areas. They offer possibilities for the exploration of both facts and imagination and creativity.

Creating cross-curricular links for language learning has the potential of creating a learning environment which caters more clearly for pupils' wider educational needs and interests. The decision to use topics, investigations, or stories to link language learning with the curriculum is inevitably influenced by several factors. These include:

the teachers: important considerations are teachers' views on language learning and teaching; their language level and confidence in trying innovations, and their knowledge of a range of suitable activity types to develop lessons and materials

the learners: their age and interests; their linguistic and conceptual level; their motivation and familiarity with different styles of learning

the learning/teaching context itself: important issues are the amount of time available; the type of syllabus and materials in use, and the attitude of parents or head teachers towards this kind of work

Starting points for cross-curricular work

According to Brown and Brown (1996) schools that decide to use a cross-curricular approach need to look at language teaching from a different angle and with broader learning aims. Starting points for this kind of language learning approach can be: *topics:* chosen to link with work already being done in the rest of the curriculum; *issues:* can include socio-cultural themes connected with citizenship, such as comparing cultural practices of different countries, stereotyping, developing cross-cultural tolerance, the environment, etc.; *skills and strategies:* focus on learning skills and strategies across the curriculum e.g. measuring, word processing, using the internet, making and interpreting charts to transfer information, using timelines to sequence events in a famous persons' or a child's life, etc.; *resources:* can be linked to other curricular areas such as Maths, Nature/Environmental Studies, Science, Geography, etc.

Topics and issues

The list below gives examples of different subjects that can be used to develop topics or issues.

Mathematics: numbers, counting and quantity (counting games, rhymes and songs), measuring, telling the time, shapes and patterns, money

Science: how seeds grow, magnetism, cogs and wheels, floating and sinking, the qualities of different types of paper, our teeth, bones and skeletons, healthy eating, sounds, science from rhymes

History: understanding chronology/the passing of time, prehistoric animals, customs and festivals from earlier ages, money through the ages

Geography and the Environment: shops and shopping, parks, sports and games, using maps and atlases, the weather and climates, volcanoes and earthquakes, the journey of a letter, road safety and environment

Cultural Studies: famous people from other countries, lifestyles and festivals around the world – similarities and differences (see chapter 10)

Art and Craft: (linked to topics, stories, etc.) drawing and printing, making masks, puppets, models, collages and posters, aesthetic appreciation

Teachers of younger children will obviously choose topics of more general interest. Nowadays you will find many examples of topics in children's coursebooks. Starting points for topics can also arise from the pupils themselves.

Task 1
Think about your own teaching and consider the following questions.

1   Are there any topics in the language coursebook you use which you could extend?

2   Are there any topics which seem more popular than others? Why do you think this is?

3   Do you sometimes think of your own topics to use for language learning?

4   Are your pupils ever involved in choosing topics?

5   What are your favourite ways of choosing and using topics? Do you find stories, songs or rhymes which link to the theme? Adapt L1 content/subject books from your school's primary curriculum? Adapt content/topics written originally in English? Use the coursebook mainly but add some extra theme-based activities? Ask the children/ monitor what their current interests are?

A useful starting point in using a topic is to make a 'topic web' which can help you pin-point the kinds of activities which could be used. You can also work out the language practice and concepts which can be derived from these activities. The general topic web for planning a topic (see Fig. 21) might provide you with some ideas, while Fig. 22 shows the detail for a project on Christmas.

Figure 23 is a mind map taken from a Swedish EFL coursebook called *Portfolio, Topic Books, Heroes* which helps pupils to plan their *own* topics where they can practise research skills. This would be especially good for the faster pupils or any who are bilingual.

Language and learning skills and strategies

School language springs from a core of thinking and learning skills which the child can transfer across different subjects. This is the case for children

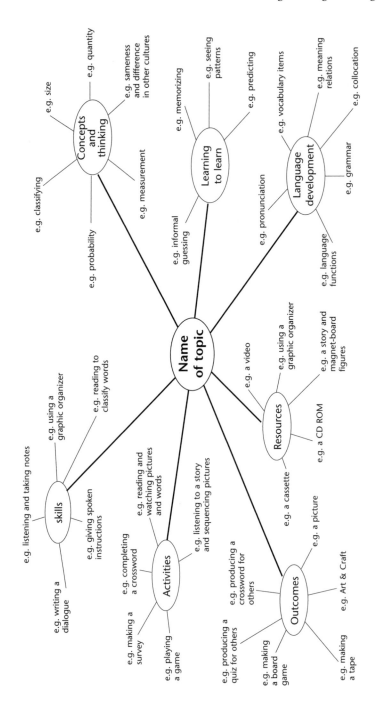

Fig. 21 A general topic web for planning a topic

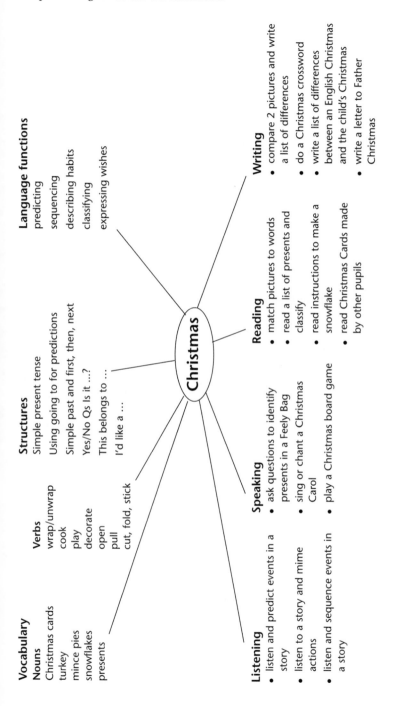

Vocabulary

Nouns
Christmas cards
turkey
mince pies
snowflakes
presents

Verbs
wrap/unwrap
cook
play
decorate
open
pull
cut, fold, stick

Structures
Simple present tense
Using going to for predictions
Simple past and first, then, next
Yes/No Qs Is it …?
This belongs to …
I'd like a …

Language functions
predicting
sequencing
describing habits
classifying
expressing wishes

Christmas

Listening
- listen and predict events in a story
- listen to a story and mime actions
- listen and sequence events in a story

Speaking
- ask questions to identify presents in a Feely Bag
- sing or chant a Christmas Carol
- play a Christmas board game

Reading
- match pictures to words
- read a list of presents and classify
- read instructions to make a snowflake
- read Christmas Cards made by other pupils

Writing
- compare 2 pictures and write a list of differences
- do a Christmas crossword
- write a list of differences between an English Christmas and the child's Christmas
- write a letter to Father Christmas

Fig. 22 Planning language for a topic on Christmas

133

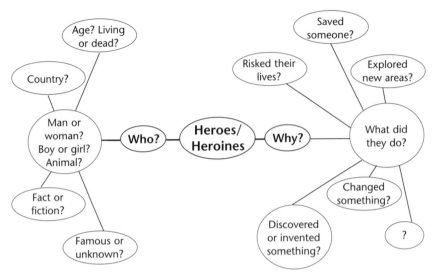

Fig. 23 A mind map for planning a topic

working both in their L1 and in an L2 when using the cross-curricular approach. Being able to use and interpret the notion *cause and effect,* for example, is a key skill children should be able to do in their first language so that they can cope with the demands of Mathematics, Geography, or Science, and so on. Developing skills in learning how to learn encourages a range of thinking strategies, such as classifying, predicting, problem-solving and hypothesising, as well as study skills, such as making and understanding charts and graphs, and organizing work. It helps to provide continuity between the learning processes established in learning English and the rest of the curriculum. (For further details see chapter 5.)

Below is a list of most of the general learning skills and strategies, which link directly to language learning skills.

- *observing* objects, actions and processes e.g. copying

- *memorizing* objects, actions and processes e.g. rote learning of spellings

- *carrying out actions, analysing* and *experimenting* with things, actions and processes e.g. carrying out investigations, surveys and experiments

- *seeing patterns and connections* between objects, actions and processes e.g. to describe, match, compare and contrast, classify, sequence, i.e. kinds of problem-solving activities

- *interpreting the symbolic representations* of information, such as the alphabet, timelines, flow charts, matrices, diagrams, maps

- *interpreting* the meaning of texts and visuals

- *reflecting on* and *evaluating* actions and learning e.g. self assessment

- *developing language awareness* e.g. sameness and difference between languages

You can see how these skills and activities link up with the eight intelligences as described in chapter 3. If these are the kinds of things pupils are being asked to do all the time in their school learning then it makes sense to exploit them further in their language learning.

Resources

Using resources from other areas of the curriculum can help children to develop confidence in using them and helps provide continuity in their learning (e.g. using an alphabet frieze, measuring cups or scales, rulers and measuring tapes, an atlas or globe, a time- or number–line). A good source of ideas is subject books in English. You may need to drop the level of the books you consider. If you want to use cross-curricular ideas with Year 5 then look at curriculum books in English for Year 3 or 4, otherwise it is likely to be too difficult. You may be able to access web sites, such as the BBC website www.bbc.co.uk/education/home and www.teachingideas.co.uk that have many useful materials and resources. The reference section at the end provides some sources for obtaining cross-curricular resources provided for children in the UK.

Task 2
The relevance to you of this list of eight possible benefits of using a cross-curricular approach will depend on your context, the age and language learning experiences of your pupils, the resources available, and so on. Read them and decide which ones seem particularly important to you. Can you add any other benefits or disadvantages?

1 It can be motivating and provide variety for the teacher and the pupil.

2 It can be used to reinforce pupils' conceptual development, for example, colours, size, shape, time, and so on.

3 It can provide consolidation of aspects of language learning in the L1 e.g. alphabetical order, word order, spelling, parts of speech, the use of dictionaries. It also helps pupils notice differences between languages, the uses of literacy, different ways we communicate.

4 The transfer of skills and reinforcement of concepts between different areas of the curriculum helps children to learn how to learn.

5 It can be used to reinforce other subjects and concepts in the curriculum.

6 Curriculum resources can be recycled for language teaching e.g. diagrams, skeletons, maps, measuring equipment, etc.

7 It can encourage collaborative teaching and planning between subject teachers and language teachers and help to reduce any feelings of isolation the language teacher may have.

8 It offers exploration of facts, imagination and creativity.

Problems and questions

Naturally, we must be aware that there are some possible problem areas when using cross-curricular work. Here we shall consider four: topic overlap and overkill; the relationship between learning facts or learning language; the balance between a product-focused approach or a process-focused approach; and the problem of finding resources.

To what extent should the topics or skills used in cross-curricular English work already be familiar to the pupils? Do teachers introduce a new concept or skill for the first time in English? Many feel that the answer is definitely not for children under eight or nine and probably not even for older pupils. Of course, this answer does not hold true for pupils working in English-medium/immersion contexts, such as in Singapore and countries with bilingual schools, who will frequently have new concepts and skills presented in a foreign language.

How many times can pupils do popular topics, such as Dinosaurs before they are thoroughly bored and demotivated? One way of choosing topics is to ask the pupils themselves. (See chapter 6 for results of a survey on favourite topics.) Teachers have to be careful that pupils do not simply copy out whole chunks of writing from topic books or the internet, without understanding what they are copying. Copying is easy to do and provides an obvious product, but it does not involve real learning or use of language and thinking. You need to think about the balance you want to create between memorizing or learning facts and gaining information from the resources you have collected, encouraging the development of language and thinking processes and skills. In our view the latter is preferable; the learning of facts will be a side-effect.

There are not many cross-curricular materials in print, although many teachers are creating their own and perhaps sharing them with others. This is very time-consuming, although for some teachers creating materials is something they very much enjoy. Some help is provided for creating and using materials and resources in the next few sections.

What skills do teachers need for cross-curricular work?

In an ideal world the skills a teacher would have in order to plan cross-curricular language teaching are given in the task below. Do not worry if you do not have any or only a few of them!

Task 3

How many of these skills do you think you have at the moment? How many would be useful or interesting to develop in the future?

1 ability to analyse the language and thinking demands of topics and lessons, to plan the language focus, including language objectives in terms of necessary vocabulary, grammatical patterns and language functions which need to be modelled and rehearsed

2 capacity to analyse the language required for activities and tasks in terms of skills or strategies which need to be modelled and rehearsed

3 ability to draw upon your knowledge about language or language processes and to use this knowledge when devising activities and tasks

4 an understanding of the principles and practice of using a wide variety of activities which support learning at appropriate levels

5 capacity to stage activities so that some draw upon the skills and language developed in previous activities to provide recycling of language and task continuity

6 an understanding of the management of learning so that key factors such as organizing and monitoring groups help support some independent learning, where appropriate

Information relating to the first skill is in this chapter. Skills two to five are developed in Part 2, while skill six is addressed in chapters 16 and 17.

Linking old knowledge with the new

As part of the pre-activity stage, children can do a mind map or concept map, or write a list of key words to describe what they already know. This can be done in the L1 at first if necessary and the key words translated into English. It can also be done through answering a set of questions in the form of a quiz, with the answers compared at the end of the topic. Or it can be done by the children writing a list of questions about the topic they would like to find answers to, or through the children making predictions and then checking for correctness.

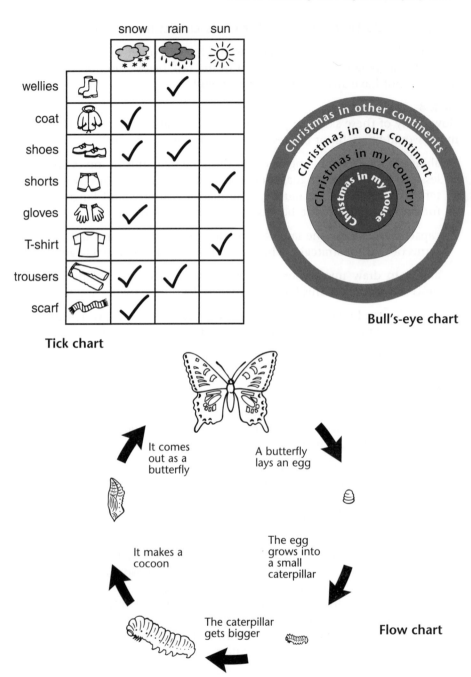

Tick chart

Bull's-eye chart

Flow chart

Fig. 24 Examples of visual support

	orange	yellow	red	green
round	orange	sweet corn	strawberry apple raspberry	apple
oval		lemon		lime
long & thin	carrot	banana	chilli pepper	chilli pepper

Grid/matrix

Which diagram is correct?

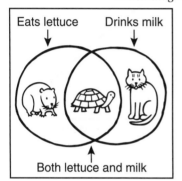

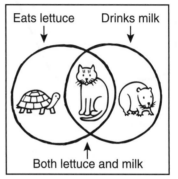

Venn diagram

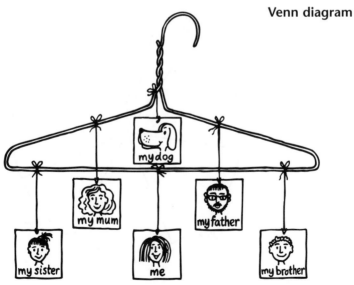

Tree diagram

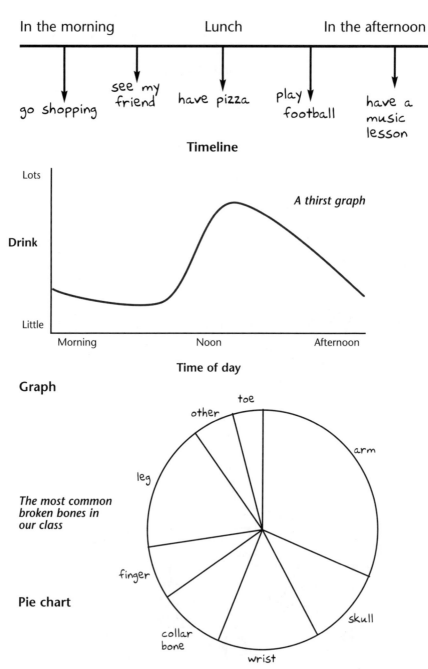

Fig. 24 Examples of visual support

Catering for learning styles

Auditory and kinesthetic support can be provided with the help of action rhymes and songs, stories, games and drama. For topics linked to Science and Maths this can be provided by engaging pupils in simple experiments or surveys where children are actively engaged in doing something (see page 145 on *Investigations into Pens*). The list of activities linked to the eight intelligences (see chapter 3) shows how we can use a whole host of activities such as word games, reading puzzles, drawings, craft work, surveys, and diagrams. The outcomes could include a drama, a set of posters, a play, creative writing, and so on. It may be useful to share these with another class, or even parents, which then provides a meaningful and purposeful context.

We have seen how many learners have a visual style which of course plays an important part in cross-curricular work. Along with the usual array of visuals, there are also other useful graphics, called *graphic organizers* or *visual frameworks*, based on the work of Mohan (1986), who works with teachers of bilingual children in Canada (for more on this see also Brewster 1999, Chamot and O'Malley 1994, Hooper 1996 and Tang 1992). These organizers help to link any background knowledge pupils have to new knowledge. Most of all, they help to structure the information which is contained in a story, or poster or description and so provide scaffolding for both language and thinking. Figure 24 shows guidelines for developing and using key visuals. Table 5 shows how these link with activities, thinking and language.

When teachers plan to use a key visual to link language learning with content learning they need to: consider the main learning and language learning focus of the lesson; analyse the thinking and language demands of the main learning expected; link this to an appropriate visual and activities; organize work in pairs or groups as appropriate; use the planned activities supported by key visuals to draw on pupils' existing knowledge, model new language, allow for rehearsal and consolidation and application of their new knowledge. These guidelines are represented by the key visuals chart (Fig. 25).

More on stories and investigations

Many stories can easily be used to tie in language learning with a wide variety of cross-curricular topics. Even if we take a less obvious area, such as citizenship and equality of the sexes, there are several contemporary fairy tales, rewritten as satires, which have this modern theme (see, for example, *The Paperbag Princess* and *Princess Smartypants*, both of which can be used to encourage pupils to think about gender stereotypes), as well as teaching new vocabulary, structures and language functions.

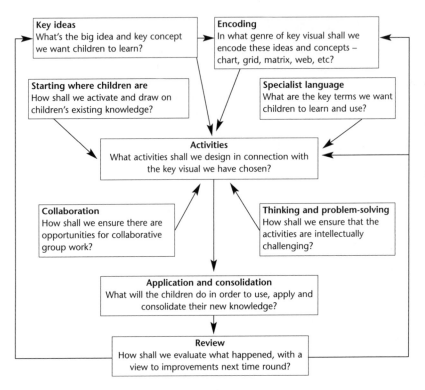

Fig. 25 Developing and using key visuals

(adapted from Cooke in BLS 1999:27)

Other stories like *The Mixed-Up Chameleon*, or *Something Else*, encourage pupils to develop tolerance towards other people by discussing sameness and difference. Two other well-known stories, such as *The Very Hungry Caterpillar* and *You'll Soon Grow into them Titch* provide a rich vein of ideas for talking about topics such as numbers, size, days of the week, food, the passing of time and the life cycle of the caterpillar. *Day and Night* has useful pictures to compare daytime activities with those done at night. This could be linked to a story like *The Owl who was Afraid of the Dark*. *Peace at Last* is a story about a mother trying to find somewhere nice and quiet and could be linked to a topic on Sounds. The possibilities are endless! For more ideas see Ellis and Brewster (2002).

Investigations and surveys

Constructivist approaches to teaching Science, current in the UK, is largely based on the pupils carrying out simple experiments and surveys,

Activity	Types of thinking	Key visuals	Key language	Examples
Matching	identifying, labelling, naming, describing, measuring, estimating, describing cause and effect/problems and solutions	flashcards; cards for Snap, Bingo, Dominoes, maps, labelled diagrams,/ diagrams with captions, tables, matrices	This goes with/matches this … These are the same/different; this belongs to; if …then … An X is a kind of …/A Y is a person who …; so	matching pictures, words, numbers, patterns, Odd One Out, words + definitions, cause + effect e.g. of Volcanoes, labelling a skeleton
Sorting	classifying, defining, generalizing, comparing, contrasting	tree diagrams, tables, tickcharts, Venn diagrams	This belongs to.. these belong together because... they are all... they are in the same family/set; these are the same/different; this is the same as /different from	classifying things under headings e.g. types of food; sorting things e.g. into objects which a magnet attracts/doesn't attract; sorting toys for girls, boys, and toys for both
Sequencing	Sequencing, describing processes and cycles, narrating events, or chronological order	time lines, flow charts, cycle diagrams, picture/diagram sequences	This comes/goes first, second, next etc. First we have/there is…; finally we have … Before Y …; we have X …; Y … comes after X …	Alphabetical order, working out the stages of something e.g. making lemonade, working out the stages of the life cycle of a butterfly, sequencing pictures from a story
Ranking	evaluating, judging size, importance etc., applying criteria, selecting, comparing	rating tables, continua, bull's eye charts	This is the most/least common/important etc. This is not so important; this is the favourite	choosing 10 things to take on holiday/ a trip to the Moon etc. evaluating their usefulness, choosing best sites e.g. for building a castle, ranking reasons e.g. why plants die

Table 5 Types of activities linked to thinking, language and visual support

referred to as *investigations*. Investigations and surveys provide a useful way of consolidating language learning and can also help to develop curricular concepts and thinking skills. Investigations can also link up with History or Geography. An investigation usually starts with a specific question, such as: Which paper is the best for writing on? How does writing on different kinds of paper compare? Which pen gives us the best value for money? Who has the biggest/smallest feet in this class? What is the most common month for birthdays in this class? How many different kinds of rubbish can we find in our playground? What can we do about this to improve our environment?

A useful procedure is to consider the following, ideally involving the pupils as much as possible:

- an interesting question, perhaps one which links to a current topic

- aspects of the question the pupils need to find out more about and where they can find the answers

- a procedure for organizing the investigation e.g. collecting things, asking questions using simple questionnaires or surveys, using worksheets based on informative texts

- the kind of language the investigation will develop in terms of new vocabulary, structures, language functions and skills

- the kinds of modelling and rehearsal the pupils will need to practise and consolidate this language

- a way of recording results/producing an outcome

Activities for useful investigations are given below.

- *Predicting, counting:* e.g. If I throw two dice six times, which number will come up the most often? Pupils predict, then discuss how to keep a simple record and compare results.

- *Measuring area, ranking:* e.g. Who has the biggest hands and feet in our class? Pupils predict the area of their hands and feet; draw around the hand/foot on squared paper; count squares (make rules about this) and rank them in order of size.

- *Measuring and comparing length and weight:* e.g. Who is the heaviest/ tallest? Is the tallest the heaviest? Children measure members of their group and rank them; class records data and draws a graph; investigation of the heaviest man in the world, using *The Guinness Book of Records.*

- *Experimenting, classifying:* e.g. Which materials are attracted to magnets? Pupils predict using a tickchart, then experiment with small objects and record their results. Results are compared with predictions.

- *Making and using maps and plans:* e.g. Who makes the most journeys in a day? Children compare the number and length of journeys each child makes in one day, e.g. to school, to the shops, to friends, etc.; draw these on maps. What would be the ideal park? Investigate local parks to make plans showing the kinds of facilities they have; children evaluate them and devise their ideal.

A specific example of 'Which is the best pen for writing and colouring?' is given in Fig. 26. Here pupils carry out a kind of consumer survey. Discuss the things that make a good pen and try to make questions using a regular language pattern such as Does it...? or How much...? How many...? Having been introduced to new language and having practised it, pupils then copy the questions and try out different pens using a star system. Once all the pens have been tested, pupils decide which is the best.

Questions	1	2	3	4	5	6
Does it write well?						
Does it draw well?						
Does it smudge?						
How many colours does it have?						
How much is it?						

Fig. 26 Investigation into Pens

Investigations and surveys give scope for learners to work at different levels according to their ability and language level. Some of the methods suggested here may be more easily adopted by primary English teachers who spend all day with one class than by those who are visiting English teachers. If you are one of this second group of teachers, the only way you may be able to do this is to work with the class teacher to find out which concepts and topics the pupils have been learning about. This will require a great deal of commitment but can lead to a greatly increased understanding of how children think and learn.

10 Culture

Learning about culture through foreign languages

Thanks to e-mail and the internet, pop music, satellite and cable TV, many young learners can experience the real value of English in their daily lives. With this trend towards globalization through improved communication, national policies on culture and education in countries like Taiwan are beginning to lay emphasis on absorbing aspects of foreign cultures. On a wider level an increasing number of countries, such as those within the European Union, include *cultural awareness* and *intercultural learning* as part of their educational and language teaching policies to promote international understanding and world peace. This is often outlined under the heading of *citizenship,* where ideas of 'education for peace' and tolerance towards others are promoted (see chapter 9).

Why teach culture within a foreign language programme?

Let us take a moment to consider definitions of two key terms, *cultural awareness* and *intercultural learning,* provided by Kubanek-German (2000:50). The first refers to 'an awareness that we are affected in our actions by culture'. The second refers to 'the ability to see oneself as part of a larger community, to contrast cultures, to be aware that a different language is embodying different cultural beliefs, behaviours and meanings'. According to Brewster et al. (1992:32) 'the role of the teacher is to encourage and help bring about this discovery, drawing attention to the fact that the differences in relation to the pupils' own habits and day-to-day lives are to be seen in a positive light. This awareness adds to the sum of pupils' knowledge of humanity and of the world'. According to Jones (1995), 'awareness of others' helps to develop an understanding of a wide range of cultural issues which include the following:

- similarities and differences between groups of different language communities
- social conventions
- things which are unfamiliar within a target language community
- stereotypes, as perceived by one linguistic group about another
- language as culture

He also suggests that this kind of cross-cultural understanding and tolerance tends to have the effect of making young people more aware of *their own* culture.

Not using foreign language lessons to also teach about culture may be a lost opportunity. However, according to Kubanek-German (2000:50), a complicating factor is that we do not have as yet a good understanding of how children form ideas and judgements about other countries and cultures. She adds that there has been virtually no research in primary ELT to consider the impact of foreign language lessons on young learners' emerging intercultural awareness nor on what processes might be involved.

Until recently the cultural dimension of language teaching programmes was rather neglected. The communicative approach tended to put the emphasis on teaching communicative functions of the language to the detriment of the culture. Literature-based foreign language study for older students often emphasised culture, sometimes to the detriment of language. Some English language materials published for the international market have depicted the target culture (i.e. American or British culture) in a way that has not taken into account the need for cultural appropriacy in their choice of topics. On the one hand we have the views of people like Maley (1999) who suggest that many international coursebooks are 'bland' and 'uncontroversial'. On the other, we have views like that of primary and secondary coursebook writer, Freebairn (2000) who discusses the need to question the assumption that learners will want to discuss more controversial topics. She also refers to writers' difficulties in finding topics which are at the same time suitable for language teaching and culturally appropriate for a wide range of contexts. Of course, these are the problems of international coursebook publishers, who aim to appeal to as wide a group of learners as possible. This is a good opportunity for teachers to supplement the coursebook so that it includes more culturally relevant topics.

Teaching culture through language

So far, we have seen how there is now a strong political will to include aspects of intercultural learning in FLL. In the past there was little systematic or explicit focus on how far to link culture and language and perhaps an uncertainty about how to teach it. More recently many materials have included an explicit focus on culture in the form of concrete activities which are carefully integrated into the language objectives of the materials (see Briggs and Ellis (1995), Ellis (1997) and Mary Glasgow Magazines at www.link2English.com). In this kind of material there is a clear focus on language and culture to produce both linguistic and cultural outcomes. In addition, some teaching material provides background cultural information in an attempt to develop cultural awareness and cross-cultural comparison (see Ellis and Brewster 2002).

What to teach

Provided it is motivating and not too abstract, early FLL has a good chance of encouraging children to take an interest and develop a positive attitude towards foreign countries and their culture. In their contact with the L2, both in and out of school, primary pupils will often learn a range of details about the target culture, especially everyday life, traditional elements of children's lore, such as songs, rhymes, games, stories, special festivals and celebrations. This can often be presented in visual form, perhaps in a specific English corner. Where possible, encourage learners to look at and use real evidence. If the pupils are very young, teachers can try to collect and use realia, such as typical food, toys or clothes. Other items might include real texts, such as books, children's comics, menus, football magazines, TV programme guides, food containers and labels, video or audio material, such as cartoons and films, or real objects such as T-shirts, football kit, and so on. Items can be collected by a whole range of people during school visits, holidays, business trips and school exchanges. The pupils themselves can collect realia for their own class and others.

This brings us to the notion of authenticity. Kubanek-German (2000:50) writes that striving for authenticity at all costs is rather naïve, as there is now so much cultural cross-over. Are *hamburgers* really German or American or British? She suggests that in the absence of real material from the target culture it is acceptable for teachers to talk about their own experiences with the target culture or to draw on that of their pupils. The question of which English-speaking culture to focus on is also worth considering. Many students today want to study American culture in preference to British culture. Perhaps with older learners there could be some consideration of the differences between these and other English-speaking cultures.

How to teach culture

The main point about linking language and culture is not to teach 'facts' about England or the USA. If we take the more current 'ethnographic' view, teachers are aiming to encourage pupils to make discoveries about culture for themselves. Here are some guidelines to consider:

- Present aspects of culture from a child's perspective.

- Use authentic materials where possible, but do not worry too much if you do not have any.

- Try to create or exploit authentic situations e.g. how an English girl celebrates her birthday (a birthday cake, candles, presents, etc.).

- Encourage the use of skills such as observing, questioning, comparing, reflecting, discussing, researching information.

- Think of the ways you can exploit the materials by focusing on specific language, simplifying and limiting the range of language.

- Think of the kinds of skills work – listening, speaking, reading and writing – which link up to the topic or activity (see chapter 9).

Observing and comparing

From the first year onwards, pupils may be introduced to fictional characters – boys and girls of their own age, their families, their friends – who feature in the sketches, stories and anecdotes contained in the teaching materials. One of the most common activities in developing cross-cultural understanding is observing and comparing life in the pupils' home country with life in English-speaking countries. This provides a very rich vein of ideas which can be explored in many interesting and creative ways. When discussing differences, teachers should be careful that they and the pupils emphasise positive opinions rather than what appears very bizarre or unpleasant. Where facilities allow, older pupils might like to make comparisons of things that are the same and different *between* English-speaking countries, for example, South Africa and the USA. Projects on comparing aspects of British and American life would be interesting, if resources allow, for twelve-year-olds with good language ability. In addition to these aspects of daily life, a certain amount of geographical or historical detail may crop up naturally in textbooks and other materials.

Starting points for teaching culture

The main starting points for teaching culture include:

Songs and rhymes These are useful for younger children and allow them to compare these English rhymes with their own. Skipping and counting rhymes are a good source. Teach some English rhymes, then ask pupils to teach you some of the ones they use. See chapter 12 for more information.

Drawings If you can make contact with another teacher abroad or have an English-speaking friend with children, you can ask them to make large drawings of some very simple things, but which tend to be strongly influenced by culture. Just asking a French, German and an English child to draw *bread* or a favourite meal (labelled) may show up many similarities and differences.

Artefacts You may be lucky enough to have an example of the latest toy which is popular in English-speaking countries. If you have one of these you can show it to the class, describe it and see if anyone else has one. All kinds of artefacts can be used.

Stories are a very appropriate way to introduce culture (see chapter 14 and Ellis and Brewster 2002).

Making contact with real people Slightly older pupils can be encouraged to carry out a range of activities, such as interviewing any native speakers available, writing requests for information, asking native speakers to provide written information, making class links with target language speakers by letter, internet, or e-mail.

Projects or topics Many of the topic-based magazines available from certain publishers make this task much easier. There is also a small but growing number of 'stand-alone' videos (and accompanying teachers' notes) which describe life in English-speaking countries. When planning a topic you could use the topic plans as outlined in chapter 9. Topics such as a typical school day, festivals, sporting personalities, pop stars, heroes, film celebrities can also be studied in the same way through whatever themes and areas of interest happen to be the subject of study.

Figure 27 below summarizes some of the ways we can introduce cultural awareness with different age groups.

Starting point	Associated material	Cultural focus	Linguistic focus	Curriculum links
A rhyme from Britain: *1, 2, 3, 4, Please come in and shut the door*	Video and activity book: *Play it Again*	Comparing a school day in Britain to own	Numbers, times, What time do you ...?	Maths Drama
A song from America: *Today is Monday*	Storybook: *Today is Monday*	Comparing weekly food customs	Food. Days of the week. What do you eat on ...?	Science Music
A song from Britain: *London Bridge is falling down*	Postcards/map of London	London Bridge through the ages Capital cities: London	Where's ...?	History Geography Music
A game from Britain: *What's the time Mr Wolf?*	Storybook: *What's the time Mr Wolf?*	Playground/ party games Meals and meal times	Meals What's the time? What time do you have ...?	Maths
A story from Britain: *The Snowman* and a finger play *Two fat gentlemen*	Video: *The Snowman*	Daily timetables Greetings	What time do you...? How do you do/Hi/Hello/ Good morning	Maths

Fig. 27 Examples of starting points for developing cultural awareness

11 Selecting materials

There is now an abundance of English language teaching material available on the market, covering different aspects of language learning and language use. It ranges from general courses, in several volumes and supported by technology, to specialized books which concentrate on one aspect of English, such as vocabulary, or one specific skill, such as listening, or books containing collections of games, songs, rhymes, etc. At the time of writing, there are now over twenty teacher's handbooks from major British ELT publishing houses on the primary market ranging from more theoretical to practical titles. (For recent reviews see Hughes 2000 and Williams 2000.) *The Keltic Guide to ELT Materials 2000* at www.keltic.co.uk lists over forty coursebooks for children and this does not include those that have come and gone over the last decade or those which have been written for specific markets. (Useful reviews of course materials for young learners include Ur 1985, Sinclair and Ellis 1992, Rixon 1992, Williams 1995.) All of these publications represent a wealth and variety of resources for the teacher to choose from and with the possibility of on-line purchasing, they are easily available. However, faced with this vast range, what are some of the key questions teachers can ask to help identify the potential strengths of coursebooks and to select the most appropriate for their particular teaching context?

Aims and objectives

Before selecting materials familiarize yourself with the aims of your teaching programme and any ministry documents that provide guidelines. The basic aim is to prepare children to benefit fully from the more formal language teaching they will get at secondary school. Psychologically, this means that they will become aware that what they say and write in their L1 can be said and written in another language. Linguistically and culturally, this means they will learn new phenomena and ways of living through different aspects of everyday life. It is important that the teaching materials used should take the child forward as directly as possible towards your aims and objectives. The objectives should be decided first, in line with the overall aims of the teaching programme, and then materials should be sought which can be related to these objectives.

Methodology

The general methodology associated with primary teaching must contribute to the general aim of all subjects taught at that level and is also an important criterion for the selection of materials. Learning activities must present and practise English in a systematic and comprehensive way so that new language items can be assimilated by the pupil. There is sometimes a tendency when working with young learners to use activities for their own sake, because they are enjoyable or because they 'work' as activities, without due regard to their value as language learning exercises. The things our pupils do in class should be interesting and enjoyable, but they should also be carefully examined in terms of their language teaching and learning potential and how they relate to what has previously been learned and what is to be learned.

Why use a coursebook?

Most teachers of English use a coursebook and there are a number of good reasons for doing so. For example, it is a useful learning aid for the pupil. It can identify what should be taught/learned, and the order in which to do it. It can indicate what methodology should be used. It can provide, attractively and economically, all or most of the materials needed. It reduces the teacher's workload. It can provide a link between the school and home.

Some teachers may have to use one coursebook only, taking their pupils through it from beginning to end and completing tests. Others may be able to use materials from several different books, adapting them where necessary and supplementing them with original material they have produced themselves. It is rare, however, to meet a teacher who does not, to a greater or lesser extent, draw on published teaching material, as producing original materials is a difficult and time-consuming process. Many coursebooks, however, are general in that they are designed to satisfy a general international market. As these courses do not have one particular group of pupils in mind, many used to take an English-speaking country as a setting along with corresponding sets of cultural values. Courses today present a much more global view of the world.

No teacher should allow the coursebook to set the objectives, let alone allow 'teaching the coursebook' to be the objective. In reality, the coursebook often becomes the teaching programme. If the teacher has established that the aims of the course and those of the coursebook are reasonably complementary, there seems limited reason for objection, although the chosen book may need to be adapted to the particular requirements of the class.

Selecting a coursebook

Different courses have different aims and claim to reach different objectives. The starting point for selecting a book for many teachers will probably be publishers' catalogues or the information on the back of the book. There is a variety of aims and methodology that abound in the world of ELT materials, so this information does not always tell us enough. It is also useful to look at the contents charts (also called course map, syllabus, or scope and sequence chart) which set out very clearly the various elements and also give insight into the methodology used. For example, if a course claims to be topic-based and communicative, but the structural items are listed first, it is possible that the publishers are paying lip-service to current trends. Read the blurbs below, then compare these to the contents tables. Are there any discrepancies?

Superworld is a complete four-level English course for children in primary schools.
- *Topic-based*
- *Child-centred*
- *Beautifully illustrated and FUN!*

Cross-curricular topics, tasks, activities, projects, games and songs
- *Make learning enjoyable*
- *Help children to use English meaningfully in a variety of contexts*
- *Develop children's critical thinking and learning skills*

Syllabus
- *Takes into account children's educational and conceptual development*
- *Provides thorough coverage and recycling of key vocabulary, functions, structures and skills.*

Title	Main activities	Language and learning skills	Cross-curricular content	Main language children use	Main receptive language	Main recycled language	Main attitudes

(Superworld, 2000, Macmillan Heinemann)

I-Spy is an imaginative four-part course for children starting English at primary school. The course develops communication skills and learning strategies, and offers a rich resource of stories, posters, flashcards, games, cut-outs, and optional activities, to cater for a range of abilities and learning styles.

I-Spy provides:
- *A spiral syllabus, to ensure thorough recycling of language*

- *Lively, original cassette materials, to develop listening skills and pronunciation*
- *Challenging, interesting tasks, to train children in learning skills*
- *Humorous, imaginative characters and cartoons, to create an enjoyable learning context*
- *The Rubbish cartoon, to encourage listening and reading for pleasure*

Themes	Main language	Vocabulary and sounds	Passwords and sounds	Communicative functions	Projects

(I-Spy, 1997, OUP)

Chatterbox *is a four-part beginner's course for children learning English in primary schools. It makes learning easy with an exciting serial story. It involves children in a variety of fun activities. It follows a carefully graded syllabus which allows for recycling of language. It gives children a thorough grounding in listening, speaking, reading and writing.*

Unit	Language items	Functions and topics

(Chatterbox, 1989, OUP)

New English Parade *is a seven-level, communicative language programme that features TPR, rhymes, songs, chants, pair work, cooperative learning, and hands-on projects. It contains cut-out Little Books for more reading, Videos and Video Guides, on per level, to surround students with natural language. Audio programme on cassette and CD includes appealing songs and chants with new melodies and voices, plus all the listening activities. Workbook Language Activities Sections for writing, grammar and language practice*

Unit	Title	Theme	Communication Objectives	Language Objectives	Learning Strategies/ Thinking Skills	Content Connections

(New English Parade, 2000, Longman)

For younger pupils:

Pebbles *is two-stage early primary English course. It concentrates on oral/aural training to provide a firm basis for future learning. Simple reading and writing is introduced in Pebbles 2.*
- *Lively/story dialogue presentation grabs children's attention and helps comprehension*
- *Vivid mix of fantasy and real-life characters appeals to children's imagination*

- *Clear syllabus progression, with lots of recyling, makes the course easy to follow*
- *Single write-in coursebook at each level means less to lose!*
- *50–70 hours of contact time per level fits your school year*

Unit number and theme	Main communicative aim	Main activities and skills	Language aims

(Pebbles, 1999, Longman)

Super Me *is a two-level foundation course for children starting English in kindergarten or the first grade of primary school. It's main aim is to give children an enjoyable experience of learning another language. It introduces children to English through a lively storyline involving three children, their imaginary friend, their dog and their teddy.*

Unit/Topic	General aims	Language Language for production Language for recognition

(Super Me, 1997, OUP)

As can be seen, these extracts highlight different approaches to English language teaching, and the terminology used in the contents tables to express aims also differs greatly. It is also useful to look to see if there is a statement of learning principles or basic beliefs about the nature of learning and teaching to children (see the teacher's books of *Superworld* and *Buzz*). Coursebooks are in no way, of course, bound to adopt one approach to the exclusion of all others and many attempt to achieve a working balance between them. Which of the above descriptions corresponds most closely with your aims and objectives? Why?

Task 1

In order to make the most appropriate choice for your context, coursebooks need to be examined carefully and compared against each other. Use the questionnaire (Fig. 28) and evaluate some young learners coursebooks you are familiar with. If possible, do this with a colleague and compare your notes. Do you agree? Do you have any other questions? Completing a questionnaire like this will allow you to compare coursebooks so you can identify which one(s) will be the most appropriate for your context.

Selecting supplementary materials

Although coursebooks may provide the majority of materials for most teachers, many like to use other materials from time to time in order to provide variety. There are a great number of supplementary materials to choose from including graded readers, authentic storybooks, songs, rhymes, and chants, games, posters, flashcards, as well as technology such as video, CDs, the internet and other CALL programmes. There are also some excellent collections of books offering photocopiable worksheets. When selecting supplementary materials, ask yourself how they relate to the language presented in your coursebook, the type of supplementary language and practice they will provide and your pupils' motivation in order to select materials that will reinforce, consolidate and extend structures and vocabulary.

When selecting supplementary materials, you can also look at authentic materials (materials not written specifically for EFL). For example, many games that children play in their L1 can be played in the L2. You may like to make a collection of children's comics, toys, posters, and so on, to decorate the classroom. See chapter 16 for ideas on classroom display.

See also chapter 14 for a list of criteria to use for selecting storybooks; chapters 12 and 13 for using songs, rhymes and chants and games; chapter 15 on the role of technology.

Producing your own materials

Producing your own materials can be time-consuming, so how often you do it will depend on the amount of time you have, the resources you have available and your particular needs. Think about some of the reasons why you may do this. For example, your coursebook does not provide enough practice; the activities, exercises, or visual aids in your coursebook may not be very interesting or may be inappropriate for your class; you want provide your pupils with a selection of different activities so that they can work at their own pace (see chapter 16); you may simply want more variety.

Making worksheets

Worksheets can be exercises and activities which are drawn, written or word processed and photocopied. If you have access to computer facilities, this will enable you to produce attractive worksheets using clip art (see chapter 15) and to store your worksheets on computer in a file directory structure so other teachers can access, use, modify and add to them. In collaboration with other teachers in your school, it is useful to create

Title ....

General questions	Comments
1 What sort of methodology does the book appear to adopt?	
2 Does one approach predominate? If yes, what are the implications of this in relation to the rest of the curriculum?	
3 How are new teaching points graded? How frequently are they introduced and how much practise material separates them?	
4 Is the organization of the course linear or cyclical? Linear – teaching points are added one at a time, each being practised before moving on to the next. Cyclical – a particular teaching point recurs in a different context to be enlarged on throughout the course. What are the implications of this to young learners?	
5 Are there any special pages for revision, self-testing, self-assessment or reference?	
6 Are opportunities for independent work provided such as through project work?	
7 Are learning strategies developed in a systematic and explicit way?	
8 What are the illustrations and layout like? Are they attractive? Are they useful or only decorative? Will your pupils like them?	
9 Does the course include any examples of authentic language and materials?	
10 What components does the course offer: (books, tests, cassettes, CDs, videos, flashcards, posters, puppets)?	
11 Is the teacher's guide easy to follow? Does it contain interleaved pages from the pupil's book?	

Fig. 28 Questionnaire for evaluating coursebooks

General questions (contd)	Comments
12 What is the socio-cultural context represented in the materials? Do they avoid sexual, racial and cultural stereotypes? Are there opportunities for cross-cultural comparison? What values are projected through the materials? What scope is there for developing citizenship education?	
13 Can you spot any notable omissions? Will you have to supplement the coursebook in any way?	
14 What sorts of demands are made on the teacher in terms of management skills and fluency?	
Specific questions Take a sample unit and ask yourself:	
15 How is each unit titled? Will it be clear to your pupils what they are expected to learn in the unit and what they have to do?	
16 How is new language presented? How is the meaning of items conveyed? Are new items related to what has been learned previously?	
17 Does the presentation of new language force the teacher to follow the unit sequence of the coursebook?	
18 How much new language is printed in each unit? Is the rate at which new material is introduced appropriate for your pupils?	
19 What kind of practice activities are there? Is there an appropriate balance between controlled and freer practice, accuracy and fluency? Are they motivating and meaningful? Do they provide opportunities for real language use and possibilities for interaction?	
20 Does the book offer L1 translation? Do you regard this as useful or not?	
21 How are the different skills treated? Are they integrated?	
22 How much variety of activity is there?	
23 How much does the course cost? Can your school or the children's parents afford it?	

Fig. 28 Questionnaire for evaluating coursebooks (Contd)

a template for producing worksheets. This will ensure some kind of standard identity and make work look more attractive and professional. Self-produced worksheets can be a great help to the teacher for organizing oral activities in pairs and small groups, and also for simple reading and writing tasks. If you do not want your pupils to write on or colour the worksheets, you must say so in advance! If they are stuck onto pieces of card and laminated they will last longer and can be used again with the same class to recycle language in different contexts or with different classes. Alternatively, if your pupils can keep the worksheets, they can personalize them by writing their name and the date, colouring them, and storing them in their English folders or sticking them in their exercise books. This involves pupils more actively in the learning task and teaches useful study skills.

When designing worksheets, think carefully about how you want your pupils to use them. For example, are they to enable pupils to work in pairs and practise listening and speaking, or to work individually and practise reading and writing? It is a good idea to try out the worksheet yourself before using it with your class. Ask yourself the following questions.

- Are the aims clear? Can the pupils see what language they are practising and why?

- Do I need to write instructions on the worksheet in English or in the pupils' L1, or can I explain the instructions orally?

- Is there enough room to write ticks (✔), crosses (✗), names, numbers, words, draw pictures, and so on?

If you do not have access to a word processor, write or draw clearly in black ink. Do not try to fit too much on to one sheet of paper. The worksheet will look cramped and overwhelm or demotivate the pupil. Focus on one language learning point at a time so that pupils are clear about what they should do and what they are practising.

It is always possible to involve pupils in making their own worksheets and this can be a useful way of linking work in the English language classroom with other subjects in the curriculum. For example, Fig. 16 in chapter 6 was made by pupils in their Maths class. This involved listening to instructions and measurements for making a grid and drawing horizontal and vertical lines. They then drew the food items and labelled them and used the worksheet to interview each other about their likes and dislikes.

Here are two examples of teacher-produced worksheets.

- **Picture dictation** (Fig. 29) The worksheet consists of a simple line drawing. The pupils listen to descriptions given by the teacher and add these to the drawing. For example: *She's got straight hair. She's wearing black stockings, she's got a broomstick,* and so on. The completed version has been labelled by copying words from the blackboard.

What is Meg wearing? Listen and draw.

Fig. 29 Picture dictation worksheet

- **True or False?** A page from a diary (Fig. 30) can be used for a true or false activity, involving pupils in listening, reading and speaking. The teacher or another pupil says for example: *The 1st of May is a Tuesday! True or false?* Pupils reply: *False! It's a Wednesday!*

True or false? Listen and read.

April 2002	2002 May
29 Monday	Thursday **2**
30 Tuesday	Friday **3**
1 Wednesday	Saturday **4**
	Sunday **5**

Fig. 30 True or false? worksheet

Worksheet features

The main features of these worksheets are:
- They are clear, simple and attractive.
- The instructions are clear or in the pupils' own language.
- Each worksheet provides an activity which lasts a designated period of time
- There are opportunities for the worksheets to be personalized, for example, coloured, labelled, and so on.
- Each worksheet practises one particular language point, for example, a structure or a lexical set, and involves pupils in different skills and possibilities for linking English with other subjects in the curriculum.

Making flashcards

Flashcards can be made by you or your pupils and can be used to introduce, practise or review structures and vocabulary. For young learners, they are very often made by using pictures but words can be used. If the latter, they should be produced in large, clear, black letters using a computer or written clearly by hand. Pictures can be drawn by you (see Wright 1996 for ideas on simple line drawings to copy) or imported from clip art on computer or photocopied. It is sometimes useful to enlarge pictures on a photocopier so the pupils can colour them. Pictures can be cut out from magazines and mail order catalogues. When using flashcards, ask yourself: Are they large enough for the whole class to see? Does the picture convey the meaning clearly?

COURSEBOOKS

Big Red Bus Lobo, M.J. & Subira, P. 1993. Macmillan Heinemann
Blue Skies Holt, R. 1999. Longman
Buzz Revell, J. & Seligson, P. 1993. Longman
Chatterbox Strange, D. 1989. Oxford University Press
Cutting Edge Cunningham, S. & Moore, P. 1998. Pearson Education Longman
early bird Vale, D. 1990. Cambridge University Press
First Steps Monterrubio, M. & Salido, M. 2000. Macmillan Heinemann
I-Spy Ashworth, J. & Clark. J. 1997. Oxford University Press
Join In Gerngross, G. & Puchta, H. 2000. Cambridge University Press
New Boomerang Blair, A. & Cadwallader, J. 1999. Santillana
New English Parade Herrera, M. & Zanatta, T. 2000. Longman
Pebbles Hancock, P. & Ellis, G. 1999. Longman
Portfolio Topic Book 'Heroes' Nihlen, C. et. al. 1999. Almqvist & Wiksell
Stepping Stones Ashworth, J. & Clark, J. 1989. Longman
Super Me Thomas, L. & Gil, V. 1997. Oxford University Press
Superworld Read, C. & Soberon, A. 2000. Macmillan Heinemann
You and Me Lawday, C. 1994. Oxford University Press

12 Songs, rhymes and chants

Children love songs, rhymes and chants and their repetitive nature and rhythm make them an ideal vehicle for language learning. Their usefulness is recognized by their inclusion in most language programmes and every primary school teacher will have their favourites. This chapter will consider the rich potential of traditional songs, rhymes and chants that have stood the test of time. There are a number of collections available on cassette or video often with attractive activity books like *Play it Again!* (Ashworth, Clark and Ellis 1996) and *Super Songs1* and *2* (OUP 1997) which allow children to hear and see the songs and rhymes being performed, which greatly supports understanding. Rhymes and nonsense verse written by contemporary poets like Spike Milligan, Colin McNaughton, Allan Ahlberg, Kit Wright and Michael Rosen, for children whose L1 is English, have a great deal of potential. Carefully selected, songs, rhymes and chants can offer a rich source of authentic input.

Why use songs, rhymes and chants?

This list of benefits for language learning has been grouped together under the main objectives of most language teaching programmes. Prioritize them for your teaching context.

A *linguistic resource*
- They allow new language to be introduced and structures and vocabulary to be reinforced and recycled

- They present familiar language in new and exciting forms and in a rich, imaginative context

- They provide for lots of natural and enjoyable repetition

- They can be used to develop all skills in an integrated way

- They help improve all aspects of pronunciation (see below)

A *psychological/affective resource*
- They are motivating and fun and help develop positive attitudes towards the target language

- They are non-threatening and the more inhibited child will feel secure when singing and chanting as a class or in groups

- They can encourage a feeling of achievement and build children's confidence by allowing children to learn chunks of language which they can 'show off' or teach to friends or to members of the family

A cognitive resource

- They help to develop concentration, memory and coordination

- They sensitize children to rhyming clues as aids to meaning

- Repetition enables children to predict what comes next and to consolidate language items

- Accompanying actions or gestures help to reinforce meaning, while channelling high levels of energy in a positive way

- The variety they provide changes the pace and atmosphere of a lesson and caters for different learning styles

- They can be compiled into song/rhyme books to help children develop good study habits

A cultural resource

- They are from authentic sources and can contribute to the cultural component of a language programme. Children can be encouraged to compare with those in their own language. See chapter 10.

A social resource

- Singing and chanting together is a shared social experience and helps to develop a class and group identity

- They can be used as the basis for a performance or show

Finally, they offer a flexible resource to the teacher. There are plenty to choose from, can be used with a variety of age groups at different stages in their language learning, can act as a starting point for devising a programme of work, can integrate with cross-curricular work, topics and stories and can complement and supplement other resources.

Pronunciation benefits of using songs, rhymes and chants

Songs, rhymes and chants are particularly useful for practising pronunciation. This includes individual sounds and sounds in connected speech but, more importantly, features relating to stress, rhythm and intonation. For more details on pronunciation see chapter 6.

Individual sounds and sounds in connected speech

Songs and rhymes are useful for showing what happens to sounds in connected speech, for example, the way that certain sounds run on together: *You're not IT!* or *All in together!* Rather complicated consonant clusters in English are often simplified, especially where a word which ends in /t/ or /d/ is followed by a consonant cluster, as in: *First by the weather* where /st/ and /by/ are simplified to /s/ and /by/.

Stress and rhythm

More important features of pronunciation, such as stress and rhythm, can also be practised in a very natural way using songs and rhymes. Encouraging children to clap the beat as they go along or say rhymes will help to develop a sense of rhythm in English.

Weak forms, where the pronunciation of a word differs according to whether it is stressed or unstressed, occur regularly in songs and rhymes. The words which are weakly stressed include.

Auxillary verbs: *Who do we appreciate?*
Conjunctions: *One went POP and another went BANG!*
Articles and some prepositions: *You eat me for breakfast*

These weak forms often practise the use of /ə/, which is the most frequent vowel in English since it occurs in many unstressed syllables. This is usually not a difficult vowel to pronounce but learners often find it difficult to know when it occurs.

Intonation

Intonation can also be practised in rhymes. See chapter 6.

Ear training

Chapter 6 referred to the need for pupils to have some 'ear-training' to help them distinguish between different aspects of English pronunciation. To do this, you can ask the pupils to listen and count how many times an individual sound or word occurs in a song or rhyme. You can also ask the pupils to listen and discriminate by checking whether rhythmic or intonation patterns are the same or different. Rhythmic patterns can be presented visually by using large and small circles or boxes, for example:

Insey Winsey Spider	O ° O ° O °
Climbing up the spout	O ° O ° O
Down came the rain and	O O ° O °
Washed the spider out	O ° O ° O

Types of songs, rhymes and chants

There are many different kinds of songs, rhymes and chants which contain different features and are used for different purposes. Opie and Opie (1967:17) suggest that rhymes can be divided into two categories: those which are essential to the regulation of games and children's relationships with each other and include dips, skipping rhymes; and those that are 'mere expressions of exuberance' and include jingles, slogans, nonsense verse, tongue twisters, scary rhymes and jokes.

Rhymes that are used for the regulation of games usually include dipping. They are used to eliminate children when deciding who is going to be a key person for a game. The players usually stand in a line or a circle and one child counts the number of counts prescribed by the stressed syllables of a short rhyme. The player that the last count falls on is then either made the chaser, and the game begins, or more often, he or she is counted 'out' and stands aside while the rhyme is repeated and a second player eliminated, and so on, until only one player remains. The player is 'it' or the chaser.

Dip, dip, dip	*Out goes the cat*
My blue ship	*Out goes the rat*
Sailing on the sea	*Out goes the lady*
Like a cup of tea	*with the big green hat*
Dip, dip, dip	*OUT spells out*
You're not IT!	*So you're not IT!*

Many rhymes are traditionally used by children to perform actions in groups, to clap together in pairs or when skipping. Here is an example of a skipping rhyme adapted for the classroom where children or groups of children stand in a circle(s), chant the rhyme and jump into the circle when the month of their birthday is called. The rhyme is repeated and they jump out again on the month of their birthday.

All in together
First by the weather
When you call your birthday
You must jump in/out
January, February, March ...

Finger rhymes or plays involve actions just for the hand and children can remain seated. For example:

Two fat gentlemen met in a lane,	*(Hold up both thumbs)*
Bowed most politely, bowed once again.	*(Bend thumbs twice)*
How do you do!	*(Bend right thumb)*

165

How do you do!	*(Bend left thumb)*
And how do you do again?	*(Bend both thumbs)*

The rhyme continues with other characters, which of course the children could choose themselves as long as they correspond with the adjectives representing the fingers:

Thin	forefingers	*Two thin women met in a lane*
Tall	Middle fingers	*Two tall police officers met in a lane*
Little	Ring fingers	*Two little school children met in a lane*
Little	Little fingers	*Two little babies met in a lane*

Riddles and jokes not only practise language but also encourage children to think. Can you answer these?

You eat me for breakfast	*I'm a very big animal*
But first crack my shell	*You see at the zoo*
If I'm fresh then I'm tasty	*I've a very nice trunk*
If not – what a smell!	*I can squirt water through*

Many jokes such as the Doctor, Doctor, Waiter, Waiter or Knock Knock type, play on words and follow a repeating pattern of statement/reply or question/answer. Older children with a higher level of English will enjoy these and can act them out in pairs as they give excellent practice in intonation.

Doctor, doctor! I feel like a pair	*Doctor, doctor! Everyone keeps*
of curtains.	*ignoring me!*
Well, pull yourself together then!	*Next please!*

Waiter, waiter! There's a fly in my soup!	*Waiter, waiter! There's a fly in the*
What do you expect for 50p, a beetle?	*butter!*
	Yes sir, it's a butterfly.

Knock, Knock! Who's there?	*Knock, Knock! Who's there?*
Tennis!	*Toucan!*
Tennis who?	*Toucan who?*
Tennis five plus five!	*Toucan play at this game!*

An excellent source of silly jokes and riddles can be obtained from the web site www.kidsjokes.co.uk

Limericks are also very popular with older children:

There once was a man from Darjeeling,
Who travelled from London to Ealing
When it said on the door
'Please don't spit on the floor',
He carefully spat on the ceiling.

Tongue twisters have always been favourites and use alliteration which makes correct pronunciation difficult and a real challenge! If they are repeated with concentration they help to establish clear speech:

> *Red lorry, yellow lorry*
> *She sells seashells on the seashore*
> *The big black bug bit the big black bear but the big black bear bit the big black bug back.*

Try the ultimate tongue twisters by Dr Seuss such as *Fox in Socks*.
Hundreds of tongue twisters can be found at the following sites:
www.geocities.com/Athens/Agora/4534
www.uebersetzung.at/twister/en.htm

Chants have always been popular in the playground and at sports events

Sausage in the pan	*Two, four, six, eight,*
Sausage in the pan	*Who do we appreciate?*
Sizzle, sizzle	*R-E-D-S! REDS!*
Sizzle, sizzle	
Sausage in the pan	

Another type of chant imitates the rhythm of a train getting up speed and often uses food vocabulary ending with *Soup* for the train's whistle.

> *Coff-ee Coff-ee*
> *Tea and biscuits*
> *Tea and biscuits*
> *Fish and chips*
> *Fish and chips*
> *Sou-oup! Sou-oup!*

A more difficult version of this type of chant is the *Song of the train* by David McCord.

Jazz chants have now become extremely popular in the young learners classroom mainly due to the contribution of Carolyn Graham's work. She puts everyday conversational English to jazz rhythms. In her book *Jazz Chants for Children* (1979:ix) she writes 'Just as the selection of a particular tempo and beat in jazz may convey powerful and varied emotions, the rhythm, stress and intonation patterns of the spoken language are essential elements for the expression of feelings and the intent of the speaker. Linking these two dynamic forms has produced an innovative and exciting new approach to language learning'. Some of her chants have now become classics like *Ernie* and *Shoes and Socks*.

Older children might find some traditional songs, rhymes and chants a little childish or uninteresting. In this case, teachers often use English pop songs, especially some of the classics such as those of the Beatles. If you look at some CDs, the words are often printed inside. Otherwise, you could listen with the children to work them out.

As can be seen, songs, rhymes and chants can contribute to the child's global development in many different ways. Table 6 gives a breakdown of some favourites to which you can add those of your own. The main overall purpose, however, is that singing, chanting and acting together is fun and it stimulates the child's sense of humour. The words and tunes to some of the songs can be found at the following site: www.bbc.co.uk/education/tweenies/songtime

When and how to use songs, rhymes and chants

Songs, rhymes and chants can be used in many different ways: as warmers, as a transition from one activity to the next, closers, to introduce new language, to practise language, to revise language, to change the mood, to get everyone's attention, to channel high levels of energy or to integrate with storytelling, topic work or cross-curricular work. (See Read 1999 for guidelines on how to use the song *There was a princess long ago* and how this can be linked into story-based work.)

Here is a flexible framework for using songs, rhymes and chants. It may not be necessary or appropriate to use each stage.

- Set the context (explain purpose, background information)
- Pre-teach any necessary vocabulary using visual aids, actions, realia, puppets, focus questions, etc.
- Play on cassette or sing or chant to allow children to listen, show understanding, familiarize themselves with the rhythm, tune, etc.
- Do further listening activity
- Work on pronunciation awareness, for example, identifying intonation patterns, stressed words or syllables, etc.
- Invite children to listen, repeat and practise by joining in and learning to sing or chant. Encourage children to use actions, mime, drama, etc. Practise several times.
- Give a written record of text: children can adapt or write their own version; listen and complete a simple gap fill; listen and sequence – children scan written phrases and put them in order; listen and sort – children have the words from two songs mixed up together and, as they listen, they sort out the lines into two groups; match pictures and lines, illustrate verses, make collages to contextualize, for example, on the beach, etc.

Main features/ types	Purpose (in addition to fun!)	Develops	Examples
Physical actions (movement, mime, skipping, clapping)	To perform actions and provide exercise To channel high levels of energy positively	Memory, concentration, coordination, vocabulary, structures, social skills	*If you're happy and you know it* *One finger, one thumb* *Hokey Cokey*
Hand actions (finger plays or rhymes)	To perform hand actions	Memory, concentration, co-ordination, vocabulary, structures, acting out	*Two fat gentlemen, met in a lane* *Tommy Thumb, Tommy Thumb*
Ring games	To perform actions and provide exercise	As above, and social development, turn taking	*Here we go round the mulberry bush*
Numbers and counting	To reinforce concepts: numbers and counting, addition and subtraction, size, shape, etc.	Memory, concentration, coordination, counting, vocabulary, structures	*10 green bottles* *5 currant buns* *10 fat sausages* *Over in the meadow* *When Goldilocks went to the house of the bears* *One, two, buckle my shoe*
Short dialogues	To learn chunks of language and dialogue that can be transferred to other situations	Awareness of language used for communication	*1,2,3,4,5, once I caught a fish alive* *Tommy Thumb, Tommy Thumb* *Who stole the cookie from the cookie jar?* *There's a hole in my bucket*
Repetition, cumulation, rhyme, onomatopoeia	To provide natural repetition and pronunciation practice of rhyming and sound words	Memory and prediction, awareness of rhyme and sounds for audio clues, pronunciation	*10 fat sausages* *One, two, buckle my shoe* *The wheels on the bus* *We're going on a bear hunt* *There was an old lady who swallowed a fly* *Over in the meadow* *In a dark, dark wood* *Today is Monday*
Contains narrative	To tell/act out a story	To develop understanding of narrative To develop memory and logical thinking (cause and effect) To develop awareness of movement and drama as songs/rhymes are acted out	*We're going on a bear hunt* *I had a little brother* *Miss Polly had a dolly* *There was an old lady who swallowed a fly* *There's a hole in my bucket* *There was a princess long ago* *When Goldilocks went to the house of the bears* *London Bridge is falling down*

Table 6 Songs, rhymes and chants

Main features/ types	Purpose (in addition to fun!)	Develops	Examples
Fits into a particular theme/topic	To consolidate and extent vocabulary sets and to explore a theme	Vocabulary and structures	*Heads, shoulders, knees and toes (the body) Old MacDonald had a farm (farm animals) I hear thunder (the weather) I can sing a rainbow (the weather and colours)*
Scary rhymes	To say a rhyme in a way that frightens the listener	Develops voice control, awareness of dramatic effect, suspense	*In a dark, dark wood*
Alliteration	To challenge pronunciation	Awareness of alliteration, rhythm, stress	*Tongue twisters Limericks Nonsense verse*
Contains a didactic message	To teach children about day to day routines	Develops awareness daily routines, punctuality, etc.	*Here we go round the mulberry bush (personal hygiene) 1,2,3,4, Please come in and shut the door (get to school on time)*
From around the world	To learn more about the world	Develops world knowledge and sensitizes children to different rhythms and tunes	*Cumbayah (America/Africa) Kookaburra (Australia) Dem Bones (America/Africa) Little Green Frog (Turkey) She'll be coming round the mountain (America)*
Refers to a famous place/landmark	To learn about the world	Develops geographical/historical knowledge	*London's burning London Bridge is falling down*
Links to a special occasion	To celebrate	To develop cultural knowledge	*Happy Birthday Mix a pancake (Shrove Tuesday) Roses are red (Valentine's Day) This is the night of Hallowe'en Remember, remember (Guy Fawkes Day)*
Predictable patterns: definitions/ descriptions, question/answer, statement/reply	To recognize patterns To challenge the mind	Thinking skills	*Riddles Jokes*

- Encourage children to compare with a similar type in their own language

- Present or perform as a whole class, in groups, in rounds, in pairs, or if there is a question and answer sequence in the song, for example, *There's a Hole in my Bucket*, one part can be sung by half the class, the second part by the other half.

Finally, children might like to make a class book or their own individual book of favourite songs or rhymes. Older ones might also like to produce their own material, such as limericks, which have a very clear rhyming pattern, or their own songs. These could be taped for other children to listen to and to complete the above activities.

Adapting songs, rhymes and chants

Many songs, rhymes or chants can be easily adapted by changing key words to fit in with a particular story or theme. The advantage of this is that children may already be familiar with the song, rhyme or chant. The finger rhyme *Two fat gentlemen* can easily be adapted to fit in with the story *The Snowman* by substituting gentlemen with *snowmen, snow women*, etc. Songs from around the world can also be easily adapted to fit in with story-based work.

Building up a repertoire of songs, rhymes and chants

To develop a wide range of songs, rhymes and chants that are suitable for the age group(s) you teach and the context in which you work, you may like to build up a record in the following way. This will help you analyse the full potential of each song, rhyme and chant and see best how you may integrate it into your syllabus. For example:

Title	Language focus	Cultural, curriculum, topic or story links	Suitable age group	Comments
1. Head, shoulders, knees and toes	Parts of the body conjunctions	Drama Physical education	5–10 year-olds	Flexible: is enjoyed by most children, can make it more challenging by speeding up and leaving out words.

Fig. 31 A record for analysing songs, rhymes and chants

13 GAMES

Children enjoy constructive play and games. They are not only motivating and fun but can also provide excellent practice for improving pronunciation, vocabulary, grammar and the four language skills. For very young children games also provide an important link between home and school which helps to make them feel more secure and confident. They usually form an integral part of language programmes and published ELT materials for young learners. In some cultures and contexts, however, games are seen as merely time-fillers and their potential for 'real' learning is not recognized. This may be true if games are not well-selected or planned, if the language they encourage is actually very limited or not very integrated with other language work, if the necessary language is not carefully prepared for or if it is not monitored while children actually play the games. Children may simply become concerned with developing strategies to play the game quickly or easily, without focusing enough on the intended language practice. To exploit games fully we need to consider carefully both the language learning benefits they may bring, and any other educational or conceptual gains. In terms of language learning, teachers need to be aware of the range of language items and skills work different games can promote and the most fruitful kinds of games to use for different purposes. There are many examples of games provided in several coursebooks, either as parts of a specific unit or as a supplementary resource. *New Stepping Stones, You and Me, Pebbles, Superworld* for example have a Resource File at the back of each *Teacher's Book* with many examples of games. There are also plenty of supplementary resources books on games, many of which have photocopiable pages. These include Gray (1996a), Gray (1996b), Holderness and Hughes (1997), Palim and Power (1990), Philpot (2000), *Classroom Timesavers* published by Mary Glasgow Magazines, Retter and Valls (1984), and Toth (1995). In this chapter we shall consider the reason for using them, different types of games, how to select games, evaluate the potential, how to organize pupils and finally, the role of the teacher.

Why use games?

First of all, we need to consider what is a game and when should we use it. Martin (1995:1) writes that it is 'any fun activity which gives young learners the opportunity to practise the foreign language in a relaxed and enjoyable way'. Games may be simple and require very little planning or may need quite a bit of preparation and the use of special materials, such as dice, boards, or picture, word or sentence cards. Some games are competitive, with teams or individuals working towards being the 'winner'. Other games are cooperative, where teams or pairs work together to achieve a common goal, such as drawing a picture or solving a puzzle. Let us now consider some of the advantages of using games.

Task 1

Here is a list of some advantages of using games. Think carefully about these in relation to your own teaching context and put two ticks in the boxes for those you think are very important, one tick for quite important and a cross by those you think are not important.

Advantages of using games	
1 They add variety to the range of learning situations.	
2 They change the pace of a lesson and help to keep pupils' motivation.	
3 They 'lighten' more formal teaching and can help to renew pupils' energy.	
4 They provide 'hidden' practice of specific language patterns, vocabulary and pronunciation.	
5 They can help to improve attention span, concentration, memory, listening skills and reading skills.	
6 Pupils are encouraged to participate; shy learners can be motivated to speak.	
7 They increase pupil-pupil communication which provides fluency practice and reduces the domination of the class by the teacher.	
8 It helps create a fun atmosphere and reduces the distance between teacher and pupils.	
9 They can help reveal areas of weakness and the need for further language.	
10. They can help to motivate and improve writing skills by providing a real audience context and purpose.	

Fig. 32 Advantages of using games

Here is a list of the language learning purposes of games.

1   They encourage the memorization of chunks of language which can be slotted into various contexts e.g. *Can I have a ...?*

2 Chunking of language provides useful pronunciation practice (as long as a good model has been provided).

3 The language needed for games may be used as part of an activity where the focus is on getting something done, rather than practising language for its own sake.

4 Language may be practised together with a wider educational or conceptual goal, e.g. using reading games to reinforce vocabulary as well as the concept of classifying, and learning more about a topic.

5 The language in a game may encourage more creative use of language in addition to simple repetition.

6 The pupils may be involved in informal language analysis and noticing of language items or rules through problem-solving and puzzles.

7 Games help to make learning more memorable and accessible by using as many approaches as possible, such as mime and movement, use of colour and patterns, or personalization.

Types of games

There are many different kinds of games which can be grouped according to the kinds of language or learning focus they have and the kinds of resources, classroom management and organization they need. These questions act as guidelines to help the teacher decide which type of game she would like to use.

1 Does this game mostly promote fluency or accuracy?

2 Does it promote competition or cooperation?

3 Does it have an educational aim, i.e. developing concepts, themes, cross-curricular topics such as citizenship, learning strategies?

4 Is it suitable for beginners or higher levels?

5 Is it a quiet, calming game which settles learners or an active, livening-up game, which stirs pupils? (see chapters 7, 16 and 17).

6 What materials, resources and classroom organization are needed?

7 Does it focus mostly on practising pronunciation, words, grammar and language functions, language skills or learning to learn skills?

Let us now look briefly at each of these questions in turn.

Fluency or accuracy?

We can divide games into two main types: *language control*, or accuracy-focused games, and *communication*, or fluency-focused games. The first type aims to practise new language items and develop accuracy, often using chunks of language which are memorized through constant repetition in the form of 'hidden' or 'disguised' language drills. In this way they provide useful pronunciation, vocabulary and grammar practice. However, Paul (1996) writes that there are many games that are played over and over to provide such practice until the children 'turn into unthinking parrots'. He suggests that children can be encouraged to discover many new words and structures *while* they are playing games in order to be more mentally engaged.

Accuracy-focused games

In these games the aim is usually to score more points than others and there is often a clear 'winner'. This kind of game may focus on comprehension (listening/reading) as well as production (speaking/writing). In this case, the child may not necessarily say anything but gets used to hearing or reading words or sentence patterns over and over again. Some of these games are also very good at training pupils' memories. An example of a game which focuses on code control and memorization is based on the formula 'I went to market and I bought ...' Here the class has to remember and repeat in the correct order a range of vocabulary and add their own examples. For example during a topic on Animals this can be changed to *I went to the zoo and I saw a giraffe*. The next child says *I went to the zoo and saw a giraffe and a tiger*, and so on. This game can be used for practising vocabulary and the simple past tense of *go*. A variation, shown below, practises the possessive. It is used after pupils carried out a survey, such as Favourite Colours. (In our survey) *Jorge's favourite colour is blue and mine is yellow. Jorge's favourite colour is blue, Anna's is yellow and mine is green.* The child (or pair) who remembers the most items in the correct order is the winner. Through constant repetition, this game provides practice in the pronunciation and meaning of vocabulary items as well as possessive pronoun *mine*. It also allows for personalization. The language for control-code games must be carefully controlled, rehearsed and contextualized, especially in the early stages, so that children are not just 'parroting' language, without understanding what it means. For example, this game can first be played with pictures of items which are drawn out of a bag, so the children receive a visual prompt to give them ideas. Later the teacher can simply have pictures of the vocabulary items displayed on the board as a memory aid. With picture prompts pupils can probably remember more, although young children

175

may only be able to remember three or four items. Later on this visual support could be withdrawn so that playing the game actually relies on and develops the memory. Even older children will probably only be able to remember up to seven items. Once the principle of the game is understood it is better to divide the pupils into groups so that they have fewer items to remember and is a way of keeping all of the pupils occupied.

Fluency-focused games

The second type of game we have referred to moves from *language control* to *communication*. This type of game tends to focus on developing fluency and collaboration with others. These games are an important part of the 'communicative' and 'activity-based' approaches and are usually done in pairs or groups of four (see chapter 4). Collaboration is achieved by trying to create a context where the pupils' focus on getting a task done together, while of course using key language, rather than simply practising language items for their own sake. The cooperative task often relies on an 'information gap'. This might include following instructions to make a drawing or follow a route on a map, such as 'Describe and Arrange' or 'Describe and Draw/Picture Dictation' (one child makes or uses a prepared pattern or drawing and explains it to a second child who cannot see it but tries to draw it). Pupils will soon learn that they need to describe things very carefully. Some games like this are often more difficult than many 'code-control' games so are suitable for pupils with slightly more advanced language. The teacher should always pre-teach the language by modelling key vocabulary or sentence patterns and providing plenty of rehearsal before pupils play the games on their own. If this is not done the pupils will probably simply revert to their L1, get the task done in the minimum amount of time without fully exploiting it or do the task while producing very little English.

Competition or cooperation?

The games we have discussed above move us on to another way of looking at games – how far is a game competitive or cooperative? Competitive games can be organized in teams, groups, pairs or individuals but they always have a winner who may be the one who has collected the most of something, or who is the first to do something, get rid of their cards or pictures or who has gained the most points, and so on. Competitive games tend to be, but are not always language control games. The Picture Dictation game outlined above is an example of a cooperative game. Here the pupils have to work together by describing, explaining clarifying, checking, agreeing and disagreeing, and so on.

176

Selecting games

Using the two main ways of classifying games there are other factors the teacher needs to consider when choosing a game.

Is it suitable for beginners or very young children?

Games for these groups need to have simple language and should be easy to explain, set up and play. Everyone should be able to participate and it should be fun. You will probably need to use more of the L1 to explain the game, although you should try to gradually introduce simple phrases which you can use over and over. The best way to ensure pupils understand is to play the game with one or two children in the front of the class as a demonstration. Always have a few attempts at playing the game before you start properly. When you play a new game for the first few times, start by giving pupils a second chance so that they are not immediately out of the game and so that the game lasts longer. If children in your group are highly competitive let more than one child be the ultimate winner. Of course the simplest vocabulary or reading games like *Snap* and *Bingo* or listening games like *Robots* (following simple instructions as in TPR) are suitable for these learners. The books of games mentioned earlier have many examples of games for children of all ages, including young beginners.

Does it settle or stir?

As discussed in chapter 7 a stirring activity engages the pupils physically or mentally so they are very active. With young children in particular you will need to use lively games to keep the children physically occupied and for them to 'let off steam'. One example is called *Pin On backs* (Paul 1996: 22) in which pupils have a card pinned on their back related to a particular topic or lexical set. They walk around the room asking *Am I a…?* at the simplest level or asking for clues, such as *Do I have a long neck?* before trying to guess.

Miming games are also useful for mentally engaging pupils. With older pupils, for example, you can use a series of cards which give suggestions for a mime, such as reading a comic, eating a hamburger, playing a computer game, etc. Pupils take a card, read it and then carry out the mime while the others guess. This can be done as a whole-class game, or once the pupils are used to it they can play in groups. Pupils can add to the cards by writing their own suggestions (you will need to monitor these carefully!). Another example taken from Roth (1998) is *The Number Game* where you say *One*, point to a child who then says *Two*, and so on.

This focuses attention on listening and trains memory and concentration. You can of course use other words, such as Colours, Animals or Clothes. A child who answers incorrectly is then OUT, although in the early stages you could let him or her have two chances or 'lives' before they are really out. *Dominoes* games are examples of physically settling games (although they are mentally very engaging). *Pelmanism* (also called *Concentration* or *Memory*) is a good memory-training language game. To play, pupils need a series of picture or word cards showing vocabulary they have recently learned. Each card must have an exact copy as this is a matching game. Each pupil or pair turns over two cards in an attempt to find a pair. The child must then say what is shown on the card; if the two cards are not a pair they must be returned to exactly the same position they where in before. The winner is the one who collects most pairs. Where the cards show words and not just pictures is excellent for training pupils to recognize quickly the written forms of words and memorize their position so they can then more easily match subsequent pairs. This is a good calming game which could be adapted to include longer phrases instead of just single words. Pupils could also be asked to match up questions with answers using the same principles.

What kind of language focus does it have ?

Teachers will be able to find a game to practise almost any aspect of language at primary level. The chart below shows how to classify some of the games we have discussed in this chapter.

What kind of resources do I need?

Games can be classified by the resources required to play them. The list below shows eight types.

1 No resources e.g. guessing games, listening games, (Listen and Do, Hide and Find, Repeat if it's True, Stand Up When you Hear ...)

2 Simple pencil and paper/blackboard games (spelling games, *Consequences*)

3 Picture games (Describe and Colour/Label/Draw/Arrange/Sequence; Picture Dictation, Mime.)

4 Word cards (*Dominoes*, Read and classify, *Pelmanism*) These practise vocabulary and may focus on the meaning and pronunciation of words, collocation or word associations such as *fighting fit*, meaning relations between words, such as opposites and word families.

Game	Vocabulary	Grammar	Listening	Speaking/ Pronunciation	Reading	Writing	Fluency/ Accuracy	Competition/ Cooperation
In my bag	clothing	present simple possessive pronoun *my*	memory and concentration	identifying and describing; linking, etc.	can be introduced as prompts	follow-up packing list	accuracy	Competition
Where am I?	various	asking and answering questions	listening for detail	question intonation, describing location *on the right*, etc.	very little		accuracy	Competition
Picture dictation	items needed for the picture, colour, size, position, instruction verbs	prepositions	listening for detail	describing position, giving instructions		written instructions for drawing could be follow-up practice	fluency	Cooperation
Pin On backs	animals	asking and answering yes/no questions	memory listening for detail	asking and answering; intonation	reading words	pupils can write the cards to be used	accuracy	Cooperation
Can You touch?	parts of the body	Using *can*	some, not central	describing ability/ inability	reading words	pupils can write the cards to be used	accuracy	Competition
Funnybones dominoes	parts of the body; connects to	simple present tense	some, not central	describing/ classifying	reading words	pupils can write the cards to be used	accuracy	Competition
Battleships	letters and numbers/ coordinates	asking and answering yes/no questions	listening for detail	identifying, describing one position	interpreting a grid	not central, pupils draw and mark a grid	accuracy	Cooperation

Table 7 Games

5   Games using Sentence Cards (matching parts of a sentence, matching questions with answers, problems with solutions, cause and effect)

6   Dice games (dice have words or pictures on them instead of numbers which pupils must name. Alternatively, the numbers on the dice can link to a list of words or actions which correspond to the numbers on the die e.g. *Follow Instructions*:1= jump twice, 2= say your name, 3= tell the time, 4= add 12 +15, 5= name 5 colour words, 6 = count backwards from 10 to 1)

7   Board games (*Five Senses*: a board with pictures of different items and 'chance' cards with instructions such as 'If you can smell this, move on two spaces' or 'If you cannot eat this, move back four spaces', and so on)

8   Games using charts or matrices (Draw and Arrange type games using an information gap, where each child in a pair secretly marks the position of things on a chart as in the traditional game called *Battleships* (Fig. 33) in which each child takes turns guessing where the objects are by naming the coordinates (e.g. A4 as on a map) and the other partner tries to make a hit by guessing the right coordinates. The hidden objects can be pirate ships, animals, treasure on a treasure island, and so on. If the partner to this child says A7 she will not have scored a hit as there is nothing in that box. The pupils need to practise finding and giving coordinates and distinguishing between *rows* (horizontal) and *columns* (vertical).

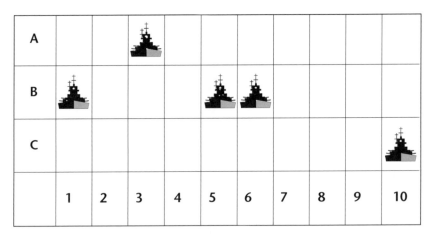

Fig. 33 Battleships

Does it have a link with a theme or other subjects?

Many games such as *Bingo* and *Dominoes*, can be adapted to link to various projects or curriculum areas. These well-known games, often played with young children at a very simple level, can be adapted for older children to fit in with various themes. For example, in the book *Funnybones* the pupils are encouraged to explore the theme of bones and skeletons through listening to the story and playing a *Dominoes* game. Here the cards are divided into two, each half has one or two words written on it. The aim is to take turns, each child putting down one card at a time to make a long line so that one half of a card matches another half of a card already on the table.

The winners are those who use up their cards first. To make this game more difficult the words which are matched up can be connected as in a real skeleton (see Ellis and Brewster 2002). So, for example, instead of just matching up *leg bone* with *leg bone*, as above, you could put down a card so that you have *leg bone* and *ankle bone* together (because the leg connects to the ankle in a real skeleton). A simpler game for younger pupils helps them practise body parts for a topic on Our Bodies. This game, *Can You Touch?* is played in small groups of three to six and requires two sets of cards of body parts. Each pupil takes the top card from the two piles (cards face down) and tries to touch one body part with the other. The pupil gets one point for each success (see Paul 1996:56).

The story *Princess Smartypants,* suitable for older children, has the theme of gender stereotypes. In this case, having listened to and worked with the story, the teacher can introduce a read and classify game called *Typical!* This game uses cards with short descriptions classified under three headings: *A Typical Princess, A Typical Prince, Not Typical.* Working in pairs, the pupils decide where statements like *usually wears beautiful clothes, is usually handsome, likes riding horses,* or *likes to rescue princes,* should be classified. The card *is usually handsome* is placed under the heading *A Typical Prince.* This kind of reading game can be adapted to discuss people and events from other cultures.

Another activity from this story uses a version of a *Bingo* game to consolidate the relationship of cause and effect/problem and solution that is contained within the story. A caller calls out some of the problems characters have in the story and the particular solutions they found to each problem. For example, problems like *the pets were too fierce* is matched on the pupils' *Bingo* card to the correct solution so *he used a helicopter.* (For further details see Ellis and Brewster 2002). Although these are particular examples linked to particular stories it is usually possible to generalize these kinds of activities to other contexts.

Evaluating the potential of games

Where possible, games should be integrated with the other language work which is taking place, for example, we have seen how games can reinforce words in a topic, Our Bodies, asking and answering yes/No questions *Where Am I?*, and so on. Teachers may sometimes use games for 'fillers' and 'light relief', but integrated practice is more educationally sound. Teachers should be able to describe and classify the kinds of language practice a game provides. They need to ensure that all of the pupils have something to do and are occupied most of the time. If they are 'out' of a competitive game too quickly, for example, pupils will have nothing to do and start being disruptive.

Teachers need to build up a repertoire of games which are useful for different stages of a lesson, such as 'five minute fillers' to finish off a lesson or wake pupils up or longer games which develop language in a more systematic way. With experience, teachers will be able to adapt games, perhaps to introduce more communication or to change the kind of vocabulary or grammar used. Teachers also need to be on their guard for games which at first sight look like fun but which do not actually provide much language focus. A useful checklist for evaluating the potential of a game is shown in Fig. 34.

Assessing the potential of games

Pupils' involvement

1 Are all the children involved for all or most of the time? Can you adapt a game slightly to ensure it is involving for all?

2 Can less able pupils take part without feeling frustrated. If not, can they work on a simpler version of the game?

3 Is the game clear, easy to explain and easy to play?

4 Ask the pupils their responses to some of these questions (in the L1).

Integration with other language work

5 In an accuracy-focused game does the language content have a clear focus? Can it be carefully controlled and graded, where necessary?

6 Do the children practise English throughout the game, or for the most part, at least?

7 Can new vocabulary be substituted into the game to fit in with other themes/ lexical sets?

8 Can recently learned new grammatical structures be substituted into the game to fit in with other language work?

9 Are the opportunities to link new language with old language in the game?

Assessing the potential of games (contd)

Pupil learning and initiative

10 How much choice and initiative do pupils have in playing the game?

11 How much can the pupils take over the role of the teacher in demonstrating or playing a part in the game? (e.g. being the 'caller' in Bingo)

12 Do pupils have the possibility of extending or adapting the game themselves?

Fig. 34 Assessing the potential of games

Selecting and setting up games is easier if they are labelled and colour- or shape-coded using categories that you find useful.

How to play games

Giving instructions

On the whole, games need to be short, easy to carry out and easy to explain. Giving instructions is a crucial stage; you may decide to do this in the L1 and then check using English (or vice versa). Keep instructions short, clear and simple and use a limited number of key phrases which the children will quickly get used to. Match carefully the language demands of the game to the language level of the class you are teaching. Plan how long the pupils need to practise newly learned language in a language control game, or whether they are ready for less controlled use in a communication game. Decide whether you play the game together as a class, or in teams or whether the pupils are ready to play in pairs or take over the role of the teacher. Make sure pupils are familiar with the necessary key vocabulary and language. Bear in mind that it may be wise to vary the choice of games so that there is a balance between competition and cooperation (although this is not so easy with young children or complete beginners). An overly competitive atmosphere in the classroom can be demoralizing for some children. The list below outlines some useful language for this stage.

> *Listen, look this way. Look at the board.*
> *Here are the instructions. Here's an example.*
> *I'd like helpers please.*
> *Show me. Repeat/explain what you must do.*
> *What's missing? What's next?*
> *Work in pairs/ teams/ groups/ on your own.*
> *Play back to back.*
> *Check you have everything you need.*

What do I do? I need ... Can I have ... ?
Team /Group 1 starts first. Get into a circle/line. Get into pairs, groups.
Throw the die. Choose your counter. Go forward/back a square.
On your marks 3. 2. 1 GO!
Counter, board, (flash)card, domino, winner, loser, touch, draw, colour,
    choose, match, collect, start, end, finish, win, lose

Use wall charts or mobiles to provide useful language. Younger children can use picture prompt cards to represent stages in a game e.g. work in pairs, match, sequence, draw. Break down the instructions into small stages, explain by showing and doing, use gesture and mime, use the board, pictures, flashcards or other material to demonstrate procedures.

Organizing the class

If the game requires teams, groups or pairs this needs to be organized quickly. Team games look like an obvious choice if you are unsure about setting up pairs or groups and if you want to work with all the pupils simultaneously. However, they can be problematic since only one member of a team is involved at a time. It is important to try and involve as many pupils as possible; whole class board games may be more participatory than team games. Elimination games can also leave some pupils standing with nothing to do. What might be better is a sort of TPR exercise where pupils simply follow instructions. It is best if the class becomes familiar with a routine to minimize disruption when moving furniture, forming groups, and so on. It is often useful to have a group leader if you want to play games in groups. This pupil will be responsible for collecting equipment, sharing it out, explaining details to the group, putting equipment away. Make sure that the role of group leader is given to different pupils so that they can all take a turn. Check everyone has understood what to do and give lots of praise.

Playing the game

Pupils must be taught the language they need to actually play each game, including the language to organize themselves. For example, pupils need to know how to check comprehension and the listener should be taught how to ask for more information or for clarification.

I don't understand. I don't know. I'm not sure. Let's check.
I've finished. Who starts? I'll start/you start. It's my turn.
Start again. Have another turn. Wait for your turn.
Wait a minute. Say that again. That's wrong. That's right. Sorry.
Don't look! Don't cheat! Don't be silly!

Have another throw. Miss a turn. Stop there.
Mix the cards. Turn over two cards. Put down a card.
I'm collecting ... Who's got ...? Do you have ...?
It matches/it doesn't match. This doesn't belong.
I've finished! It's a draw! (i.e. there are two winners/ equal points).
I've/We've lost, I've/We've won. I'm the winner!/We're the winners!

The teacher's role

While the pupils are playing games the teacher has a key role in observing and listening, monitoring pupils' language, giving prompts and explanation where necessary, noting pupils' language difficulties which may need re-teaching, and so on. Try not to over-correct the children if this is likely to spoil the flow of the game or reduce their enthusiasm. Make a note of how long the game takes to play for future reference and whether you need to improve on the instruction-giving stage. You will soon find out from the children which games they really enjoy and over time you will not only be able to gauge which ones really seem to work, but you'll understand why they work!

14 Storybooks

This chapter discusses why and how storybooks can be used, offers criteria that can be used when selecting storybooks, describes a story-based methodology and suggests ways teachers can improve their storytelling techniques.

Why use stories?

The educational value of using storybooks and storytelling has always been undisputed throughout the world. EFL teachers of young learners are now more familiar with an acquisition-based methodology, and recognize the true value of using storybooks and storytelling as a way to create an acquisition rich environment and ideal learning conditions which provide comprehensible input, or language a little beyond the child's current level of competence (Krashen 1981:103). Hester (1983), Garvie (1990) and Ellis and Brewster (1991) wrote about the benefits of using stories with children. Subsequently, many of the major coursebooks for young learners *Buzz*, *I-Spy*, *Pebbles*, *Superworld* have incorporated stories, some of which are simplified versions of well-known fairy tales, fables or stories inspired by modern classics. There have also been a number of handbooks for teachers that deal solely with this technique notably Wright (1995, 1997), Zaro and Salaberri (1995) and Gerngross and Puchta (1996). In addition, various magazines and newsletters for teachers have devoted whole issues to the subject of storytelling and children's literature, *jet* (1993) and *CATS* (1999 and 2000), and there are numerous websites to consult for the latest news on storybooks. See for example, http://hosted.ukoln.ac.uk/stories and http://www.realbooks.co.uk.

Children enjoy listening to stories in their L1 and understand the conventions of narrative. For example, as soon as they hear the formula, *Once upon a time ...*, they know what to expect next. For this reason, storybooks can provide an ideal introduction to the foreign language as it is presented in a context that is familiar to the child. Stories can also provide the starting point for a wide variety of related language and learning activities. Here are some further reasons why teachers use storybooks.

- Stories are motivating, challenging and fun and can help develop positive attitudes. They can create a desire to continue learning.

- Children can become personally involved in a story as they identify with the characters and try to interpret the narrative and illustrations. This helps develop their own creative powers.

- Linking fantasy and imagination with the child's real world, they provide a way of enabling children to make sense of their everyday life and forge links between home and school.

- Listening to stories in class is a social experience. Storytelling provokes a shared response of laughter, sadness, excitement and anticipation which is enjoyable and can help build up confidence and encourage social and emotional development.

- Listening to stories allows the teacher to introduce or revise vocabulary and structures, exposing the children to language which will enrich their thinking and gradually enter their own speech.

- Listening to stories helps children become aware of the rhythm, intonation and pronunciation of language.

- Storybooks cater for different learning styles and develop the different types of 'intelligences' that contribute to language learning, including emotional intelligence.

- Storybooks provide ideal opportunities for presenting cultural information and encouraging cross-cultural comparison.

- Storybooks develop children's learning strategies such as listening for general meaning, predicting, guessing meaning, and hypothesising.

- Storybooks address universal themes beyond the utilitarian level of basic dialogues and daily activities. Children can play with ideas and feelings and think about important issues.

- Stories can be chosen to link English with other subjects across the curriculum.

- Storybooks add variety, provide a springboard for creating complete units of work that constitute mini-syllabuses and involve pupils personally, creatively and actively in a whole curriculum approach.

- Storybooks offer positive concrete outcomes in the form of games, competitions, quizzes, drama, songs, projects, book making, etc.

- Learning English through stories can lay the foundations for secondary school in terms of learning basic language functions and structures, vocabulary and language-learning skills.

Selecting storybooks

Readers

Up until quite recently many of the storybooks used in the young learners ELT classroom were adapted and simplified versions of popular fairy tales, fables, nursery rhymes or specifically written stories. These books are commonly referred to as readers and are often produced to supplement the syllabus of a particular course where the vocabulary and structures are carefully graded and sequenced. Usually they are intended to be used by the pupil working alone to develop reading skills, rather than by the teacher for reading aloud to the children and as the starting point for other related language learning work. Often series of readers were not always very attractive or interesting. However, many publishers are now producing greatly improved readers such as the Penguin Young Readers series (www.penguinreaders.com).

Authentic storybooks

During the 1990s many EFL teachers began using authentic storybooks, also termed real books, which are written for children whose L1 is English, but can also be suitable for those learning English as an L2, if carefully selected. The language is not selected or graded. Many, however, contain language traditionally found in most syllabuses for young learners. The advantage of using authentic storybooks is that they provide examples of 'real' language and offer a rich source of authentic input, especially in terms of vocabulary. Authentic storybooks can be very motivating for a child as they experience a strong sense of achievement at having worked with a 'real' book. Furthermore, the quality of illustration is of a high standard, appealing to the young learner, and aiding general comprehension.

Types of storybooks

Teachers can select from a rich source of existing children's literature: stories that children are already familiar with in their L1. However, a criticism often aimed at using real books is that the language may be too complex and the content too simplistic for the age group they are aimed at. In a foreign language, however, children are often very happy to accept stories which they may reject in their L1. Furthermore, carefully selected storybooks can be interpreted on many different levels based on the child's age, conceptual and emotional development and all round experience, and can be exploited in many different ways. Teachers have used *The Very Hungry Caterpillar*, first published in 1970, which has become 'an international superstar on the EFL front' (Rixon, 1992:83), with children in nursery, primary and secondary school.

Criteria for selecting storybooks

Care needs to be taken to select authentic storybooks that are accessible, useful and relevant for children learning EFL. Some stories are linguistically less complicated than others. This is partly to do with the language used in the text, the length of the story, the amount of repetition, and the use of illustrations and layout. A common feature of narrative is the simple past. Some teachers may feel that they do not wish to introduce their pupils to this tense in the early stages of their learning. However, many stories begin with the formula *Once upon a time there was a ...* This indicates that the story is going to describe past events and actions, which is a natural feature of narrative and many stories would sound unnatural and distorted if this was changed. Furthermore, children will be concentrating on the meaning of the story, not on why and how the simple past is used. Their previous knowledge of narrative conventions in their L1 will have, to some extent, prepared them for its use in the target language. When selecting storybooks, other factors such as time, your pupils' conceptual level and ability to concentrate should also be considered. Generally speaking, many authentic storybooks are flexible for use with a variety of ages and levels, depending on how you exploit the story and wish your pupils to respond, but do not waste the full potential of some stories by using them with children too young. Real success depends on having the right story for the linguistic and conceptual level of the children. What criteria, then, can a teacher use? Figure 35 breaks down the main objectives of most language teaching programmes into criteria which are further translated into questions you can ask yourself. The objectives overlap to some extent, as indicated by the arrows.

Obviously, different storybooks contain different features, but all good storybooks contain a number of those in Fig. 35. If, however, after having selected a story you realize that it does not appeal to your pupils, it is advisable to adapt your plan of work or even abandon the story altogether. The most important objective is to develop appreciation and enjoyment of literature.

Using storybooks

Introducing and exploiting storybooks successfully in the classroom needs careful planning. Although most children are used to listening to stories in their L1, understanding a story in a foreign language can be

Category	Keywords	Questions
Level	vocabulary structures/functions	Is the level accessible? Does it provide an appropriate level of challenge? Does the story contain examples of rich vocabulary to provide comprehensible input?
Literary devices	repetition/cumulative content rhythm/rhyme question/answer dialogue/narrative humour/suspense predictability/surprise onomatopoeia/alliteration contrast metaphor/simile	What literary devices does the story contain? How will these help pupils understand the story, participate in the storytelling, improve their pronunciation, encourage anticipation and memorisation, enrich their language, maintain their concentration and add to their enjoyment?
Content/subject matter	relevant interesting amusing memorable length values	Will the story engage my pupils? Is it relevant to their interests? Is it amusing and memorable? Does it address universal themes? Is it possible to read the story in one go or can it be broken down into parts? Do we agree with the values and attitudes projected in the story?
Illustrations/layout	use of illustrations/layout attractive/colourful size target culture	Do the illustrations synchronize with the text and support children's understanding? Will they develop children's visual literacy? Are they appropriate to the age of my pupils? Are they attractive and colourful? Are they big enough for all the class to see? Do they depict life in the target culture? Does the layout (split page/lift the flap/cut-away pages, speech bubbles/no text) support children's understanding and maximise their interaction with the story?
Educational potential	learning to learn cross-curricular links world/cultural knowledge conceptual development learning styles/intelligences	How does the story enable children to become aware of and develop their learning strategies? Can the story link in with other subjects across the curriculum? What can children learn about the world and other cultures? Does the story develop and reinforce any concepts? Does the story and related activities accommodate different learning styles and bring into play different intelligences?

◄---- LINGUISTIC ----►

◄---- PSYCHOLOGICAL ----

◄--- COGNITIVE ---

◄---- CULTURAL ----

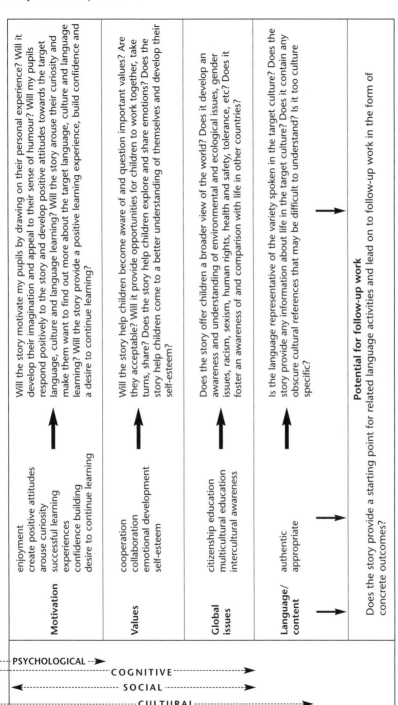

Fig. 35 Criteria for selecting storybooks

hard work. Simply reading a story aloud to a class without preparation could be disastrous, with a loss of pupil attention, motivation, and self-confidence. Pupils' enjoyment will increase enormously if we ensure their understanding is supported in several ways. Pupils will also need to feel involved and relate the story to aspects of their own experience. This takes gradual preparation which could spread over several lessons.

Storybooks and the coursebook

Storybooks can be used to provide extra language practice by supplementing and complementing a coursebook. For example, if you have just covered a unit about Animals, you may like to read your pupils an animal story. Or, if you have just covered a unit which has introduced a particular language function and structure, you may like to read a story which shows how this language is used in another context, making learning more varied, memorable and fun.

Storybooks as an alternative to the coursebook

If you do not have to adhere rigidly to a particular coursebook, storybooks can also be used as short basic syllabuses in their own right. Six or seven storybooks can be worked on throughout a school year. This would mean spending about four to five weeks on each story and between six to ten lessons per story, if the class has approximately one and half to two hours of English per week. In this way, storybooks can provide the starting point for all kinds of related language learning activities and offer a novel alternative to the coursebook.

A methodology for story-based work

As our starting point to designing a plan or programme of work is a storybook, we already begin with some of the crucial ingredients that can contribute to successful language learning with children:

- Input of authentic language so that children are exposed to the true complexities and richness of the language in order to work out meaning, and how language works through opportunities to experiment and hypothesise.

- Memorable, child-centred contexts from which language arises naturally so language is a means to an end, rather than an end in itself.

- Interesting and enjoyable content or themes which are motivating and develop positive attitudes.

- Opportunities to learn other things in addition to language through linking work with other areas of the curriculum. This also involves developing appreciation of literature.

- Opportunities to learn how to learn through organizing lessons which provide opportunities to develop learning strategies (see chapters 5 and 17).

We suggest applying the model presented in chapter 5 (Fig. 9) as it provides a framework for incorporating the above and is based on the familiar three stages usually associated with skills-based work. This model can be activated at three different levels to plan a programme of work constituting a mini-syllabus which can include up to 6–10 hours of work around a storybook, to plan individual lessons and activity cycles within lessons (see chapter 17). Figure 36 summarizes the procedures for planning a programme of work around the story *The Kangaroo from Woolloomooloo*, a repeating and rhyming story about a child's visit to the Sydney Zoo where he meets a variety of animals native to Australia. Full story notes for this story can be found in Ellis and Brewster (2002). This framework can be applied to any story and enables children to perceive a clear progression of work from pre- to post-story-telling activities leading up to a concrete outcome.

What is storytelling?

The challenge of any storyteller is to maintain the listener's interest and attention. Telling a story brings out a person's individuality and personality. Some people are natural storytellers. Most of us are not but we can all become good storytellers through practice and rehearsal and by becoming aware of techniques we can use to bring a story alive.

Reading or telling stories?

There are advantages and disadvantages of both reading a story aloud or telling a story and the two are closely interlinked. The beauty of a written story is that everything is provided. You are using the story as a guide; after you have read it and used it in the classroom several times you will probably be able to remember it by heart. So try to know the story well enough so that you are not reading words directly from the page, and can almost tell it without looking at the words. Do not read with your head down and look at the pupils frequently. We feel that reading a story aloud for most teachers is probably less daunting than telling a story, which puts an enormous burden upon the memory and their linguistic skills.

General procedures for planning story-based work	Stage	Story *The Kangaroo from Woolloomooloo*
• Decide on your learning goals (linguistic, cultural, cross-curricular, citizenship, etc.) and main outcome(s) • Decide if you need to modify the story in any way • Decide how long you will use the storybook for • Decide what storytelling techniques you will use. Will you read it all the way through in one go or can it be broken down into shorter, manageable sequences? • Decide how you may need to make the content accessible to your pupils by: contextualizing the story, introducing main characters; relating the story to the children's own experience; activating children's prior knowledge pre-teaching language that children will not be able to infer from the context, visual support, etc. • Decide which materials you may need to prepare • Decide how you are going to explain the aims and main outcomes to your pupils so they know what is expected of them	**1** **Plan** **Pre-storytelling activities** →	• To learn the names of native Australian animals and to produce short descriptions. To make a zig-zag book of Australian animals • No modification required • Between 6–8 hours about 6 lessons • The story will be read all the way through. Encourage participation through repetition of the refrain and question and prediction of animals and rhyming words • Show cover: *What's this? Have you ever seen a kangaroo? Where? Where do kangaroos live?* Elicit names of other Australian animals children may know • Locate Australia on a world map. Find Sydney and locate Woolloomooloo as an inner city area of Sydney. Ask general questions about Australia and comparison with own country as appropriate • Flashcard games to learn the names of animals • Prepare animal flashcards and sentence joining activity and dominoes • *We are going to listen to a story about a boy who visits the Sydney Zoo, and then make our own zig zag book of Australian animals and learn how to describe them.*

General procedures for planning story-based work	Stage	Story *The Kangaroo from Woolloomooloo*
• Decide how you are going to arrange your classroom for storytelling so everyone can see you and the storybook • Decide how, when and how many times you are going to read the story again for specific purposes	2 Do While-storytelling activities →	• Listen and repeat names of animals and refrain. • Listen and predict names of animals and rhyming words via visual clues • Listen and sequence (children are allocated an animal and stand in line as their animal is read) • Listen and match (animals to words) • Listen and remember (rhyming words)
• Decide which activities you are going to create to consolidate language introduced through the story • Decide which activities you are going to create to extend and personalize language from the story • Decide how you are going to get children to review work done and evaluate main outcome(s)	3 Review Post-storytelling activities →	• Pronunciation focus: card game to recognize number of syllables in words • Memory game: card game to find rhyming words • Matching activity: join the sentences which match • Guessing game: children listen to short descriptions and guess animal • Identifying musical instruments • Class survey: *Can you play the flute?* Etc. • Song (based on traditional Australian song) to consolidate language • Australian animals dominoes to consolidate animal and rhyming words • Book making: zig zag book of Australian animals to consolidate, review, extend and personalise language. Display children's work.

Fig. 36 A framework for planning story-based work

195

Using recorded versions of stories

Some stories are available on audio cassette or CD-ROM and these can be extremely useful for the following reasons:

- The voice provides a pronunciation guide for certain words as well as for sentence stress, intonation patterns and rhythm. It may also illustrate a number of storytelling techniques, such as disguising the voice for different characters, intonation patterns and rhythm, alternation of the pace of the voice, and so on.

- It allows pupils to hear English spoken by someone else.

- Some recordings contain amusing sound effects which are motivating and can support children's understanding and help them guess the meaning of unknown words.

It is important to bear in mind that listening to recorded version of a story can become a mechanical and passive activity unless it is set up in a way that actively involves pupils in listening tasks. Chapter 7 describes a number of while-listening activities.

We suggest you read the stories aloud as often as possible to your pupils rather than use a recorded version, and especially the first time they hear a story. This is important because it allows you to develop a personal, shared rapport with your pupils and to involve them actively in the story. You can help make the story come alive through use of intonation, gesture, mime, and so on, and by focusing pupils' attention on the illustrations to help them infer meaning. Reading a story aloud to your pupils yourself is more flexible than using a recorded version as it allows you to anticipate when to stop and ask pupils questions so that they can relate the story to their own experience. It allows you to repeat a part of the story immediately if you sense the pupils have not understood, to encourage them to repeat or to predict what happens next, to join in, to clarify a language item or cultural detail, or to refer to some other work you have covered together. Finally, it allows you to deal with a distracted child.

Using storytelling techniques

Once you feel confident with the story text, consider the different techniques you can use to provide further support for your pupils' understanding.

- If they are unfamiliar with storytelling, begin with short sessions which do not demand too much from them and over-extend their concentration span.

- If possible, have younger children sit on the floor around you, making sure everyone can see you and the illustrations and can hear you clearly.

- Read slowly and clearly. Give your pupils time to relate what they hear to what they see in the pictures, to think, ask questions, make comments. However, do vary the pace when the story speeds up.

- Make comments about the illustrations and point to them to focus the pupils' attention.

- Encourage your pupils to take part in the storytelling by repeating key vocabulary items and phrases. You can invite them to do this by pausing and looking at them with a questioning expression and by putting your hand to your ear to indicate that you are waiting for them to join in. Then repeat what they have said to confirm that they have predicted correctly and, if appropriate, expand by putting the word into a full phrase or sentence.

- Use gestures, mime, facial gestures to help convey the meaning.

- Vary the pace, tone and volume of your voice. Are you going to whisper to build up suspense? Are you going to introduce an element of surprise by raising your voice?

- Pause where appropriate to add dramatic effect or to give children time to relate what they hear to what they see, and to assimilate details in the illustrations.

- Disguise your voice for the different characters as much as you can to signal when different characters are speaking and help convey meaning.

- Make sound effects where possible.

- Ask questions to involve children *What do you think is going to happen next? What would you do?*

- Do not be afraid to repeat, expand and reformulate. This increases opportunities of exposure to the language and gives children a second (or third) chance to work out the meaning and have it confirmed. If you need to walk around the class to show children the pictures, repeat the text again and again.

Here is a short transcript taken from *The Snowman* to demonstrate some of the above techniques. The extract is when James shows the Snowman around his house. They go upstairs and visit his parent's bedroom. The class of eight- and nine-year-olds had only had eight hours of

English classes. Key vocabulary had been previously introduced. Notice how the interaction takes place entirely in English, the involvement of the children and the amount of repetition which provides further input and positive reinforcement for the children.

Teacher:	James said, Let's go … *(the teacher uses a slightly questioning intonation to invite pupils to complete the phrase. She points to the picture and also raises her hand in an upwards movement to prompt pupils and elicit upstairs.)*
Pupils:	Upstairs.
Teacher:	Upstairs. Let's go upstairs … *(the teacher smiles and nods, repeats the keyword, then repeats and expands by putting the key word into a complete phrase)* And James said at the door
Pupils:	Shhh! Be quiet!
Teacher:	Yes. Shhh! Be quiet! Just like I say to you! *(the teacher confirms and repeats using mime and sound effects and then relates it to the children!* This is my … *(slightly raised intonation to signal that she wants the children to provide the next word and points to the picture)*
Pupils:	Parent's bedroom.
Teacher:	Good. My parent's bedroom. This is my parent's bedroom. *(the teacher praises, repeats and expands)* And in the bedroom the Snowman put on a … *(the teacher points to the picture and elicits tie)*
Pupils:	Tie. A tie.
Teacher:	A tie. Yes. Like Benjamin. *(The teacher repeats and confirms then relates it to one of the children who is also wearing a tie)*
Benjamin:	And Meddy. *(Benjamin points out another pupil who is wearing a tie)*
Teacher:	Oh, yes. And Meddy. Meddy's wearing a tie too. Right. And some … What are these? *(She points to the glasses)* Do you remember? *(Children have forgotten)*. Some glasses. A pair of glasses. *(Teacher supplies the word in order to maintain the children's interest and pace. She puts her hand to her ear to signal that she want children to repeat.*
Pupils:	A pair of glasses.
Teacher:	Good. And a pair of … *(teacher points to trousers and invites pupils to provide word)*
Pupils:	Err. Blue jeans.
Teacher:	Blue jeans? *(the teacher wants the children to say trousers. Pupils learned blue jeans for the trousers James was wearing and they are over-generalizing. She does not say they are wrong but invites them to reconsider by comparing)*. Are they the same as

James's? *(Teacher turns back the pages and shows pupils a picture of James in his jeans. Then points again at the trousers the Snowman is putting on)* What are these?

Pupils: Trousers. *(Pupils remember!)*

Teacher: Good. Trousers. A pair of trousers. *(Teacher praises. Repeats and expands).* And a ... *(pointing to the hat)*

Pupils: a hat.

Teacher: and a hat. Good. *(repeats and praises).*

You might like to record yourself reading a story aloud and use the self assessment questionnaire suggested below.

Evaluating your storytelling skills

Figure 37 offers a technique you may like to use to develop your confidence and to identify which areas you need to improve. The self-assessment task follows the three stages: plan, do and review. You may also like to record yourself reading a story to your pupils and use the self-assessment questionnaire (Fig. 38) again afterwards.

Organizing a book corner

Most primary school classrooms have a book corner where pupils can look through books of their own choice and at their own pace, so it is a good idea to include copies of storybooks used in the English class. In this way, children can look at them at their leisure. This will provide an introduction to the written word in English. Furthermore, a stimulating book area will also promote a positive attitude towards reading and create enthusiasm among children for books.

Setting up a book corner

If you do not already have a book corner in your class or would prefer to set up a special one for English, you may find the following tips useful.

- A bookcase or shelving is ideal but a table or cardboard boxes covered in coloured paper can be used to display and store books.

- If possible, display books with the cover showing. This is more attractive and makes selection much easier.

- Try to involve your pupils as much as possible in the organization of the book corner. Looking after a book corner encourages children to take responsibility for the care of books. The class could elect book corner monitors who keep the book corner tidy.

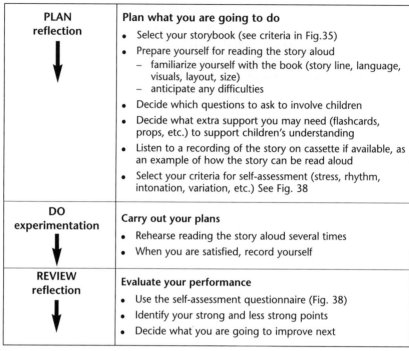

PLAN
reflection
	Plan what you are going to do
	• Select your storybook (see criteria in Fig.35)
	• Prepare yourself for reading the story aloud
	   – familiarize yourself with the book (story line, language, visuals, layout, size)
	   – anticipate any difficulties
	• Decide which questions to ask to involve children
	• Decide what extra support you may need (flashcards, props, etc.) to support children's understanding
	• Listen to a recording of the story on cassette if available, as an example of how the story can be read aloud
	• Select your criteria for self-assessment (stress, rhythm, intonation, variation, etc.) See Fig. 38

DO experimentation	Carry out your plans • Rehearse reading the story aloud several times • When you are satisfied, record yourself
REVIEW reflection	Evaluate your performance • Use the self-assessment questionnaire (Fig. 38) • Identify your strong and less strong points • Decide what you are going to improve next

Fig. 37 How can I improve my storytelling skills?

Self-assessment
1   **Pronunciation.** Did I have any problems with any vowels or consonants?
2   **Stress.** Did I have any problems with stress in individual words or in sentences?
3   **Rhythm.** Did I read too slowly or too quickly? Did I pause in the right places?
4   **Intonation.** Did I sound interesting or boring and did I vary my intonation where appropriate? Did I use the appropriate intonation for questions, statements, lists, and so on?
5   **Variation.** Did I vary the pace and the loudness of my voice where appropriate? Did I disguise my voice enough for the different characters?
6   **Pupil participation.** Did I pause in the correct places and use appropriate intonation to invite my pupils to join in? Did I ask the appropriate questions to encourage my pupils to predict what comes next?
7   **General impression.** How did I sound in general? Clear? Expressive? Lively?
8   **What do I need to improve?** What shall I focus on next week?

Fig. 38 Self-assessment questionnaire

- Decorate the corner with any work done by the pupils which has been inspired by stories read to them in class.

- Bring your pupils' attention to other books in English or in the L1 related to a topic you are covering.

If it is feasible, allow pupils to have open access to the book corner. This will encourage them to use it as often as possible without feeling they have to use it at specific times. If your pupils may borrow the books, you will need to devise a lending system. A simple system is to use an exercise book in which pupils write their names, the title of the books, date borrowed, and date returned. Decide how long the lending period should be. It is useful for pupils to keep a personal record of books they have looked through or borrowed. You could design a record card (Fig. 39). The information recorded can be written in English or in the L1.

Class Library – Pupil Record Card							
Name _____ Class _____							
Title/author	Date borrowed	Date returned	Comments	Title/Author	Date borrowed	Date returned	Comments

Class Library – Pupil Record Card						
Name _____ Class _____						
Title/author	Date borrowed	Date returned	Type of book	Main characters	Useful vocabulary and information	Comments

Fig. 39 Pupil record cards

Effective organization and imaginative display of your book corner both play a vital role in helping your pupils develop a positive attitude towards books, reading and the foreign language. Similarly, you could provide a poster to keep a class record of books read.

Associated activities

There are several activities which can follow on from regular book reading.

Drawing and colouring

Children can redraw the characters, create maps showing where the story takes place, think of other possible cover illustrations, and so on. The results of their efforts can be kept and then used as collages or posters to decorate appropriate areas of the book corner. Alternatively, pupils could make a folder of their own work.

Handicrafts

Pupils can be encouraged to create their own masks, hats, models of streets and buildings, etc., inspired by the characters and places in the books they have enjoyed. Activities of this kind present an ideal opportunity for developing oral comprehension through the language used for giving instructions.

Songs and rhymes

Very often, the themes developed in stories are to be found in various songs and rhymes. See chapter 12 for further suggestions.

Vocabulary activities

Pupils can create their own 'Picture Dictionary', based on words from the stories they have read or heard. They can work individually or pool their efforts to illustrate the words, either by drawing pictures themselves or by cutting pictures out of magazines or catalogues. They can choose whether to arrange the words alphabetically or thematically. For further suggestions, see chapter 6.

This chapter has shown that using stories and the technique of storytelling provide an acquisition-rich learning environment for our pupils and an all-round curriculum approach. There are a number of considerations facing teachers when selecting stories and the potential of each story needs to be evaluated carefully for a specific group of learners. The accompanying methodology offers a gradual progression from general understanding of the story to tasks which consolidate, extend and personalize the language and content presented through a story in the form of concrete outcomes. Reading stories aloud also needs careful preparation and rehearsal in order to fully support our pupils.

15 Technology

When using technology we need to consider how best it can be used and how it can complement our classroom-based work so it becomes integrated into our overall plan of work. First we shall consider how technology can contribute to our pupils' learning. Then we will look at a methodology for using different types of technology including video and computer assisted language learning (CALL) which covers the use of word-processing, CD-ROMS, authoring programmes and the internet.

The benefits for young learners

Technology can contribute to the global development of our pupils and complies with the psychological, linguistic, cognitive, social and cultural objectives of most language teaching programmes. Figure 40 highlights some of the benefits of using technology.

Using video

There are a number of videos that have been made specifically for the ELT classroom which are accompanied by activity books and teacher's guides or accompany coursebooks. One of the most well-known is *Muzzy in Gondoland* produced by the BBC in the 1980s but still used widely. Although it is accompanied by other components including activity and workbooks, the coursebook *Buzz* was produced later to link into the video. *Chatterbox* is accompanied by *Wizadora*, episodes about the antics of a witch. More recent courses with accompanying videos are *New Boomerang, Join In* and *New English Parade*. In addition to courses, a number of supplementary videos are available with songs and rhymes like *Play it Again!* Ashworth et al. 1996). *We're Kids in Britain* (Ellis 1997) presents cultural aspects of life in Britain from a child's perspective. The accompanying activity book invites children to compare these with their own cultural experience. Finally, Oxford University Press have made ELT video adaptations of the award-winning storybook *Winnie the Witch* and the Oscar-winning Wallace and Gromit animated films, *The Wrong Trousers* and *A Close Shave* all of which come with pupil's and teacher's books.

There are also a number of authentic sources of suitable videos but you must check copyright first.

- Animated stories: *Spot* series, *The Very Hungry Caterpillar, Funnybones, The Snowman, Rosie's Walk*, etc.

Technology – the benefits for young learners

Psychological	Children find it fun, motivating and stimulating. It provides variety.
	It appeal to childrens' sophisticated tastes.
	It caters for children with different learning styles, can provide successful learning experiences and therefore develop confidence and positive attitudes to the foreign language and to language learning.
	It can be used to reward pupils for work they have done. For example, if pupils have worked hard on a story in class you can show them an animated version on video or they can use a CD-ROM version for pleasure.
Linguistic	It combines sound and vision and provides a full context for language so children see language in use making it more accessible and memorable.
	It shows all factors of communication, including non-verbal communication.
	It can develop all skills and introduces or revises new words and phrases.
Cognitive	It develops the child's curiosity and provides up-to-date information.
	It heightens childrens' powers of observation and awareness of visual and audio clues as aids to meaning.
	It enables children to maximize their abilities to infer from context.
	It develops motor skills, keyboard skills, information and research skills as well as independent learning.
Social	A class working together on a video of an animated story or a video extract is a shared social experience. Pupils working together on a computer program will develop collaborative skills as they take turns using the keyboard and help each other complete a task.
Cultural	It takes the child outside the classroom into the real or fantasy world.
	It helps bridge the culture gap by providing background cultural information.
	It helps bridge the credibility gap – children can see what it's really like in an English-speaking country.

Fig. 40 Benefits of using technology

- TV children's programmes

- Documentary: e.g. BBC *World of Wildlife*: although linguistically difficult, short sequences can be used with the necessary preparation and very specific while-viewing tasks to focus childrens' attention

- Nursery rhymes: excellent cultural input to bridge the credibility gap as pupils see children singing and performing songs and rhymes

- Self-made videos: it is very motivating for children to watch a video of themselves acting out a story, singing songs, etc. These can be used at school open days.

A video-based methodology

The familiar three stages as described in chapters 5 and 7 can be applied to using video: pre-, while- and post-viewing. Following this three-stage methodology allows you and the pupils to get the most out of a video sequence and transforms passive viewers into active viewers. A video sequence or extract can be as short as two minutes or longer. This will depend on your reason for using video. Each stage will include some or all of the following:

Pre-viewing/Plan
Planning and preparing for active viewing will include:

- contextualizing the video sequence
- motivating pupils to view
- focusing the pupils' attention on the topic or specific language items
- activating prior knowledge about a topic
- making predictions about content and language
- eliciting or pre-teaching key language
- explaining the reason for viewing and purpose of task

While-viewing/Do
There are three main reasons for viewing:

1 *Global viewing or viewing for general understanding:* children do not see videos as language learning devices and are very reluctant to have an extract interrupted or broken down by teachers. Children need to see a whole video sequence or extract shown straight through first so that they can follow and understand the global meaning. After that the teacher may go back over the sequence or extract and exploit it in order to focus on particular aspects of language and content. If a sequence is carefully selected it allows you to maintain interest and suspense and encourage children to predict what happens next.

2   *Viewing for detail:* this usually requires children to focus on something very specific and they may require a physical response such as putting up a hand each time they see a specific item or hear a specific word or structure. The following typical activities are taken from Ellis (1997):

- Watch and complete the picture (to practise vocabulary for food)

- Watch and number (put things in sequence to practise vocabulary for playground games)

- Watch and tick (choose from a selection of items to practise vocabulary for means of transport)

- Watch and draw (draw items on a picture to practise prepositions of location)

- Watch and write (write numbers for children's ages)

- Watch and sort (sort items into different stockings to practise vocabulary for Christmas presents)

These activities only require children to tick, number, draw lines and sometimes complete a picture. The teacher can aid this process by using the pause button and playing the short sequence again for a second viewing or for pupils to check their work.

3   *Viewing for pleasure:* see below

Post-viewing/Review

Activities to provide opportunities for language presented and practised through the video sequence to be consolidated, extended and personalized or to provide opportunities to research further information can include: recording information, comparing information, crosswords, spot the difference, craft activities, drawing, writing instructions or recipes, sequencing, questionnaires and quizzes, surveys, labelling, designing a poster or a badge, reading and colouring, playing a game and reviewing work done. At the end of pupils' hard work, allow them to view the video again for pleasure.

Video room management

As with any classroom aid it will only fully contribute to the learning process if the teacher is in control of equipment and has fully planned and integrated video-based work into a lesson. Here are some tips to aid this process:

- Familiarize yourself with the video player and the remote control. Practise several times.

- Watch a sequence several times before showing it to your pupils so you know where you will want to pause, to ask questions, etc.

- Practise using the pause button, rewind, etc.

- Always check your equipment before you start your lesson. There is nothing worse than building up children's motivation ready for viewing, then when you start to play a sequence, you find you have forgotten to switch on or have not found the right place.

- Make sure all pupils can see and hear the video.

- Make sure pupils know what they have to do while viewing and why.

- Use the pause button to give pupils time to complete a task and always be prepared to give pupils second or third viewing if needed.

Using computers

The purpose of this section is to provide guidelines on how CALL can complement and reinforce classroom-based learning. It does not look at the technical side of computers because there are so many differences and the field is changing and developing so rapidly. A number of recent publications on the use of computers will make useful reading if you wish to pursue this area further (Eastment 1999, Teeler and Gray 2000, Windeatt, Hardisty and Eastment 2000, Dudeney 2000, Sharma 1998).

Computer facilities in schools will vary enormously from one per school to one per classroom to a fully equipped computer room. Experience has shown though that without the necessary technical support, using computers can become frustrating for yourself and the pupils and extremely time-wasting. If you are in a school where there is one computer per class, you can organize part of your classes where pupils divide into groups and move around doing different activities, so each group will get a turn to work on the computer. Alternatively, you could use one computer with the whole class if you are able to project the screen. In this way, you could elicit from the pupils and invite individual pupils to operate the keyboard. Some teachers may work in a school which has a computer room which is fully operational with no technical hitches where pupils can work in twos or threes per computer. It is important that pupils understand that using computers is for learning and not for play! The following methodology can ensure purposeful and productive computer sessions.

A computer-based methodology

Applying the three familiar stages to using computers allows us to use a methodology as follows:

Before using computers/Plan

- Plan work you will do with computers so it integrates into your over-all lesson plan and is not a simple 'add-on' or time-filler

- Establish ground rules: it is important that children respect hardware and software and are made responsible for hanging up headphones, tidying the room, respecting the mouse and keyboard, etc.

- Pre-teach computer related vocabulary: *screen, mouse, headphones, keyboard, click on, go back, scroll up/down*, etc.

- Contextualize work and get pupils to focus on the topic

- Prepare pupils linguistically and conceptually for the activity type, demonstrating as appropriate

- Make sure that children working together on a computer understand that they are to take turns, share and help each other as necessary

- Explain purpose of a computer activity: to practise, to draft, to produce final work for a display, to reconstruct, to spell, to revise, etc.

While using computers/Do

- Make sure pupils respect rules!

- Make sure pupils stay on task (a back turned and they may be into a another programme or website!)

- Make sure pupils carry out their task while you monitor, help, guide and advise as necessary

After using computers/Review

Depending on the task, pupils should:

- complete work in the classroom
- check work, record scores, complete evaluation sheet
- collate work that has been produced by computer
- display work
- compare their work with others
- review what they have done and why (see Fig. 42 for a sample record sheet)

CALL options

Word processing packages

Most computers come with a CD-ROM and word processor. The word processor allows pupils to practise their writing skills and take pride in the presentation of their work, especially creating materials for project work and displays. *Creative Writer* is a desktop publisher/word processing package for children produced by Microsoft. Children can produce different types of writing for different purposes such as letters, cards, menus, book reports, etc. It comes with a spellcheck and children can import illustrations, backgrounds and borders. It is ideal for developing an awareness of the writing process and layout, as pupils have to produce various drafts of their work before they complete the final 'product' on *Creative Writer*.

CD-ROMs

The range of CD-ROMs is increasing rapidly although at the time of writing, there is a need for more specifically created CDs for young EFL learners. Some coursebooks are accompanied by a CD-ROM of video clips, songs and activities although there is no complete course on the market as yet. Delta's *Listen and Learn English* offers a set of games designed to help children working towards the UCLES Young Learner English Tests. *WordBird's Wordland* (Perrett 1995) is a vocabulary development package which can be used to consolidate and extend vocabulary presented through coursebooks, topic work and stories. It is grouped into 20 topics representing over 400 words. There are games to develop reading, listening, observation and spelling, and songs including a karaoke version. The graphics are attractive and *WordBird* rewards each answer. There are also a number of dictionaries on CD-ROM such as Longman's *Zak's Wordgames* and *Oxford Interactive Word Magic* which are both links to young learner dictionaries but have the advantage of sound and animation.

Some stories exist on CD-ROM for example *Winnie the Witch* and *The Fish Who Could Wish*. These CD-ROMs can be used to extend a story presented in the classroom with activities which can be used by groups of two or three children working together at a computer or by children working individually. The accompanying handbooks of instructions explain a range of different activities. *Winnie* teaches the vocabulary of the rooms of the house, colours, furniture, etc. *The Fish Who Could Wish* consolidates vocabulary related to under the sea, such as *fish, sharks*. Adjectives and nouns of shapes are used in an imaginative rhyming story.

Finally, there is a wealth of informational CD-ROMs created for native-speaker children and produced by trade publishers such as those by Dorling Kindersley (www.dk.com) which can link in well with topic-based and cross-curricular work. (See also www.brainworks.co.uk)

Authoring programs

An authoring program allows teachers to create their own exercises, allowing great flexibility as exercises can be designed to be used with near beginners to higher level pupils. The authoring suite from Wida Software (www.wida.co.uk) for example, provides a range of programs that can be used to successfully complement classroom-based work and provide excellent opportunities for pupils to consolidate their learning. They include gap filling, matching, multiple choice, vocabulary and sequencing activities.

One of the most popular is a text reconstruction activity called *Storyboard*, where a short text (authored by the teacher to suit the level of his/her pupils) is entirely obliterated on screen, each letter of each word being replaced by a blob, leaving only the title, punctuation and spacing intact, all of which provide pupils with important clues. Pupils reconstruct the text by guessing single words. When a correct word is found it is printed in the place wherever it occurs in the text. Help options are available and it is also possible to provide visual and audio clues. It can be used with a variety of levels building up writing skills from word and sentence level to short text level. Pupils enjoy the challenge it presents and as they work together on reconstructing a text, they are developing social and collaborative skills.

Storyboard can be used after language has been introduced and practised from a unit in a coursebook or after a topic, a story, a song or rhyme has been presented in class and pupils are confident and familiar with the language. For example, the teacher writes a short summary of a story or copies the words of a song or rhyme and enters the text into the authoring program. The text can range from about 50 to over 100 words depending on the pupils' level and ability to concentrate. For example here is a short summary of the story *The Kangaroo from Woolloomooloo.*

> *A visit to the Sydney Zoo*
> *One day a boy goes to the Sydney Zoo in Australia. He sees lots of Australian animals, a kangaroo, a bandicoot, a koala, a rainbow snake, a crocodile, a goanna, a wombat, a cockatoo, a dingo, a magpie and a platypus. A goanna is a type of lizard and a dingo is a wild dog.*

(54 words)

If the first word that children enter is *a,* this word will appear everywhere it occurs in the text, that is 14 times! As children become familiar with *Storyboard* they very quickly develop strategies for attacking the blobs, such as entering common function words, using the title to predict content, remembering key vocabulary and phrases, remembering sequences, etc. A scoring facility tells them the number of words in the text so they can see how many words they have found and how many they still have to find which adds a game-like dimension to the activity.

The internet and how to find appropriate sites

The Web can be a useful tool for project work, topic and story-based work in the young learners classroom and e-mail is a wonderful way of encouraging children to read and write to other children all over the world.

Many sites are regularly updated and well-designed. To find worthwhile material, we need to bear in mind certain criteria and know how to use search engines and web directories efficiently. For example, *Google* is a search engine and we use this when we know exactly what we are looking for, such as a work, a phrase or a name. *Yahoo* is a web directory and we use this if we are looking for something more general, such as a subject or a topic. Probably, the best piece of advice is to go on personal recommendations or sites recommended in books and journals. Generally speaking, children are more likely to pay attention to sites which include plenty of images which will support their understanding of the accompanying text. There are many beautiful sites for children, and simple tasks with specified outcomes can be created to guide them through a site.

When selecting sites for use in the young learners classroom it is useful to bear in mind the following criteria (adapted from Eastment 2001:102):

Accuracy:	Is the information correct?
Authority:	Is it clear who wrote the page? Is there an e-mail address to contact?
Currency:	Is the information up-to-date. Do we know when the page or site was last updated?
Presentation:	Are the pages attractive, not too detailed and cluttered, not too text-based and easy to find our way around?
Visuals:	Are there plenty of images which support the text?
Sound:	Do any sound effects, music, speech, support children's understanding?
Relevance:	Is the content relevant to our pupils? Does it link into our classroom-based work?

Usability:	Is it possible to design a task that will focus our pupils' attention and guide them through the site?
Language level:	Is the language accessible for our pupils' level? Does it provide our pupils with an appropriate level of challenge so they can overcome any difficulty by using appropriate strategies? Does it avoid too technical, idiomatic or culturally specific language? Will children be able to extract specific information from the text with the support of a task?
Education potential:	Will our pupils learn useful information from the site?
Potential for follow-up:	Is it possible to download material from the site that pupils can use to make displays, class magazines, projects, etc.?

Once you have found sites you are satisfied with, bookmark these or add them to your favourites. Please note, however, that websites can change frequently in both content and design, so sites and accompanying task sheets may need checking before use and updating accordingly.

Web safety

The open nature of the internet means that there are some materials which are inappropriate for viewing by children. It is, therefore, extremely important to protect your pupils from distasteful sites which the random nature of search engines can sometimes reveal. If possible, your computers should be equipped with a program like *Net Nanny, Cyber Sentinel* or *Cyber Patrol* which are designed to filter out unsavoury content, words and phrases and will not let surfers connect to banned sites. However, even with a filter, it cannot be guaranteed that an inappropriate site cannot be accessed. It is advisable not to allow your pupils to use a search engine unless authorized and supervised by you, or unless it is a child-safe one such as *Yahooligans, SafetyNet* or *Ask Jeeves for Kids*. Children should always be supervised in a computer room and it should be arranged so that computer screens are facing inwards so the teacher standing in the middle can glance around quickly and always see what the children are doing. It is also worth considering having an Acceptable Use Policy (AUP) which is a document signed by pupils and parents detailing how the internet can and cannot be used. It sets out specific consequences – usually the suspension of computer privileges for pupils who disobey a teacher's instructions. Such action is a precaution and can protect you, the teacher, the pupils and the school from embarrassing moments. The site http://safety.ngfl.gov.uk provides information on many aspects of web safety including sample AUPs and letters to parents as well as links to other school sites in Britain. (See Etchells 1999.)

Making use of the internet

The internet lends itself particularly to communicative and task-based learning and links extremely well into project, topic and story-based work. Here are some of the uses that can be made of the internet by young learners:

- Reading and following instructions and answering questions. A task such as the one in Fig. 41 involves the children in working through a series of instructions and answering specific questions. It could be related to a project on Dinosaurs as well as linking in with story-based work such as *Meg's Eggs*. The task develops a number of skills and strategies including skimming and scanning, using visual clues to support understanding, reinforcing alphabet skills, using prior knowledge and reinforcing geographical knowledge of continents, and reinforcing concepts of size. Afterwards the pupils could check their answers with each other and the teacher, collate them and produce a dinosaur display.

---

www.enchantedlearning.com

Dinosaurs

1 Click on Zoom Dinosaurs. Put your cursor on the dinosaur. What can you see?
2 Click on Dinosaur Dictionary. Click on D. Then click on Di. Find Diplodocus. Click on Diplodocus. Where was Diplodocus found? Name the continent.
3 How long was the neck of Diplodocus? How long was the tail of Diplodocus?
4 Go back. Click on S. Then click on St. Find Stegosaurus. Click on Stegosaurus. How many bony plates did Stegosaurus have?
5 Where was Stegosaurus found? Name the continents.
6 Go back. Click on T. Find T.rex. Click on T.rex. What does Tyrannosaurus Rex mean?
7 How long was a T.rex tooth?
8 Go back. Click on F. Find footprints. Have any dinosaur footprints been found?
9 Find feather. Did any dinosaurs have feathers?
10 Click on All About Dinsosaurs. Could dinosaurs fly?

Fig. 41 An internet task

- Accessing a site such as the one above to produce a quiz for other pupils based on the model above.

- Looking for specific information connected to a topic. It is useful to discuss in advance and agree on questions that will guide pupils through a site.

- Doing language activities. There are many sites that now include activities for younger learners. See for example www.learnenglish.org.uk/kid_frame.html

- Creating a school website. This is an ideal way for children to tell the world about themselves and their school and to find out about other children and schools around the world. It is an ambitious project and requires knowledge of how to create websites or help from a willing technician. However, it can lead to twinning with a school and all kinds of project work which can provide ideal opportunities for cross-cultural comparison. See web projects/keypals on the IATEFL Young Learners web site http://www.countryschool.com/younglearners.htm

- Writing to keypals. These are the electronic equivalent of penpals and allow children to make direct contact with another child of their own age and interests anywhere in the world. An excellent starting point is www.eduweb.co.uk

A useful book by Sperling (1999), although not written for young learners, provides 30 topic-based chapters many of which could be easily adapted, for example, First Meeting, Amusement Parks, Animals, Food, Games, and so on. There is a workbook and a companion website which provides links to the Web pages needed to complete the activities in the workbook.

Computer management

A well-planned session with computers that links into classroom-based work should not allow children either the time or inclination to, for example, change activity or surf the Net. Here are some basic steps to follow to ensure responsible and effective computer room management:

- Establish ground rules for using computers.

- Make sure pupils know what will happen if they disobey.

- Always visit a site before using it with your pupils and if you are satisfied, bookmark it so you can access it quickly.

- Check (or, if possible, get a technician to do this) that computers are switched on, in good working order, headphones are working, CD-ROMs you wish to use are installed, or a website is already accessed.

- Ensure that pupils understand the purpose of their work with computers.

- Never allow a child to access a link or download anything unless authorized and supervised by the teacher.

- Always give children a task to focus their attention.

- Restrict use to a limited time.

It is a good idea for a school to record work done on computers in a record sheet like the one in Fig. 43 so its use can be monitored. This also helps us to think about and plan our work with computers carefully using the three stage methodology to ensure that it is fully integrated into our classroom-based work. Older pupils can also be given a record sheet Fig. 42 to encourage them to reflect on what they did and how they did it as well as how their work with computers can consolidate their classroom-based learning.

Technology and professional development

Finally, don't forget the role that technology can play in your own professional development. You can join discussion groups for example, www.tefl.net or the one available through the IATELF young learners special interest group www.countryschool.com/younglearners.htm, download materials and lesson plans, find out about the latest publications, and so on. Volume 55 (2001) of the *English Language Teaching Journal* has a series of features on websites for the language teacher.

This chapter has shown that technology can play an important role in contributing to children's learning. It can offer children a rich and memorable learning environment with the possibility of developing many linguistic skills as well as more global skills such as keyboard and other IT skills that will help them in their future studies. It does require, however, careful planning in order to integrate CALL into regular teaching as well as careful management to ensure responsible use.

**Computer Work
Pupil Record Sheet**

1 Name   _____

2 Date   _____

3 Class   _____

4 Materials used _____

                             _____

                             _____

5 Did you work   a) alone? _____

                    b) with a classmate(s)? _____

  If b), did you discuss the activity in:

                    a) English? _____

                    b) your language? _____

6 How did the software you use help you with your English?

    _____

    _____

    _____

    _____

    _____

7 What are you going to do next?

    _____

    _____

    _____

    _____

8 What did you enjoy about working on the computer?

    _____

    _____

    _____

    _____

Fig. 42 A Pupil Record Sheet for computer-based work

Date	Name of teacher	Class level	Pre-CALL preparation	CALL used (CD, internet, authoring program etc.)	Objectives	After-CALL follow-up

Fig. 43 A Teacher Record Sheet for CALL

16 Classroom management

In this chapter you will be encouraged to think more carefully about classroom management skills in relation to three main areas: creating and maintaining motivation, maintaining classroom control and discipline and organizing learning activities. Classroom management will also be influenced by your teaching style, the amount of pupil independence that is acceptable in your context, the amount of competition and cooperation you establish in your class and the role and use of the L1 in your class.

Motivation

Motivation is a term which in the past has been used quite loosely. For example it sometimes refers to feelings, a goal, a mental process, a certain type of behaviour or a personal characteristic. More recently, motivation has been seen as a set of beliefs, thoughts and feelings that are turned into action. According to Dörnyei (1998:117), 'motivation has been widely accepted by both teachers and researchers as one of the key factors that influence the rate and success of second/foreign language (L2) learning'. Being motivated to learn a language is the first impetus. At first the novelty factor may be enough to carry children's learning forward. But feelings of enjoyment, challenge or success will need to continue for many years if the difficult task of learning a language is to be achieved. If children now learn English from the age of six or nine, they may well be learning it at school for up to nine years. If the pupils are not enjoying their lessons, the teacher's job is much harder. We have already discussed the fact that young children will not necessarily have the same kinds of motivation as adults. In some countries pupils will be all too aware of the benefits that knowing English can bring, such as a better job or better opportunities for studying abroad. However, for young children these reasons will not be relevant to their immediate, day-to-day concerns. Cajkler and Addelman (2000), suggest that, in order to keep levels of motivation high, language teachers should adopt a 'critical attitude' to the activities and tasks they use and the expectations they create. This is done so as to develop a healthy questioning of the work they prepare for their pupils and the schemes of work they follow.

We have already referred to the need to provide a classroom atmosphere which promotes pupils' confidence and self-esteem so that they can learn more effectively and enjoyably. This echoes two key factors in motivating learners that Dörnyei describes. The first is how far a learner expects to be successful in doing the task, the second is how much the learner thinks being successful in doing the task is important. Judging how far a learner will have feelings of success comes partly from their past experiences in learning, partly from the kinds of judgement they have made about their own abilities and partly from their feelings of wanting to feel good about themselves, known as *self esteem*. Children seem quickly to become aware of their position within a class and tend to know whether they are one of the 'clever' pupils at school or not. Studies show that where classes are divided into ability groupings, the children know whether they are in the top ability group or not, even if the groups are given innocent names like Tigers, Leopards, Lions, and so on. If children have had very negative experiences with language learning, or feel they are not good at language learning, they may underachieve even if they actually enjoy it.

Classroom control and discipline

Here we shall consider five main areas that help to create an effective learning environment.

Establishing routines

When children enter school they are faced with a new set of social routines and relationships which even a kindergarten may not have prepared them for. According to Nelson (1977) children develop *scripts*, or *mental maps*, to understand routines in their lives in the same way that adults do. As adults we know what to do in a doctor's surgery or in a job interview, both of which can be stressful situations if we do not know what to expect. In the same way, children learn how to cope with the demands of school and the stress of being in a large class, receiving little individual attention and facing unfamiliar rules and conventions. Young children gradually become familiar with established classroom routines that help to make them feel confident. Anxious or immature learners will tend to react negatively to changes in the normal classroom pattern, so it is a good idea to develop familiar patterns with young learners in their first year of schooling. If children in your school learn English at a very young age, teachers need to be careful not to speak too much in English. The children may become very bewildered and uncomfortable if the teacher talks to them all the time in a strange foreign language. Gradually introducing pupils to use English for a short period of time through songs or rhymes will help to ease them in slowly.

Finding a balance

Children very quickly work out which teachers are inconsistent in their standards of discipline. Some are very authoritarian, and this may be part of the normal classroom culture, but a classroom with little discipline may descend into chaos where nothing is learned. Finding the right balance between order and flexibility is very important. The most effective environment for learning is often found in a classroom where the teacher is firm but kind and encouraging so that pupils, especially very young children, feel confident and happy. One way of establishing this is quickly getting to know the pupils' names, as this will help to create a secure and friendly atmosphere. It will also enable you to control and discipline the class much more effectively, as it helps to identify who should respond in class, it aids the organization of learning activities and it helps you to identify troublemakers more easily. You will have to decide whether you are going to address the pupils by their original names or whether you want to give them special English names. You may like to ask the children to vote for their preference. Many primary classes have fewer than thirty-five children; learning names for larger classes can become quite problematical. A four-point action plan could be:

- Copy out class lists and the names of children you commonly put into groups; write their names on any piece of work you collect or display.

- If you call a register, look at the children as they respond.

- Ask the children to write their names clearly on a piece of card which they place on their desks. Collect them, then distribute them at the beginning of each lesson.

- Keep a seating plan of the class. At first you may wish the children to remain in the same seats, although it would be a pity to let this organizational convenience dominate your decision to let the children work in different groups once you know their names.

Children generally like to work within a framework where the boundaries of acceptable and unacceptable behaviour are reasonable and consistent so that they know where they stand. You will need to decide what you consider acceptable behaviour in the light of the general ethos of the school, the age of the pupils, the size of the class and your personality. You may find that in order to establish your authority a clear indication needs to be given early on of your classroom rules and your determination to keep them calmly and fairly. The number of rules you make should be kept to the minimum and the reason for having them should always be explained to the children. They will probably focus on the encouragement of reasonable behaviour and sociability. Older children could be involved in making up a set of classroom rules, perhaps under a list of Dos and Don'ts, which they, and you, have to observe! You may like to draw up a class contract with your class at the beginning of a school year (see Greenwood 1997:11 for an example).

Getting the pupils' attention

With young pupils you may need to establish a signal for getting the pupils' attention. This may be when you say FREEZE! RIGHT! or clap, or use a musical instrument, or knock on the desk, and so on. Quickly start an activity such as an action song or rhyme to create a momentum and keep them occupied. When you want to gain the attention of the whole class you can also try these steps:

- Firmly name the children still talking: *Jules and Michelle, stop talking please* and maintain eye contact. As soon as the children become quiet, give a short verbal instruction, such as *Let's begin.*

- Start a well-known activity or routine or give instructions for a new activity to keep the pupils' attention. Keep eye contact with talkative children for a while to show them their behaviour is being monitored.

- Wait for quiet before beginning a new activity.

- Once these routines have become established you should be able to cut down on the amount of time you spend disciplining pupils.

Finding an acceptable noise level

Once the lesson has started and the children are working on tasks that you have set, you may find the children becoming noisy. If the children are engaged in communicative activities to develop fluency in pairs or groups, the noise level will inevitably rise. Most language teachers would find this acceptable, as long as the talk is 'on-task'. If the noise level rises too much, pick out the noisiest group, name one of the children in the group and gesture them to quieten down. Remember that the noisier the teacher is, the noisier the children will become. Sometimes the noise levels rise because the tasks you have chosen are not clear, are too easy or too difficult. If so, you may need to re-think the activity.

Giving praise

You can quickly establish good relationships with your pupils by praising good behaviour, commenting on good work, making helpful suggestions and encouraging pupils' efforts. This is important in setting the right atmosphere, providing a good model for your pupils to follow and boosting your pupils' confidence and self-esteem. However, if you constantly over-praise pupils, it may become valueless. Some of the kinds of pupil behaviour you might want to encourage and praise include:

- thinking before answering, trying something difficult for the first time, achieving something difficult, persisting with a difficult task

- sharing with others or helping a classmate, working well together

- listening and following directions well, using English correctly or creatively, making a big improvement

- observing classroom rules, putting classroom materials away, completing homework on time

The kind of English to praise young learners will have to be quite simple, especially in the early phases. You can simply use words like: *well done, brilliant! superb, good reading/writing/spelling; what a good listener/speaker/reader/writer/speller, what neat work, very good behaviour/manners*. If you want to praise older pupils in a slightly more sophisticated way, especially in the early days when you are establishing a routine with a class, it may be useful to use the L1 occasionally. You might say things like: *You must be proud of … See how you have improved in … You have worked so hard.*

In summary, what you are trying to do when giving praise is: pinpoint what you like by being specific; give praise with sincerity and enthusiasm in a variety of ways; use praise consistently and frequently, especially when the pupils are first learning something; praise groups or the whole class as well as individuals; vary to whom you give praise (i.e. not always just the 'best' in the class) and look for and name at least two children who are doing what you want to avoid 'favouritism'.

Organizing learning activities

Find out the textbook your pupils used with their previous class teacher, what topics they have studied already and found particularly interesting, what kinds of activities they liked, etc. Ask about hobbies, clubs they may be in, their favourite games, toys, sports, TV programmes, music, and films. This will help you to build up a picture of topics and activities that you can draw upon in your lessons to make them interesting or to supplement the textbook. When children endlessly repeat activities on the same topics or when language activities are pitched at the wrong level or are too mechanical, they are liable to become frustrated and noisy. In some contexts pupils' main motivation is to pass English tests and they may be less willing to engage in activities which they think do not prepare them for these. In these cases, teachers must determine an appropriate balance between teaching to the tests and other language learning.

Dealing with bilingual pupils

Some pupils in your class may already speak English well because they have an English-speaking parent, may have lived in an English-speaking country or may holiday in such countries. Some children may also have extra English lessons outside school hours and will have more advanced levels of English than the rest of the class. If these pupils' learning needs are not catered for, they may become bored or disruptive, which is a pity as their skills can be seen as a bonus. Use strategies for encouraging these children to: 'show and tell' some of their experiences in the country of the target language; explain the instructions for games to groups or even act as the teacher in demonstrating a game; help others in groups (only where this pupil has the right attitude and does nor ridicule slower learners, etc. and where this does not happen too much so the pupil becomes bored and resentful); make recordings of stories or other listening activities; write stories, instructions or descriptions for other pupils to read and act upon; make games which require sentence cards or board games and 'Chance' cards; test pupils, e.g. spelling and complete individualized work at a higher level

It generally means making higher demands on and having higher expectations of these pupils and not allowing their work to become sloppy (see more in the section below on mixed ability classes).

Managing pair and group work

Berman (1998) suggests that very young learners prefer working alone and can be reluctant to share. Imposing pair or group work on pupils who are not yet ready for it can sometimes have a negative effect, so be aware of this when trying it out for the first time with children under the age of seven. For some activities it is often easier and more fruitful to organize work in pairs than in groups where pupils can easily work with the person next to or behind them. Alternatively pupils can work 'back to back', especially where they are working with an information-gap activity using different sets of information, or working from information you have pinned on walls. This information could take the form of large pictures, charts or graphs which one child asks questions about and the other answers, for example, in a guessing game using pictures.

There are several ways of organizing groups to work together. The easiest is to ask pupils who sit near one another to form a pair or group.

Another method is to use the children's choice. Such friendship groups are probably the most popular with pupils and these may work well. On the other hand, they may encourage pupils to become easily distracted from their task and their talk may be 'off-task'. With all groups you will have to be careful about determining how well the members of the groups will work together. It is also important that groups do not always remain the same as they may not contain a good mix of gender or ability levels or the children may become bored with working with the same people all the time. The group members you select may either mix or match the ability level in a pair or group. When quicker learners work in mixed ability pairs or groups it may be necessary to provide extra activities for these pupils after they have finished the main activity.

Other ways of organizing pupils into groups include choosing group members using features of a project the pupils may be doing, or language they have just learned. For example, while doing a project on Birthdays groups can be organized by month of birth, those born on odd days of the month and those born on even days. In using pair work or group work, preparation and discipline is important as the teacher is not so centrally in control. Pupils need training in how to work in pairs or groups, especially if the English lesson is the only time in the school day when this happens. Pupils need to get used to starting and stopping when you tell them to (use some kind of sound signal); switching quickly from one activity to another with minimum noise and disruption; working quietly on activities and listening carefully to instructions. The rules you may have established with pupils should include ways of working in groups. A move to more independent learning also changes the role of the teacher and pupils and has several implications for the way you organize resources, monitor the tasks different children work on, the kind of learner training you provide and the way you record progress. Pupils need to be clear about your expectations.

The effects of different kinds of classroom activities

Teachers need to anticipate the effects on their pupils of different kinds of activities. Activities which usually engage and stir pupils are those where the learners are physically or mentally active and thus more involved in their learning. These include activities which involve reasoning or imaginative thinking skills such as problem-solving, puzzles or information gap, matching or sequencing with pictures or words, ranking to list things in order of importance. Some activities occupy the learners physically e.g. paper and pencil activities such as listen and drawing, completing charts, copying, games such as action songs and rhymes. On the other hand, there are activities which usually calm and settle pupils, for example when using mechanical routines such as to start or end the class. Teachers sometimes use writing tasks simply as a way of calming pupils down, which is fine as long as writing is not *always* seen as a way of maintaining classroom control. Here are some general principles for using *stir* and *settle* activities. How far do you agree with them?

- Start a lesson with a settling activity to calm pupils down if they seem very lively or restless. If they seem very tired or lethargic at the beginning they may need waking up with a lively, stirring activity.

- Make sure lively, stirring work returns to something calmer and more settling.

- Make sure everyone has something to do, especially in group work.

- Avoid activities which are emotionally or intellectually 'empty' or meaningless, e.g. too much copying or repeating.

- Try not to have a sequence of only settling or stirring activities throughout the whole class. Sandwich something lively between calming activities.

For more on this see chapter 17.

The mixed ability class

Many textbooks assume that all your pupils are at the same language level, whereas the average classroom is normally of very mixed ability. When a lesson has gone badly the checklist below may help you to pinpoint difficulties which may have arisen because of your organization of learning activities:

- Was the task given to pupils too difficult? Did you explain the task carefully enough or give sufficient practice or models to follow? Would more pictures or charts or tables make the task more manageable?

- Was the task rather boring and mechanical with too little contextualization or focus on meaning? Some practice is bound to be repetitive but if it is disguised, as in a survey or game, or if older children know it is leading to more purposeful language use, it may become more motivating.

- Was the task too easy? The pupils may have done similar work before and finished the task more quickly than expected.

- Was there too much 'dead time'? If there is not a sufficient range of tasks at different levels, the able learners will always finish more quickly, while the slower learners may cope with the task by finishing it quickly but in a very superficial manner.

- In each lesson there should be a *core* of the most important concepts, skills and language that should be straightforward enough for everyone to do. You may then need *extension activities* to challenge the more able pupils and more *support activities* for the less able. Making activities that cater for different levels is called mixed ability teaching or 'differentiation'. To do this successfully, teachers can organize differentiated learning activities by considering seven key factors:

1 *The text used*: for young children, listening to a simple spoken text is usually easier than reading the text in English. Later on, reading a simple text while listening is often easier than simply listening to a text by itself. Pupils can read different versions of a story, e.g. the text can include more or less complicated details, many or no pictures, mostly direct speech or mostly narrative. You may record the story onto cassette so that young pupils can listen and read at the same time.

2 *The task used*: pupils can work on the same topic but the tasks can be graded in difficulty. Playing *Dominoes* is easier if the cards have words and pictures rather than words alone. Playing *Bingo* is easier than '*Opposites Bingo*' where you have to cover the opposite of the word called out.

3 *The support provided*: some pupils can be provided with extra help, such as a checklist, a substitution table with useful phrases for producing writing, a chart with notes under headings for producing written work, picture cards, posters,etc.

4 *The outcome demanded*: writing something is of course more difficult than just talking about it; a drawing with a simple caption is easier than re-telling a story. Performing actions is easier than speaking out loud.

5 *The ability group used*: we have discussed earlier ways in which ability groupings can be organized.

6 *The range of activities used*: teachers who are aware of pupils' differing learning styles (visual, auditory, kinaesthetic) can ensure they use a variety of activities which will cater to all these styles (see chapter 4).

7 *The choice of activity*: older or more linguistically developed learners may be allowed to choose which activity they would like to

pursue according to their own interests. They can choose which kind of task they are interested in, which skill to use, which topic it is based on and what kind of outcome they would like to produce (a picture and writing, a survey, a graph, a board game etc.). This requires a bank of materials or suggestions, organized into sets and colour-coded or labelled. (see more on creating resources in Part 3)

Here is an example of how to do this. If pupils are asked to ask riddles about animals for other pupils to guess, most children will find this easy once you have provided some examples. Others will need more support, often in the form of visuals to provide scaffolding, such as large pictures of various animals, perhaps labelled with body parts such as *legs, long tail* can be placed on the walls for pupils to refer to, as well as model sets of questions and answers for pupils to use. You can also break down the task into smaller sub-tasks by providing some form of organizer, such as a tickchart. Figure 44 is an example for riddles such *as I'm thinking of an animal with no legs. What is it?*

	No legs	2 legs	4 legs
lion	✗	✗	✔
snake	✔	✗	✗
elephant	✗	✗	✔
hen	✗	✔	✗

Fig. 44 Tickchart for asking riddles

What you are doing in providing more support is choosing a selection from the following kinds of *scaffolding:*

- breaking down the learning sequence into smaller steps
- simplifying the language, narrowing the range of possibilities
- using more spoken language before moving onto written language
- translating abstract concepts into more concrete ones
- using physical movement
- using more audio-visual support
- providing a greater variety of activities

More able pupils can apply skills and knowledge to different situations or contexts; engage in more problem-solving; be encouraged to draw on a wider range of vocabulary; be encouraged to draw on a wider range of language functions; do more written work, often in the form of products that other children can use and be encouraged to do more finding out and 'research' using a range of resources.

Time management

Even experienced teachers can be over-optimistic about how much can be done in a lesson or despair that they will ever have enough time to work through a scheme of work or syllabus. It is very useful to train yourself to plot realistic timings for the completion of certain activities; this avoids having to rush, which may lead to inattention or ineffective learning. On the other hand, you may be left with time to spare at the end of the lesson, in which case you need to have some activities 'up your sleeve' which might include songs, rhymes, games or puzzles. It is useful to build up a repertoire of these so you can select one that revises language or fits in with your current teaching focus. When ending a lesson, here are several points to bear in mind:

- Plan, so you do not have to stop in the middle of an activity.

- Finish work on the main teaching point a little early rather than late; you can always find an activity to fill up a few minutes.

- If you want to give out homework, take time to explain it beforehand and give an example. Avoid squeezing it in at the very end of the lesson.

- Plan a teacher-led review session at the end of each class. (See chapter 5.) Try to give praise and encouragement about what the children have achieved during the class. With older pupils you can review the language or learning focus you have concentrated on that lesson.

Classroom organization and layout

Careful planning of your classroom is very important as it helps to create an organized and secure atmosphere. In an ideal situation, you would be able to organize the classroom in the way you think is most effective for children's learning. In practice you may not have total freedom to reorganize the layout of the classroom in the way that you would wish. However, if you have some possibilities of doing this, here are six points for you to consider:

1 A grid plan made to scale is especially useful if you have a large class

squeezed into a small area. Round tables take up more space than square or rectangular tables.

2   Think carefully about whether you want the children to sit in rows or groups. Primary schools often have tables arranged in groups to seat four to six children, which makes pair and group work easier.

3   If you decide to have a 'teaching base', make sure you have a clear view of the whole room. Although you may have a base in one place, you could try varying your actual teaching position. Montgomery and Rawlings (1986) suggest that there are 'action zones' where children who sit closest to the teacher concentrate more and work harder; you need therefore to vary the action zones by changing position or, alternatively, by changing at periodic intervals the children who sit close to you. Don't put troublemakers at the back of the classroom!

4   A story corner for younger children is also a good idea. See chapter 14 for setting up a book corner.

5   You may also like to include a listening or computer corner which is screened-off by cupboards or screens to provide a quiet corner for listening to cassettes of stories or pre-recorded listening activities or for working on a computer activity. With older, more reliable children, a quiet listening corner can sometimes be set up temporarily in a corridor or cloakroom outside if there is no space in the classroom. If you do this, the children must know how to operate the cassette on their own and must have clear instructions on the task they are to perform. This task should have a definite outcome, such as a drawing or pictures to sequence and should have been demonstrated and practised beforehand. Make it clear that you will tolerate no misbehaviour as it leads to automatic withdrawal of their right to work unsupervised.

6   Make sure you include some areas to display children's work, using notice-boards, screens or a table. The layout of the room can be varied and sections remodelled by the use of simple screens, such as large sheets of corrugated cardboard to make moveable walls and partitions. This can also be used for displaying pupils' work.

Keeping teaching records

Teaching records are a kind of teaching log, memory aid, or reminder of the language points or the stories and topics which have been covered in a term. The information can be a record for the teacher alone, or with older children can also be made public for the whole class to see and to use. Large wall charts can show which language functions, structures, or vocabulary children have been taught with accompanying questions such as *Have you put some new words in your dictionary? How many new words did you learn this week? Can you say .... in English?* Charts can also show which pupils have completed particular activities, especially where these are free choice or optional. For example, if the class has worked on a story like *Princess Smartypants* (see Ellis and Brewster 2002) there may be a 'free choice' lesson with five different activities which the children can choose from. The children can sign their names alongside different activities (see Fig. 45).

Charts are also useful for keeping track of homework activities. Older children may also be encouraged to keep a personal record of work they have done which summarizes the language and learning skills they have covered.

Activity	Names
1 Plan a drama retelling the story.	*Luis, Ana, Jorge, Maria, Aracelita, Guillermo Jesus*
2 Find out about and design coats of arms.	*Carlos, Nelita, Enrique, Beatriz, Ricardo*
3 Find out about royalty and make a magazine.	*etc.*
4 Rewrite the story with a different ending.	*etc.*
5 Make up spoof characters, draw and describe them.	*etc.*

Fig. 45 Storybook activity record card

This chapter has tried to illustrate some of the ways teachers can reflect on, and perhaps improve, their classroom management skills. It is hoped that developing confidence in these skills will make teachers more effective and less stressed.

17 Lesson planning

Rivers (1981:484) reminds us that 'A lesson is not a haphazard collection of more or less interesting items, but a progression of interrelated activities which reinforce and consolidate each other in establishing the learning towards which the teacher is directing his or her efforts'. Bearing this advice in mind, this chapter aims to develop a more critical awareness of the lesson planning process.

Ur (1996:213) describes a lesson as follows: 'A lesson is a type of organized social event that occurs in virtually all cultures. Lessons in different places may vary in topic, time, place, atmosphere, methodology and materials, but they all, essentially, are concerned with learning as their main objective, involve the participation of learner(s) and teacher(s), and are limited and pre-scheduled as regards time, place and membership'. A lesson is also often characterized by certain rituals or routines depending on the rules of a school or a teacher's own preferences and teaching style. Think about any special characteristics a lesson has in your context.

What is a good lesson?

Task 1
What do you consider constitutes a 'good' lesson? List your points and then compare them to the ones given below from teachers at a recent seminar in Paris. Do you have any other points?

A good lesson is adaptable and flexible; is a back-up system; has clear objectives; has a variety of activities, skills, interaction, materials; caters for individual learning styles; has interesting, enjoyable content; has an appropriate level of challenge and is well prepared, well planned and well timed.

The points above are in no particular order, but all participants agreed that advance planning and good timing were essential. One participant felt strongly that without a controlled and disciplined learning environment none of the points listed above bore any relevance, which highlights how lesson planning is closely linked to classroom management (see chapter 16).

Why plan a lesson?

Children learn more easily when they know what to expect in a lesson and what the teacher expects of them. It makes them feel more secure and more confident. It also enables them to predict situations and the language and behaviour likely to be used in them. There are many ways of planning a lesson and each teacher has his or her own style and preferences but often tend to use more or less the same model or pattern for each lesson, although in some contexts there may be a set format which teachers have to follow. A model or format, however, represents the basis of a routine which can be followed in each lesson with the aims and activities being slotted into the model. After a few lessons children get to know the routine and feel comfortable. If the teacher stages the lesson carefully and gives explicit signals to the children so they know when they move on to the next stage, they will often make preparations themselves and therefore become more responsible for their own learning. The security of knowing what to expect next enables children to concentrate on an activity. A class that is used to a routine is calm compared to a lesson that is 'a haphazard collection of more or less interesting items' where children do not know what to expect next. Finally, children do know when a teacher has or has not spent time thinking about and planning a lesson, as an unplanned class results in disruption and poor learning. Consequently, this filters back to heads as well as to parents.

A well-planned lesson makes a teacher feel more confident and professional. A lesson planned in advance in all respects, with clear aims, clear statements of how the aims are going to be achieved, how time will be managed for each stage, how the class is to be arranged, which visual aids and technical aids will be used, materials (books, photocopies) prepared in advance, means that a teacher can give full attention to the pupils before, during and after the lesson, and to parents should they have contact with them. It follows, that the same teacher will go through a similar process of reflection after a lesson asking themselves what worked well, what worked less well, what they would do differently another time. This process helps teachers monitor their teaching and identify their strong and weak points as well as evaluate their pupil's learning and form the basis for future planning. It is therefore an important aspect of evaluation and self-development (See chapter 20). Finally, lesson planning provides accountability by providing a record of work which can be shown to school authorities, inspectors and parents, or used by another teacher who may have to substitute for the class.

What is involved in the lesson planning process?

As River's states, a lesson is a carefully planned and managed event which needs a framework: a beginning, a middle and an end. The lesson planning process is a complex one which includes a variety of aspects that intertwine. We will now consider the different aspects of the lesson planning process, in order to find practical solutions to these problems.

What is my syllabus?

Basically, a syllabus provides a list of the language items that are to be taught, how they are to be taught, in which order, and how long it should take to teach them. Whether teachers are working with their country's national syllabus, a syllabus designed by a course or their own syllabus, they must know what the long-term objectives are, and how these are to be achieved. Many teachers use a course which will define the syllabus for one, two, three or more years. If this is your case, you still need, however, to decide how best to use the course, how each lesson links to the next and builds up to the overall aims and how to teach each lesson. Does the syllabus provide enough hours of work for your school year? Will you need to supplement the course in any way? How much work does each unit provide?

The syllabus is provided through the contents page, the course map or a scope and sequence chart. Study this carefully to find out how the course is structured. Courses will express their aims in different ways depending on how they are organized as discussed in chapter 11.

The accompanying teacher's guide to a course will usually provide detailed guidelines on how to teach each lesson but you may prefer alternative ways of approaching a lesson than those suggested. Above all, a course should be used as a menu from which you choose, rather than a recipe which you follow rigidly. Initially, less experienced teachers are likely to follow a plan closely but, with more experience, will learn to adapt coursebooks and lessons in a much more flexible way according to the pupils' needs and interests. Be ready, however, to depart from your course when the needs of your pupils, or syllabus, do not correspond with what is offered by the course.

What are my learners' needs?

In the EFL classroom, there is often a lot of pressure on the teacher to produce immediate, tangible results in terms of concrete linguistic outcomes, and teachers may feel responsible if new language is not produced each lesson. The needs of the children and how they learn must be considered first so that teachers achieve a balance between the language aims of the syllabus and the needs of the children, which involve their all round general education. A major consideration when planning a lesson, then, is how to provide optimal conditions for learning so children are motivated and interested in learning, understand what they are being asked to do and why, get plenty of meaningful exposure to the language, get plenty of variety and are allowed to work at their own pace, experience success, feel confident and secure to try out language, have plenty of opportunities to use language, and opportunities to review and reflect on what they have done and why. The Plan-Do-Review (see Fig. 9) model presented in chapter 5 helps the teacher to set up such conditions for learning.

Other aspects to be considered are the lingusitic and cognitive demands of language activities. We need to ensure that the tasks we ask our pupils to carry out in the language classroom are ones which, with a reasonable degree of effort or challenge, can be completed successfully. This means that we need to be able to evaluate tasks and materials in terms of the linguistic and cognitive demands they make on our learners, and to be aware of the kinds of tasks pupils can cope with at specific stages of their development. Tasks and activities should neither be so simple that they provide no challenge or learning experience, nor so difficult that they frustrate and demotivate. Analysing tasks in this way allows us to judge whether the level of demands made on learners is appropriate, but also to identify the types of demands made and to thus plan our lessons more confidently. Some tasks or activities are also more suitable for some learning styles or intelligences than others (see chapter 3). Finally, if our pupils are taking an examination at the end of the year, does the syllabus adequately prepare them or will it need supplementing?

What content areas, materials and methodology can I use?

If you are using a course this will define the content areas, provide the material as well as suggest the way things should be taught. However, you need to evaluate whether the subject matter or content, material and the methodology is entirely appropriate for your pupils. The methodological approach to teaching English may contrast starkly to the way other subjects are taught and children may not understand the teacher's reasons for using activities such as songs, games, pair work, stories, role-plays and may regard them as 'not serious' and an opportunity to relax and have some fun. Some may become disruptive and disrespectful. Although it is our intention to create an enjoyable learning environment for our pupils, it must, nevertheless, be one that they perceive as purposeful. Methodological preparation as defined in chapter 5 can help pupils understand the reasons for your choice of a certain methodology, but you may also decide to modify this slightly by adapting and supplementing your materials to keep more in line with their expectations. Ask yourself also whether the content, materials and methodology in the course are culturally appropriate? Do you need to provide material related to the topic which is more familiar to your pupils?

How can I structure a lesson, select, sequence and time activities?

A lesson can vary in length from as little as 15 minutes to as long as 120 minutes depending on the context in which you work. The typical structure of most lessons consists of three main stages: a beginning, a middle and an end. Depending on the length of the lesson, the middle may consist of one, two or more activity cycles. Whatever the length, pupils need clear signposting (see chapter 5) so they understand how a lesson progresses from one stage to the next and from one activity cycle to the next, gradually working to the stated goal. We need strategies such as those described in chapter 16 for dealing with mixed level classes.

The selection and sequencing of activities throughout a lesson needs careful consideration. Chapter 16 discussed the effects on pupils of different kinds of activities, those that *settle* children either positively in the sense of calming them or negatively by boring them into some kind of unresponsive stupor, and those that *stir* pupils in the sense of either stimulating or unsettling them. When selecting an activity we need to know more than what language learning it will encourage. We must also be aware of what general behaviour it is likely to encourage. This will help us judge if the activity or sequence of activities is a good choice for a particular lesson or group of pupils. We also need to consider the *involvement* factor when selecting and sequencing activities. Maclennan (1987:196) gives the example of a guessing activity where pupils have to guess what is on a flashcard. She explains that while this activity scores high on mental involvement it scores low on the *occupying* scale as probably only one pupil and the teacher is talking at one time. Copying, however, scores low on mental involvement but high on actual occupation and therefore has an important contribution to make to a lesson as a whole.

When selecting and sequencing activities, we also need to think in terms of variety, although varied activities put together in no particular order can result in confusion on behalf of the pupil. We therefore first need to think of how we can offer variety, and secondly how best to combine different activities.

- Types of activities: problem solving, listening to a story, singing a song, a guessing game, a word puzzle, a role-play, a picture dictation, a physical response activity, etc.

- Types of interaction: teacher with whole class, teacher with individual pupils, pupil with pupil; whole class working in pairs or groups

- Language skill: although much of the work that takes place in a young learners class in the initial stages is based on listening and speaking, we also need to introduce reading and writing and vocabulary work to offer variety and gradual exposure to the written word

- Tempo/pace: some activities may be fast moving such as a team game and others slower and quieter such as colouring or copying words

- Stir/settle, involve/occupy (see above)

- Difficulty: some activities are more fun and lighter while others are more demanding and require greater effort and concentration

- Level of pupil responsibility: some activities require pupils to work independently of the teacher and use their own initiative, while others require pupils to do as the teacher says

- Classroom arrangement: it is possible to vary the seating arrangement of your classroom from time to time to facilitate certain types of activities: tables arranged in groups if you are doing group work; a horseshoe allows a space in the middle for physical activities; leaving a space at the front of the class is useful for storytelling sessions where children sit around the teacher to listen, etc. It is also a good idea to vary the places children sit depending on the activity. Vary criteria for forming pairs and groups, for example, friendship, ability, fast or slow finishers, random, age, boys, girls, etc.

- Materials: if possible, vary these, so pupils are exposed to a variety of input. Supplement your core materials with stories, videos, games from authentic sources, if possible

The way you sequence your activities in a lesson will depend on the different factors mentioned above, but some general guidelines you may like to consider are:

1 Begin and end the lesson so that children perceive their English lesson as an 'event' which has a specific structure: a beginning, middle and an end. A clear beginning and an end also allows you to inform pupils of your aims and to summarize what you have done so they leave with a clear idea of what they can now do and a sense of achievement.

2 Depending on how long your lesson is, consider putting harder activities earlier as pupils will probably be fresher and more energetic.

3 Decide at which point it is best for your class to be lively. It is sometimes difficult to calm a class down once they have been involved in a lively, fun activity. It is important that pupils are quiet at the beginning and end of a lesson so they are attentive when you inform them of the lesson's aims and also during the review session at the end.

4   Think carefully about transitions from one stage or activity cycle to the next. How are you going to manage this and what language are you going to use? (See chapter 5.)

5   End on a positive note. Make sure pupils leave your class with a sense of achievement and self-esteem. Sum up and praise what the children have done well. Build in a short routine fun activity for leaving the class which can be linked in some way to the content of your lesson, for example, a password that children have to remember and/or spell, or an instruction: *Children who have a dog can go! Children who are wearing something red can go! Children who have got a brother can go!* This ensures that pupils are listening attentively!

Good time management skills facilitate the smooth running of a lesson. Knowing about the linguistic and cognitive demands that certain lessons make on your pupils will help you judge how long an activity is likely to take. If you see the activity is taking longer than you anticipated but children are participating positively and producing purposeful language, be flexible and allow them to finish. If, on the other hand, the activity is taking longer because it is too difficult either linguistically or cognitively, stop the activity and help the class complete it together. If some children complete an activity sooner than anticipated be prepared with extra materials or activities for fast finishers, or reassure slower learners that they can complete the activity later or at home. Always set a time limit for an activity so children know how long they have got. Time your lesson carefully so you leave five minutes or so at the end to review and summarize work covered. There is no point beginning another activity five minutes before the lesson is to end even if it is on your plan. The key to effective lesson timing is good planning and flexibility.

How can I write a lesson plan?

There is no 'correct' way to write a lesson plan, but it should give a clear picture of *what* you intend to do (your aims) and *how* you intend to achieve them (your procedures). To start off, you may find it helpful to use a lesson planning/record sheet like the one in Fig. 46. The linguistic aims are listed starting with grammatical structures, language functions, vocabulary, pronunciation, and skills. The ordering of these aims can vary according to the focus of your language materials, for example, depending on whether they are structurally-based, activity- or task-based, topic-based, etc. The learning to learn aim follows as, although not purely a linguistic aim, it will be closely interrelated with language learning activities. By listing the learning to learn aim after the linguistic aims, it can be derived naturally from and incorporated into language

Lesson Planning/Record Sheet		

Date _____ Class _____ Length of lesson _____

Materials _____

Aims	Plan (what I intend to do)	Record (what I actually did)
Grammatical structures		
Functions		
Vocabulary		
Pronunciation		
Skills		
Learning to learn		
Other: Social, psychological, cultural, educational/ cross-curricular, citizenship education		
Classroom arrangement		
Assumptions		
Anticipated difficulties		
Evaluation: Did I achieve my aims? What worked well? Why? Why not? What would I do differently next lesson? Why?		

Fig. 46 Lesson planning/record sheet: aims

	STAGE	ACTIVITIES			MATERIALS	TIME
		PLAN	**DO**	**REVIEW**	Activity cycles	
P L A N	**Beginning the lesson** • Warm up • Review work covered in previous lesson • Inform pupils of lesson aims					
D O	**Activity cycles** Plan / Do / Review	Provide a context. Familiarize topic. Activate prior knowledge. Motivate. Introduce and practise new language. Explain purpose of activity/task.	Children do activity/task and experiment with and use target language. Teacher monitors and helps as necessary	Children consolidate language from previous stage by extending and personalizing. Teacher runs review session to evaluate activity and performance.		
	Activity cycle 1					
	Activity cycle 2					
	Activity cycle 3					
R E V I E W	**Ending the lesson** • Round up, review and summarize lesson • Set homework • Routine fun activity					

Fig. 46 Lesson planning/record sheet: procedures

239

work as appropriate, but does not override the language learning aims of a lesson as the main goal of language teachers and children remains language learning.

As the teaching of children is concerned with their all-round general education, there are other aspects to take into consideration when planning a lesson. In addition to purely linguistic aims we also need to consider more global aims or non-linguistic aims which contribute to the child's all-round development and reinforce their learning across the curriculum in general. These aims in addition to learning to learn, are usually achieved through the methodology, for example, a group work activity will develop social skills, or through the focus of the materials, a story can develop the theme of environmental awareness. These additional aims include the following:

- Social – how is what I am doing helping pupils develop peer respect, collaborative skills, communication strategies such as listening to each other, turn taking, etc.

- Psychological/Affective – how are my methodology and materials contributing to the development of self-confidence, self-esteem and positive attitudes and values?

- Cultural – what are my pupils going to learn about the English-speaking world and other world cultures?

- Educational/cross-curricular – how does the content of my materials reinforce and contribute to my pupil's general knowledge and learning across the curriculum?

- Citizenship education – how are my methodology and materials contributing to the development of my pupils as future aware, responsible and tolerant citizens?

It would be unrealistic to plan a lesson which incorporates all of these aims, but it is important to be aware that as language teachers we are contributing to these to a lesser or greater extent.

Once we have defined our aims, we need to decide *how* to achieve these. The procedures page in Fig. 46 applies the Plan-Do-Review model presented in chapter 5 to the overall lesson structure and individual activity cycles within the lesson. This provides clearly defined stages and combines the development of metacognitive and cognitive strategies. The different stages on the plan include:

Plan: Beginning the lesson
Warm-up: This could take the form of an informal chat, ritual activities like taking the register, writing the date on the blackboard, talking about

the weather, etc. It may include singing a song or chanting a rhyme of the pupils' own choice which provides a good transition for the children if they have come directly to English class from a main subject class in their own language. This helps them 'move into' English and to get in the mood. Bear in mind the type of behaviour an activity is going to evoke, the stir or settle factor.

Reviewing of work covered in previous lesson: This is to consolidate language learned in the previous lesson and may provide a base for input of new language. It can be very useful as it encourages pupils to reflect on what they learned and did in the previous lesson. It can also provide you with valuable information about what your pupils learned and what was significant to them in the lesson and if you need to do further revision before moving on.

Informing pupils of the lesson aims: Think about the language you would use to explain the aims of the lesson, for example, *Today we are going to ...*

Do: Activity cycle(s)

An activity cycle involves children in a learning task which incorporates the Plan-Do-Review sequence. A lesson will include one or more activity cycles that have some kind of connection and purpose between them. Children must be able to see how activities contribute towards the goals stated at the beginning of the lesson.

- **Plan: Activity cycle(s)**
  This stage allows you to set the context of the lesson so the pupils see its relevance, to draw upon and activate pupils' prior knowledge, arouse their curiosity and motivate them and to set up an activity. You may use a variety of techniques such as elicitation, showing a picture, playing a guessing game, playing a flashcard game. Whichever technique(s) you use, it must allow children to think about what they are going to do, predict content and language and be clear about the language they are going to practise and learn. This can be done through highlighting the vocabulary or structures and getting the class to repeat as a whole, in groups or as individuals until they feel confident. You may write the key language on the board or put visuals on the board to aid children's memory. Encourage pupils to interact with you by asking questions, *Can you explain again, Can you repeat please.* Explain also the purpose of the activity that will take place in the next stage.

- **Do: Activity cycle(s)**
  This stage will involve the children in an activity or task which enables them to experiment and use the language practised in stage

one. Explain and demonstrate an activity yourself or ask other pupils to demonstrate so everyone is clear. This is your chance as a teacher to ask yourself *Can my pupils use the language/do what I have just set up/practised/explained?* It is also your pupils' chance to ask themselves *Can I use the language that my teacher has just got me to practise?* You may monitor the activity, evaluating and helping as necessary. Your pupils' performance may well indicate a need to modify what you had planned to do next. If you notice that they have had problems which are due to linguistic difficulties, you may decide to back track here and reinforce the language again before moving on.

- **Review: Activity cycle(s)**
  This stage is likely to include an activity or activities which enable the children to consolidate, extend and personalize language introduced and practised in the above two stages. The focus in this stage will be more on the use of spontaneous language in which children have some choice and control over what they say, and they may well be working independently in pairs or in a group. There may well be a concrete outcome at this stage eg, to produce a labelled picture, to make something, to complete a worksheet etc. This stage will end with a review to evaluate the activity and the children's performance as well as to revise what has been practised. Depending on the review, it may well lead back into or on to another activity to provide further practise of language introduced in the plan stage of the first activity cycle.

Review: Ending the lesson

Give a rounding up, overall review and summary of the lesson, a confirmation of the aims of the lesson and review of pupils performance. Give pupils any homework explaining what they must do and when you want it. You may prefer to explain homework earlier on in the lesson if it relates to a particular aspect you have been working on. Use this stage as an opportunity to remind your pupils of their homework. Also use this short stage as an opportunity for social chat.

This type of plan offers a framework with plenty of scope for flexibility. However, as stated above, a lesson plan can only indicate what you intend to do in a lesson. What you actually do and what actually happens may differ for a number of reasons. The key factor is to be flexible and adapt your plan if necessary so that you respond to your pupils' needs during the lesson. It is then useful to reflect on how and why your lesson differed to your plan and make notes in the Record column (What I actually did). This will then provide an accurate record for monitoring your lessons and for accountability purposes.

How can I evaluate a lesson?

Allow some time after a lesson to reflect on what happened in your class. Be honest in your self-appraisals. To simply say, 'I think it went well' or 'The lesson was fine' tells you nothing. Probe deeper and ask yourself why. Here are some questions you might ask yourself.

- Did I achieve the aims stated on my lesson plan? If not, why not?
- Was my lesson different from my plan in any way? How and why?
- How did I move from one stage of the lesson to the next? What did I say to the class?
- Did I keep to my timing? If not, why not?
- Were my pupils active and involved in the lesson? Why? Why not?
- Did my pupils learn what I set out to teach? How do I know?
- Did my pupils respond positively to the materials and in English?
- Were there any problems? If yes, why?
- What would I do differently next time? Why?
- What did I do better this time than ever before?

To help in evaluating your lessons you may like to tape- or video-record your lessons, ask your pupils to comment on your lessons, or if possible, invite a colleague to sit in on a lesson and observe. Afterwards, answer the questions above individually, and then come together and compare your comments. Finally, lesson planning differs from teacher to teacher and each teacher has their own preferred way of planning a lesson. As teachers gain in experience and confidence their plans probably become more informal. However, it is a useful exercise to continue to write more detailed 'formal' plans from time to time and to evaluate them afterwards, as this will enable you to think about your teaching in a systematic way and is an important aspect of professional development (see chapter 20).

18 Record keeping and assessment

In this chapter we will consider three main aspects of record-keeping and assessment: the reasons why it is used at primary level, features of the teaching and assessment cycle and finally, various types of assessment.

Issues in assessing pupils' language development

Assessment at primary level can be described as an attempt to analyse the learning that a child has achieved over a period of time as a result of the classroom teaching/learning situation. Assessment does not need to be based on a particular task nor is it always expressed as a percentage or mark. It may include a teacher's subjective opinion of the achievement of a child in terms of attitude, participation and cognitive development. Assessment may also be assessed 'relatively' in that the progress of an individual child can be measured against his or her individual starting points and abilities, instead of being compared with the skills and abilities of other children. As yet there is very little research on how different forms of assessment may affect young pupils' learning of English. The list below shows some of the issues in the assessment of language which concern many teachers today.

1 Is there a minimum age or optimum age for introducing formal assessment?

2 To what extent do different kinds of assessment encourage and challenge pupils or demotivate them?

3 Are there different personality or ability types which respond better or worse to different kinds of assessment?

4 What form and techniques of assessment might be considered most effective for different age bands and levels within the primary sector?

5 How far do the different forms of record keeping and assessment provide sufficient information for teachers on how pupils learn a foreign language effectively?

We have very few answers to most of these questions at the moment but more and more research is being carried out and there may be more guidance on these issues in the near future. A lot of interest has been shown recently in finding out the sorts of achievements pupils at primary level show after several years of language. If children all over the world are now spending more time learning a foreign language, governments, teachers and parents need to know how effective this learning is and be reassured of what exactly young learners are able to do, or even should be expected to do in the foreign language.

Why keep records of progress and assess pupils' English?

You may think this is a silly question – of course teachers should keep records of progress and children should be assessed. However, your answers to this are likely to be greatly influenced by cultural views on teaching and learning at primary level. Each region will have its own views on what is considered 'good practice' in record-keeping and assessment. Some countries, such as Japan, regularly test young pupils on their learning, a process which may begin at nursery or kindergarten levels. Assessment practice in different countries is influenced by several factors, such as regional educational policy and practice for the primary curriculum, views on teaching and learning, views on what it means to 'know' a language and the views of central groups of people, such as ministry officials, school principals, teachers and parents. In most countries, however, assessment of some kind is seen as part of the normal planning, teaching and assessing cycle.

School-based language assessment has been defined by Rea-Dickens and Rixon (2000:89) as 'the collection of data on language use by pupils in classroom language learning'. The data might include regular records based on observations of pupils' oral or written performance in class or homework tasks, or information based on oral or written tests. However, this definition does not include any reference to what then happens to this data or the reasons for collecting it. To return to our initial question of *Why assess?*, we can say that there are five main reasons:

1 *formative:* to increase motivation by making assessment a part of the continuous learning process

2 *summative:* to give pupils feedback on their progress or achievement at a particular point in time, often done formally through tests of various kinds

3 *informative:* to give pupils, parents and other teachers feedback on progress or achievement

4 *diagnostic:* to monitor individual pupils' needs and help identify pupils who need special support

5 *evaluative:* to identify pupils' levels of achievement and select or order pupils according to merit, to check the effectiveness of teachers, teaching materials or teaching methods

(adapted from Cajkler and Addelman 2000)

In the Rea-Dickens and Rixon survey (2000:89) most teachers used assessment to inform their classroom planning and action, while a minority were required to assess pupils for administrative purposes. Eighty-six per cent of teachers in the survey prepared classroom assessment themselves, with or without the help of a coursebook.

Another issue to consider is what happens to the results of the collection of data on progress and achievement and who has access to these results. Some schools may produce class lists, especially for older pupils, which rank each child's performance. This information is very public and may be considered very inappropriate in some countries. In other schools each child will receive an individual report card with grades or marks for each subject and perhaps a few written comments. This is more private and is usually only available to the child's immediate family. In yet other schools pupils will receive an individual record which details progress or achievements which refer to particular skills but do not include grades or marks. Much information is also provided for parents in the form of work the child takes home or information given by the teacher on parents' evenings at school (see chapter 19).

The teaching and assessment cycle

In some contexts assessment plays an extremely important part in the teaching and learning process and may even heavily influence the way the pupils are taught and the kinds of activities they do. In other contexts assessment plays a smaller part in this cycle. Figure 1 starts with the aims and objectives of teaching a foreign language (see chapter 1) and how this feeds into the syllabus and course description. This then influences the methodology used (see chapter 4) and the type of learning outcomes (see part 2). The pupils are then assessed using criteria which are shaped by the expected learning outcomes. The kind of assessment the teacher selects has specific techniques and procedures which lead to different ways in which the results are recorded and then evaluated. The evaluation of results may lead to a further re-evaluation of the aims and objectives of the programme and so the cycle continues.

The aims and objectives of foreign language learning include the learning of specified language structures and vocabulary and the development of the most relevant language skills. As we saw in chapter 1 they may also include wider educational and social goals, such as developing a positive attitude to learning the target language and developing awareness and respect for other languages and their culture. An interesting finding in the survey of assessment by Rea-Dickens and Rixon (2000) is the way in which most assessment practice rarely examines motivation or attitudes and nearly always focuses purely on language items and skills. Let us now consider each of four different kinds of assessment.

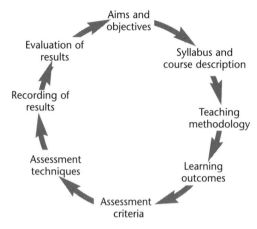

Fig. 47 The teaching and assessment cycle

(adapted from Cajkler & Addelman 2000)

On-going record keeping and formative assessment

Many coursebooks have a mix of both on-going and end of year assessment (*formative* and *summative*). In *Blue Skies,* for example, the teacher's book says on page 144 that 'careful assessment and recording of the students' progress is important as it allows you to take remedial action. Teachers may select tasks to provide informal assessment information, but day-to-day monitoring of students' performance will give the best results'. On-going or formative assessment may increase pupils' motivation by making the monitoring of pupils' progress and achievement a part of their continuous learning process. If pupils can see the progress they are making it can help to raise their self-esteem and confidence, which is very important with young children. Of course the opposite can also happen, especially if a teacher focuses mainly on what the pupil *cannot* do rather than focusing on what the child *can* do or is good at. Teachers need to be sensitive to young learners' emotions and feelings if they want to create and nurture their pupils' enjoyment for FLL. Where a teacher notices a pupil's weaknesses these can be dealt with constructively by converting them into a set of learning targets for the future. Formative assessment provides feedback and information on pupils' performance over time and can provide a more rounded view of the child's learning than 'one-off' performance on a test. We all know how hard it is to be labelled by the results of a test on a day on which you performed badly because you were not feeling well, or you had some emotional upset. Continuous assessment helps to overcome this kind of 'snapshot' result, but it can, of course, be quite subjective and may be influenced by the teacher's relationship with a particular pupil. Continuous assessment can also be used by the teacher as a diagnostic tool which is used to monitor individual pupils' needs and to help identify any pupils who need special support. Keeping records of pupils' progress might also provide useful information to evaluate a new method of teaching or new resources you are trying out in your classroom.

What might record keeping or continuous assessment look like?

An important part of a teacher's duties is keeping track of her pupils' progress. This may be a formal or informal process. If it is a formal process the school will probably have official forms to complete for each child. These may consist of checklists of language items or skills which the teacher ticks or comments on. The records may focus on grammatical points, such as tenses or prepositions; word sets, such as clothes or animals; or components of language skills, such as listening or reading. If informal records are kept then teachers can keep a recording notebook where they write down some comments about pupils' progress and difficulties, strengths and weaknesses over time. For very young children comments might focus on: the child's concentration span when doing listening activities or handwriting, motivation levels for different activities, willingness to use English when singing songs, saying rhymes or playing games, or ability to work individually, in pairs or in groups.

These can be recorded on a 'continuum chart' which is filled in over time (see Fig. 48). The teacher can colour in the appropriate box showing the child's development and date it to show progress over time. In an unpublished survey of learners in Hungary who considered they had 'failed' at their English language learning the most important characteristic they highlighted was the need for perseverance – the motivation to keep on trying. A continuum chart for this feature might look like this:

Gives up a task at the first sign of difficulty		Sticks at a task as long as there is some reward		Keeps trying even if difficult but success is likely

Fig. 48 A continuum chart

Again, this can be ticked or coloured in using different colours at different times of the year to account for any changes. These comments can then be transferred to individual record cards (with the pupil's name and the year) at regular intervals. For younger children teachers can also use a simple *recording ladder* for individual pupil's literacy or oracy development. On the ladder there is a list of language items, language skills or strategies that are coloured in by the teacher when she thinks the child is capable of using them. If a different colour is used for each term everyone can see at a glance how much progress has been made over the year. See Fig. 49 for an example of a recording ladder for early spelling and handwriting.

Copies letters neatly and correctly only when watched
Copies letters neatly and correctly independently
Can spell a small number of familiar words accurately
Can use a simple picture dictionary or word book
Can spell accurately most words in the coursebook units covered so far

Fig. 49 A recording ladder

Records can consist of a checklist of learning targets which can be ticked to give a yes/no answer. These are easy to do for vocabulary and grammatical items once they are learned. The teacher must decide of course what she means by 'learned'. This could just mean that these items have been taught, which is less helpful, or can refer to specific evidence of learning, such as 'can produce a range of colour words in speaking and writing' or 'can use these adverbs correctly in a spoken sentence'. Checklists like this can provide more detail if the teacher uses a five-point scale, such as the acronym, NOFAN. This stands for Never, Occasionally, Frequently, Always, Naturally. The final stage shows how far pupils have internalized and mastered aspects of language or a particular language skill. The NOFAN acronym can also be used on a checklist for speaking: Uses one word utterances, Puts two words together, Uses a chunk or phrase, Uses simple sentences, Uses coordinated sentences.

Record cards, perhaps based on observation sheets, can include the pupil's name, the year and term or semester and a range of marks or comments on the pupil's written work or homework (see Fig. 50). The main thing is that record keeping should be simple to do and the records

RECORD CARD FOR STORYTELLING

Name

Year

Comments

Listening

Shows global understanding when a story is read aloud

Can listen for specific information

Predicts what comes next

Infers meaning

Uses audio and visual clues as aids to meaning

Recognizes words in context

Can follow instructions

Understands classroom language

Speaking

Participates in storytelling sessions by repeating key vocabulary and phrases

Pronounces intelligibly

Participates in oral activities and tries to use new language

Uses communication strategies

Uses classroom language

Reading

Shows global understanding of language in context

Can read for specific information

Predicts what comes next

Infers meaning

Uses contextual clues as aids to meaning

Recognizes words in context

Can follow simple written instructions

Can match simple dialogues with characters

Fig. 50 Example of a record card   *(adapted from Ellis and Brewster 2002)*

easy to find. Some coursebooks have review units at regular intervals to give pupils and teachers an idea of how much they have learned. They may also include some self or peer assessment, which we shall return to later. Figure 50 shows an example of an observation sheet that can be used to keep an individualized record of each child's progress with story-telling, which can be adapted for more general purposes.

Other ways of monitoring progress is to keep a sample of the child's work in a 'profile folder'. The pupils might sometimes be involved in choosing their own pieces of work for their folders. Folders like this give a very clear idea of a child's achievements as well as areas for further development and can be part of the evidence a teacher uses when discussing progress with parents.

Classroom testing and summative assessment

Many coursebooks include a selection of tests to provide revision of work covered, sometimes in addition to the teacher's records of progress. A great deal of the typical end of term or programme assessment consists of traditional paper and pencil tests. These are very convenient to use and are usually fairly quick to carry out with the whole class and to mark. Although they provide an incomplete or snapshot picture of the child they are particularly good for testing certain aspects of language learning, such as memory and recall. In *You and Me,* Book 1, for example, the formal tests assess knowledge of and ability to read vocabulary items, such as numbers or everyday objects, the ability to read and match questions with answers, the ability to spell words, write simple sentences which test knowledge of grammar and create a simple dialogue.

Pupils may also be assessed on their listening skills, such as when asked to follow simple instructions or do simple dictation. Formal assessment of oral skills, however, is less common as this can be time consuming, especially in larger classes. Formal tests are less useful for providing information on learners' willingness to communicate, take risks or their ability to get their meaning across, even if the language is full of mistakes. However, we need to recognize that formal testing is an important part of the learning process and aims to be more objective than more informal record keeping procedures.

Assessment procedures

A teacher may have to write end of term or year tests herself or she may be preparing learners for tests from outside, such as some of the international tests for young learners. The aims of these tests may include testing relevant and meaningful use of language and testing fairly and accurately.

Task 2

Look at this list and add any other characteristics which you think are important in designing tests. In your opinion, which of these characteristics are the most important? The University of Cambridge makes these claims about the characteristics of their tests:

We want our tests to be:
- *fun for children to take so the tasks are varied and some look like games or puzzles*
- *attractive and colourful to look at so all tasks are based on colourful graphics*
- *interesting in content so topic areas which are relevant to children's lives are chosen e.g. school food, animals*
- *encouraging and confidence building so the tests are short and plenty of time is allowed for each task; the tests have a simple format with simple instructions for the learners*
- *relaxed and non-threatening so all listening tasks are heard twice; speaking tasks are activity-based; oral examiners can give lots of encouragement*

An important issue is how far tests reflect the aims, objectives and methodology of the language programme and how far they are different. The kinds of activities contained in the tests may not reflect the goals of the language programme but teachers may still feel obliged to 'teach to the test'. Although the teachers may have the goal of communicative competence for their language programme, the tests do not always reflect this approach. This mismatch between teaching and assessment was often found in the survey by Rea-Dickens and Rixon (2000), which showed that the content of many tests focused on grammar and vocabulary items, often using gap-filling and multiple choice which are easy-to-mark procedures. The tests did not often focus on the ability to communicate in speaking or writing and often ignored listening and speaking skills. This, in fact, is something the teachers themselves commented on. This may, of course, happen because testing pupils' speaking skills can be difficult and time-consuming with a large class. Young learners in the early stages are not always expected to develop literacy skills in the L2 but may spend a lot of time singing songs, saying rhymes or dialogues, playing games, listening to and participating in storytelling. These activities are also rarely focused on in tests. A further finding was that many classroom paper and pencil tests focus on testing language items at word or sentence level and rarely focus on longer stretches of language (discourse level). As a result pupils are not often asked to do things like listen to a short description and draw a picture or to listen to a story and sequence pictures. We have seen from chapter 2 that young children are skilled at interpreting language using a variety of clues, such as using the physical or visual context, their knowledge of the world, or by working out speakers' intentions. Many tests for primary EFL, by contrast, seem to assume that young learners cannot do this and can only operate at the level of individual sounds, words or sentences. Rea-Dickens and Rixon warn that if we always present a limited view of language which operates only at word and sentence level this does not take account of the language skills young children have been 'programmed' for when they instinctively make use of their Language Acquisition Device (see chapter 2). Some tests are beginning to use longer texts and make increasing use of all four skills.

Let us now turn to examine the kinds of activities which could be used in classroom testing which, as well as the more usual word and sentence level activities, also draw on these four features:

- testing simple language *skills* as well as specific structures or vocabulary items

- testing listening and speaking as well as literacy

- testing by making use of learners' background knowledge such as predicting content from pictures or a list of words

- testing using longer stretches of language, such as dialogues, short descriptions

Assessment activities

Many intelligence tests, tend to focus on the first three kinds of intelligence: *linguistic intelligence, logical-mathematical intelligence* and *spatial intelligence*, which ignores the potential of learners with different kinds of intelligence. This also tends to be true of language tests. Tests often deal with the four classic skills separately, although often, of course, the skills are combined together in some way. Increasingly, some published tests for young learners include simple tasks such as drawing, colouring, labelling, and so on, which reflect the kinds of activities used in the typical primary classroom. Below you can see a list of the types of activities that can be used in tests. You will notice that they are very similar to the kinds of activities recommended in part 2 and are in line with 'good practice' in testing techniques and activities (see Heaton 1990). Some of these activities can be done with the whole class or in smaller, informal groups, which may be easier with younger children if the class is not too large.

Listening
Listen and discriminate between sounds
Listen and point to things or follow instructions
Listen and select the appropriate pictures
Listen to a description and draw or colour a picture
Listen to a description and label a picture
Listen and match two pictures or a word and a picture
Listen and sequence pictures, words or sentences
Listen to a description or story and tick items on a simple chart
Listen and take simple notes
Listen and complete gaps in words or sentences
Listen to a narrative and trace a route on a map or plan
Listen and select the correct response (multiple choice)

Speaking
Listen and repeat words that rhyme or have the same/opposite meanings
Listen and repeat only things which are true
Sing a song, say a rhyme or poem from memory
Do pair work tasks, such as simple problem-solving
Speak from picture prompts
Finish off a sentence
Pass on a telephone message
Play a guessing game
Listen to a story, sequence pictures and then retell the story

Reading
Do simple reading games at word level like Odd One Out
Read a rhyme, poem or part of a dialogue aloud
Read vocabulary items and group them into families
Read a description and label a drawing or diagram
Read a description and colour or draw a picture
Read letters and rearrange them to produce words/sentences
Read and match pictures to written labels or two halves of a sentence
Read and transfer simple information onto a chart
Read and follow instructions to make something or retell them
Read and answer multiple choice, true/false or comprehension questions

Writing
Rearrange and copy letters to spell a word
Read a description and write labels or captions for pictures
Complete a crossword
Fill in gaps in sentences to test grammar or vocabulary
Write speech bubbles for characters from a story or dialogue
Transfer simple notes on a chart into sentences

Answer simple questions in written form
Correct mistakes in a sentence or text
Write sentences from picture prompts

Grammar and vocabulary
Listen or read then change from singular to plural, etc.
Fill in gaps with the correct grammatical or vocabulary item
Correct grammatical or vocabulary mistakes in a sentence
Correct the word order in a sentence
Read or listen to lists of words and classifying them
Sequence time expressions such as *today yesterday tomorrow*
Use picture prompts to contrast things using comparatives, tenses etc.

You will find that some tests have a set of fairly random sentences which do not connect together. Other, more effective tests, build up a sequence of sentences within an exercise which then fit together to make a short, coherent text. The assessment criteria used by the University of Cambridge detail the *levels of attainment* children may reach. In the listening and interaction tests, for example, *level one* shows that a child 'understands some of the questions and requires a lot of support', whereas level three, the highest level, shows that a child 'understands all questions, with some support and can also ask for help/clarification when needed.' If one of the aims of introducing language learning at a young age is fostering a positive attitude then we must ensure that the whole experience is not destroyed by unrealistic expectations in assessment. This is especially true of primary level pupils whose self esteem and confidence should not be damaged by an over-emphasis on tests and their results.

Whether you use formative or summative assessment children need some idea of their progress. This can be done through spoken discussion or written comments. Some companies produce useful stickers and stamps for primary classrooms which give praise and encouragement and recognition of effort, progress and good behavior. These can be used on a drawing or piece of writing and include things like: *Outstanding, Brilliant, Superb, Lovely Work, What a Star!* (see www.superstickers.com). Some coursebooks like *You and Me* also include stickers for children to monitor their progress, while other coursebooks now include end of unit self-assessment sheets.

Peer group assessment

Peer group assessment is where the pupils become involved in monitoring others' progress. It can be a useful type of formative assessment for older children, perhaps those ten years old and over. This may depend on how many years they have been studying English and what their usual experience is of assessment in other parts of the curriculum. The teacher will have to explain to the class that the point of doing this kind of activity is to support their peers and not humiliate or bully them. She will have to select the pairs of learners who work together very carefully to check that they can work well together. It is not useful to have a very dominant child working with a rather timid or passive child. If this selection is done carefully pupils can sometimes be better at explaining things at the child's level than the teacher and this may help the assessment process to be less intimidating. Other advantages are that: it is motivating for pupils to become involved in the process, it can be time-saving for the teacher, pupils receive more individual attention than otherwise, and it may sometimes help in classroom control.

The teacher can help pupils with the kinds of comments they make, which are probably going to be more useful if they are done in the pupils' L1. One golden rule for commenting on a pupil's work is to make sure that peers always start off with something positive, for example, talking about something they liked or thought was good. Students can be provided with a few stock phases such as: *The story/characters was/were funny/interesting/exciting. The beginning/middle/ending was good. I liked the beginning/middle/ending/characters/action.*

Self-assessment

According to Cajkler and Addelman (2000), self-assessment is not as successful or as convincing as peer assessment although it is an important part of learning to learn. The reason for this is the belief that the more pupils are encouraged to be responsible for their own learning and assessment, the more they will understand what is expected and try hard to achieve it. Pupils can be asked to assess their performance in general classroom activities by completing comments (in their L1) such as: *I have enjoyed ... because ... I am good at ... because ... Today I learned ... I have done some good work in ... I am best at ... I need to improve at ...*

If self-assessment avoids becoming too mechanical, but is used carefully and in conjunction with other types of progress monitoring, it can be an effective and useful exercise for pupils. For more about self-assessment see chapter 5.

19 Parental involvement

As more and more children are learning a foreign language at an early age either in mainstream schools as part of the curriculum or in out-of-school clubs or private schools, parents are increasingly asking how they can become involved in and support their child's language learning. Research has shown (McConkey 1985:13) that children benefit in many different ways when their parents are interested in and involved in their education, and there is plenty of evidence too that most parents want to be involved. At least two in three is the commonly cited figure. Furthermore, child psychologists such as Bruner have described parents as 'the only true educators'.

This chapter provides suggestions on how to work with parents and ways of fostering parental involvement in order to establish a partnership between parents, teachers, children and the school. This involves helping parents formulate realistic expectations and informing them about the language learning process. A variety of ways of doing this are described.

Working with parents

The most important people that teachers see besides their pupils are their pupils' parents, and teachers of primary children come into contact with parents more often than teachers of other age groups. However, working with parents is not always easy. Teachers need to be prepared and willing to take on this additional aspect of parent care as part of their day-to-day role, by making themselves available to talk to parents about what their child is doing and why, and to regularly update them on their child's progress. Teachers need to know how best they can do this in order to capitalize on parents' eagerness to support their children's learning and to encourage less eager or confident parents. There is, however, very little provision on training courses to equip teachers with the appropriate attitudes, interpersonal skills and strategies for working with parents or on how to best involve them in their child's learning. The ultimate objective of encouraging parental involvement is to develop a partnership between teachers and parents of mutual understanding in order to maximize their child's learning time.

As a starting point, it is useful to ask yourself how your school currently deals with this issue. What steps does your school take to involve parents in their children's learning? How are parents informed about your language programme and methodology? How effective is the system of written communication between school and home? Does your school arrange meetings for parents? What efforts are made to keep in touch with those parents who fail to attend the meetings? How does your school carry out the registration and induction of children and parents who are new to the school? How are parents encouraged to support their children's learning at home? What provision is there to 'train' parents to do this in the most effective way? Are parents encouraged to help in the school or help in classrooms? Are there any ways of improving what you already do? What new initiative do you think your school should develop? (Adapted from Sullivan 1988:138.)

Most parents see the provision of English in schools as vital for giving their children a better chance for the future. However, unlike other subjects such as L1 development, Maths, History, Geography, Science, etc., where parents share a common language and possess some content knowledge, helping their child with a foreign language can be problematic if they do not speak any or only a little of it. They may feel insecure, inadequate and unable to support their child's learning. These parents need to understand that they can still provide an enormous amount of support and encouragement for their child.

Other parents may have unrealistic expectations in terms of results, about how much and how fast their child can learn, because they evaluate progress solely in terms of linguistic outcomes. It is quite common for parents to expect their child to become bilingual after a year of classes (this may represent not more than thirty to sixty hours tuition). Part of the teacher's role, therefore, is to help parents formulate realistic expectations, as this type of parent is also likely to make the most noise and blame a school for a perceived lack of progress if such results are not achieved. Parents also need to understand that the teaching of foreign languages to young learners contributes to their global development and also offers important personal, cognitive, cultural, social and affective gains, although these are more difficult to perceive and to evaluate.

Modern communicative language teaching methodologies may also differ from the way parents themselves learned a foreign language, and from the way children are taught other subjects at school. Parents often have strong views on how languages are learned and how they should be taught. These views are often based on their own experiences of foreign language learning, good or bad, successful or unsuccessful. They may perceive modern methodologies as 'less formal', 'not serious enough', 'less disciplined' and their value may be questioned. To allay such fears, these parents need 'methodological preparation' as defined by Dickinson and Carver (1980:2). This includes explaining about the foreign language learning process, methodological approaches and materials, what the aims of foreign language teaching are and how they are to be achieved so they understand what is going on in the classroom and why. It goes without saying, that pupils also need this preparation so they can explain to their parents what and how they have learned in a meaningful way (see chapter 5).

Fostering parental involvement

In the field of English language teaching, the issue of parental involvement has recently been receiving more attention as reflected by the inclusion of guidelines in the introductions to teacher's books of some major courses. Vale in *early bird* (1990) an activity-based English course, provides a model letter to be translated (if necessary) and given to parents at the beginning of the course, which explains the methodology used in the coursebook. *Super Me*, *Pebbles* and *Superworld*, among others, provide short guidelines on how to foster parental involvement.

Providing 'parent training'

Parent training is not a new concept. Like learner training it is another strand of the movement in education and language teaching which has been advocating the development of an awareness of learning and, ultimately, autonomy as an educational goal. A need for parent training has surfaced recently due to the challenging demands made by parents in today's competitive market place. The main focus of parent training is to help parents understand how their children can learn a foreign language and how they can support them.

There are a variety of ways of delivering parent training all of which have an informative and awareness-raising purpose. Whatever the delivery mode, the content should, as far as possible, relate to the specificities of each learning context.

Course brochures and guides

Course brochures and parent guides allow a school to state its pedagogical objectives and to explain its methodological approaches. A written record can be read by parents at their leisure and at their own pace and they can reflect on the content. Parents can share the information with other members of the family or with other parents. It can also be used to form the basis of a discussion with the teacher. Written documentation provides no doubt about the school's approach to language teaching and can also act as a safeguard for the school. Brochures or guides should be written in clear, accessible language and avoid jargon. They can also contain attractive photographs, examples of pupil's work, and quotes from teachers and parents. If necessary, they should be produced in the home language.

Open days
Open days are usually organized to allow parents or prospective parents the opportunity to visit a school, meet and talk with teachers and other parents and pupils, visit language classrooms and look at pupils' displays of work. They may even offer the possibility of watching a demonstration lesson. Teachers will be able to answer questions, give brochures or guides to parents which will provide a written record of objectives as described above.

Meetings
Parents are busy people and it is not always possible for them to find the time to attend meetings. A school may organize one meeting a year at the beginning of the school year, a meeting each term or more regular meetings. Whatever your school decides, try to organize meetings at times you know are convenient for most parents. Give plenty of forewarning so parents have the opportunity to organize their work and home life around the meeting. The meeting allows the school to explain its pedagogical objectives and approaches and the possibility of illustrating these with video extracts or other visual aids. Keep to the time you have allotted for the meeting. Do not overrun – this can be very frustrating and is a sign of poor preparation or decision making. Build a question/answer slot into the meeting. A break in the middle of the meeting or at the end with drinks will allow parents to discuss issues informally.

The advantages of meetings are that parents can learn from other parents as each ask different questions or make different suggestions and meetings allow parents to take a wider perspective and possibly acquire a broader understanding of how children learn.

Courses or workshops
Courses for parents can be general or address very specific aspects of foreign language learning. They can be one-off or serial (several meetings organized over a period of time). As stated above, parents are busy people and the one-off course, for example, a three-hour course one evening or at the weekend may be an important parent-convenience factor. To get the most out of your course, advertise it well in advance, state clearly its objectives and the content and the mode of delivery, for example, talk/demonstration, workshop, audience participation, etc. All of this helps parents build realistic expectations. You may wish parents to conduct a short pre-course task or read an article before attending. Course handouts are also very useful as they enable parents to concentrate and listen instead of having to take notes. Bibliographies allow parents to follow-up areas of personal interest afterwards.

Courses will differ from country to country depending on the needs of parents. The British Council's network of teaching centres run a variety of courses (see www.britishcouncil.org). For example, a course in Singapore may focus on raising parents' awareness of standard English grammar and identifying common errors in use; raising awareness of the features of English phonology and providing strategies for helping children improve their pronunciation; and equipping parents with strategies for helping children improve their writing in examinations. In Korea, a course may focus on giving practical suggestions on how parents can help their children learn and demonstrating common classroom activities (dialogues, dominoes, pelmanism, vocabulary card activities, alphabet games). Parents are given copies of the games to take home and use with their children. In France, a three-hour course may address How do children learn languages (L1 and L2)? What is a good language learner? How can I formulate realistic expectations for my child? How can I help my child? What materials and techniques can I use?

It is useful to examine the ways in which children acquire an L1 and L2. As a starting point, parents may like to complete the quiz in chapter 2. Furthermore, parents are often unaware that, in addition to the favourable human environment they provide in the home which is essential for interaction between parent and child to take place, they also use intuitively a range of effective strategies (known as caretaker speech) to draw their children into the use of the L1. (See the transcript in chapter 14 where the teacher is consciously using these strategies).

It is also a useful exercise to ask parents to think about what makes a good language learner and to consider the characteristics their own child possesses. This will help parents identify their child's learning style and understand that learning a foreign language brings together a variety of skills and 'intelligences' in addition to purely linguistic ones. (For further information see chapter 3 and Rubin 1975.)

An understanding of the differences and similarities between first and second language acquisition and, in particular, the conditions for learning (see chapter 2), as well as identifying the characteristics their child possesses, can help parents to formulate more realistic expectations for their child's language learning.

Although parents may be very good at praising and encouraging their children, they are often unsure as to how they can help their children in practical terms and feel insecure, tending to think it is much more complicated than it need be and that they will have to invest a lot of time and money in finding and buying resources. First, by brainstorming the type of materials parents can use they will soon realize that many are part of their everyday household paraphernalia and clutter! Secondly, a demonstration of a variety of activities (Fig. 51), many of which will

Activity	Ages	Parent skills and language required	Child skills and language developed	Materials	Situation
1 English corner	All	No specific language required. Time available and resourcefulness	Interest and curiosity. Cultural awareness and knowledge. Vocabulary and language of explaining: *This is a …* *This is a packet of tea. People in England drink a lot of tea.*	Table, notice-board, bookcase (stamps, postcards, tickets, maps, books, dictionaries, cassettes, videos …)	Language time. Visitors' time: explaining things to other members of the family or to visitors
2 English project	All	No specific language required. Showing interest and helping with researching and organization	General and cultural knowledge, organizational skills, vocabulary and related language	Pictures from magazines, reference materials, internet	Language time
3 Bingo	4 +	Ability to act as caller and pronounce vocabulary items correctly	Listening, selecting, matching, word recognition, vocabulary	Picture or word boards + cards	Language time. Play time
4 I spy with my little eye something beginning with …	6 +	Ability to pronounce alphabet in English, Vocabulary	Observation, guessing, recognition of initial sounds, spelling, vocabulary	none	Language time. Journey time. Play time. Bath time
5 I went to the market and bought a/some …	4 +	Vocabulary	Memory, vocabulary sets (food, clothes, toys) concentration, speaking and pronounciation	none	Language time. Journey time. Play time
6 Labelling	5 +	Willingness to allow household objects to be labelled!	Interest and curiosity, copying and writing. Household vocabulary	Labels	Language time. As appropriate
7 Storytelling	All	Ability to read story aloud and to use 'caretaker speech' including good questioning techniques	Listening, predicting, memory, vocabulary, structures, general and cultural knowledge, social skills	Illustrated storybooks and/or accompanied by cassettes	Language time. Bed time. Journey time. Story time
8 Songs and rhymes	1/12 +	No specific language required, willingness to join in and sing!	Interest, motivation, pronunciation and rhythm, vocabulary and structures, social skills	Traditional songs and rhymes on cassette or video	Language time. Bed time. Journey time

Activity	Age	Description	Focus/skills	Necessary ingredients	When
9 Cooking	3 +	Knowledge of national dishes, cakes, biscuits, etc.	Interest, motivation, cultural knowledge, cooking skills and related vocabulary and structures		Language time Meal times
10 TV/video	1 +	No language required Time to share viewing with your child	Interest, motivation, pronunciation, cultural knowledge, vocabulary, structures	TV (satellite) cartoon network, videos	Language time Rest time
11 Handicrafts Making activities Picture dictionary	2 +	Language for giving instructions: *cut here, fold here, paint here*, etc.	Interest, motivation, cultural knowledge, vocabulary and structures	Coloured paper or card, boxes, glue, sticky tape, etc.	Language time Play time
12 Reviewing work from school	6 +	No specific language required. Willingness and time to review work, show interest, encourage and praise	Reflecting, revising, memory, confidence, interest, motivation	None	Language time Homework time
13 Collecting English in your environment	4 +	No specific language required. Good observation in the home and outside	Observation, interest and curiosity, language awareness, vocabulary sets: clothes, food, toys, technical equipment social sight vocabulary, etc.	None	Language time Shopping time Walking time
14 Drama, role-play puppets	2 +	Ability to produce simple dialogues relating to situations that are relevant and meaningful to the child	Motivation, speaking, functional language, awareness of use of language for communication, social skills	Simple props, puppets, Acting out of stories	Language time Play time Story time
15 Dictation: traditional and other	3 +	Varied for basic colours and numbers to short texts	Listening, writing, confidence, communication strategies, *Could you please say that again*, etc.	Paper, colours, dictionary	Language time
16 Definition game	4 +	Ability to give simple definitions: *It's green and round. You can eat it.*	Motivation, guessing, language of defining: *It's + adjective. You can + verb/You use it for + gerund*	None	Language time Journey time

Fig. 51 Activities and techniques to support children's learning at home

already be familiar to parents, will not only boost their confidence but also provide a useful repertoire to take home and use with their children, by integrating them into different situations related to family life. The situations range from a specific 'language time' to natural situations such as visitors time, play time, journey time, bed time, etc. The 'language time' is a systematic session planned by the parent which will help a child understand that a language needs to be learned and practised in the same way as any other subject. Sometimes 'language time' can be integrated into some of the above 'natural' times. Whatever, if a parent senses their child is not receptive on a particular day it is probably best not to insist and to postpone the session until a more appropriate moment. However, both child and parent should regard 'language time' as a commitment. 'Language time' need not last for more than ten minutes (or less) depending on the age of the child. (For further information see Dunn 1994.) The chart highlights the parent skills and language required and the child skills and language developed. The child skills developed contribute to the global development of children and include skills other than linguistic as mentioned above. The materials required are also listed. It can be seen that many of the activities can be used with a range of ages, and the level of parent language required varies from a little to a good level, to show that however small a parent's contribution they can support their child's learning.

At the end of this course, parents are invited to complete a personal action plan so they can put into practice what they have learned from the course.

Courses allow parents to investigate areas of interest in depth and, as above with meetings, to learn from each other and establish a feeling of group solidarity:

> *The course was very interesting and provided me with a great deal of information and answers to certain questions that I had asked myself. It was very interesting to listen to the other parents talking about their problems and to listen to their questions which complemented mine.*
>
> *The participation of other parents contributed a great deal to the interest and value of the course. The handouts were very useful.*
>
> *(feedback from Paris course, October 2001)*

Handbooks
There are now a number of excellent parent handbooks and newsletters that parents can read in their own time (Baker 2000, Crystal 1986, De Jong 1986, Dunn 1994, Harding and Riley 1986, Taylor 1984, The Bilingual Family Newsletter, *REALBOOK News*). There will also be local publications in home languages that you will know about and wish to

recommend. Short bibliographies can be given to parents at registration, at meetings, at courses or by teachers. These bibliographies can also include home study materials, many of which are produced by local publishers with parents' guidelines in the home language. There are also detailed Parent's Notes for the *Muzzy* videos (Webster 1989).

Dispelling common misconceptions or fixed attitudes

You may often hear parents express a variety of misconceptions or display fixed attitudes. Try to dispel these by informing and explaining or asking why parents feel the way they do. Such misconceptions could also form the basis of discussion groups or meetings. Common misconceptions include some of the following:

My child is bilingual. Parents sometimes overestimate what they believe to be their child's level. This may be because many parents living in monolingual countries often use the term 'bilingual' rather freely. They are under the impression that living with two or more languages is exceptional. However, over half the world's population is bilingual, so bilingualism is not rare which often comes as a surprise to such parents. Furthermore, bilingual means different things to different people. It is a term that is difficult to define and many definitions derive from a view of bilingualism which is idealized: *The bilingual is someone who speaks two languages perfectly.* In fact, bilingualism is a matter of degree depending on a number of different factors. Bilingualism is a term which is used when referring to 'natural' users of two (or more) languages developed in parallel (if not necessarily to the same extent or for exactly the same functions) because of early 'natural' exposure to them, most often because of family circumstances (for example, parents using two or more languages in the home, or a family moving to an English-speaking country where the child is educated in an English-speaking school).

My child is gifted/My child is useless. These comments reflect parents perceptions of their child's ability to learn an L2. Most schools will recognize each child's individual potential as a foreign language learner, and encourage the development of the different intelligences (Gardner 1993) required in foreign language learning. A link between intelligence and foreign language learning has been reported by several researchers. However, 'intelligence' as measured by IQ tests may identify high academic ability but are often poor predictors of other forms of intelligence. Learning a foreign language is an all-round ability involving a variety of skills and strategies which enable the learner to read and write, learn grammar and vocabulary as well as develop communication and social skills. If a child has been identified by an intelligence test as gifted, this does not necessarily mean he or she will find foreign language learning easy as many different forms of intelligence contribute to success in foreign language learning. Equally, if a child has been identified as a weak learner, it does not mean that he or she cannot learn an L2. Research has shown (Lightbown and Spada 1993:112) that learners with a wide variety of intellectual abilities can be successful language learners. Probably the most important factor in a child's language learning, however, is motivation and success. The more one succeeds, the greater one's motivation; the greater one's motivation, the more one succeeds. Parents can help by showing an interest in their child's work and praising all efforts however great or small.

But my child's got karate at that time ... If you work in a private school where a child comes for out-of-school activities, it may sometimes be difficult to find a mutually convenient time for the child to attend English classes. Parents need to understand that learning an L2 is a long-term investment. It is going to take a lot of time and hard work. Therefore, the earlier a child begins systematic foreign language learning, the more time he or she has to achieve a desired performance level. However, whenever the start, optimal conditions (see Rixon 1999), regular practice and reviewing are essential to maintain the level already achieved and to make further progress. FLL is a complex process and one of the main reasons for failure is a lack of continuity. If an English class does not coincide with the time a parent has requested, and it is not possible to rearrange one of the activities, then parents must be aware of the consequences and decide which is the priority for their child.

But I hear the teacher speaking (Spanish) in the classroom. As teachers, if we have a class that shares a common L1 which we also speak, we sometimes use this for very specific reasons to facilitate learning of the foreign language. However, if parents hear the L1 being spoken in the classroom they sometimes misconstrue the reasons for this, as they may feel very strongly that the 'no L1 rule' is the best way for their child to learn the target language. Teachers need to explain to parents, either at meetings or in a parent's guide, why the L1 may sometimes be used as a tool to facilitate L2 acquisition (see chapter 20).

Arranging special events
Parents enjoy being invited to a school to see examples of work produced by their children or to attend a special event. These provide an ideal opportunity to forge strong parent/teacher/school links. Think about the type of special events which are/could be possible for your school. Give parents plenty of prior notice so they can organize

themselves. Find out if any parents can play a musical instrument as they may be able to provide musical accompaniment at a presentation. Some parents are also very willing to film a performance. Here are a few suggestions:

A Book Fair: Support the local book trade and invite a bookseller to come to your school to sell books. Make sure a few teachers are available to advise parents on the most appropriate books/levels for their children. If possible, invite an author or illustrator to talk about his or her books, tell stories, run a workshop, etc.

A Celebration: Organize a celebration to coincide with a festival that is appropriate for your context. This could be a Christmas pantomime, a play, a party, a presentation of songs, the acting out of a story, etc.

An end of term/school year party: involving any of the above, plus the presentation of certificates, if appropriate.

Celebrate topic or story-based work: If you are working around topics or stories, build up to an exhibition or display of writing, artwork, projects and handicrafts to which parents and friends are invited. (See Ellis and Brewster (2002) where suggestions are provided for concrete outcomes related to story work.)

Providing parent care

Parents are our customers and as professionals we must take great care to think about the relationship we develop with them and the service we offer. Some teachers welcome dialogue with parents while others avoid it because they may feel threatened or attacked or they may simply prefer to keep a social distance. We can provide quality parent care by implementing some or all of the following actions:

- Arrive in class ten minutes early to greet parents and make yourself available for questions.

- Establish a system for communication to take place between teachers and parents, for example, a small notebook.

- Make sure parents receive regular information from class teachers or the head in the form of letters, information sheets, termly reports, meetings, etc.

- Provide a suggestion box for parents to leave questions or suggestions.

- Share information with parents and explain what you are doing and why. Develop mutual respect.

- Build in regular review sessions into your classes so that children understand what and how they have learned and can explain their lesson to their parents (see chapter 5).

- Try to dispel and break down common misconceptions or fixed attitudes (see above) by informing and explaining.

- Invite parents to look at children's work in the classroom.

- Suggest ways parents can help their children at home (see Fig. 51): by asking their child what they have done in English; looking at their English books; asking children to sing songs or to repeat rhymes; asking their child to teach them some English and showing an interest in any materials they have produced, praising their children regularly so they feel proud of what they are doing.

- Organize and invite parents to special events.

- Share information and communicate your skills to parents.

- Listen to parents and consult them as well as be consulted.

- Be honest about your feelings so that parents can be too.

- Ask questions and be prepared to answer questions.

The above suggestions can contribute to encouraging parental involvement, enabling parents to become partners in learning so they can maximize their child's language learning opportunities through self-help, encouragement and mutual understanding between themselves, their child and the school.

PERSONAL AND PROFESSIONAL DEVELOPMENT **PART 5**

20 Planning for the future

So far we have considered the aims and methodology of teaching young learners. Part 5 considers your own personal and professional development.

Personal and professional development: why it is important

The challenge for all primary teachers of English is to have the knowledge, skills and sensitivities of a teacher of children and of a teacher of language and to be able to balance and combine the two successfully. When thinking about your personal and professional development it is useful to bear this in mind, and we have broken it down into the following two categories:

Language development goals: Whether English is or is not your L1, you may feel you need to reflect on when to use the L1 and when to use English in the classroom. If you are a teacher for whom English is not your L1, you may feel a need to improve your English for classroom use as well as for your own personal use.

Skills and techniques development goals: This relates to aspects of teaching methodology which you may wish to develop: planning lessons, storytelling, handling discipline, using technology, etc.

As we gain more experience, it follows that we expand our repertoire of teaching techniques, we understand our pupils' needs better, we are better able to control our pupils, we become more self-confident and, ultimately, we become more effective teachers. However, you may find you have ups and downs in teaching: perhaps in the beginning you will feel very keen and enthusiastic but later become rather tired, bored or frustrated (or vice versa)! It may sometimes be hard to keep your level of enthusiasm and motivation high. Furthermore, the teaching profession can be a solitary one and teachers often complain of feeling isolated. The supportive atmosphere experienced at teacher training college or university and the regular contact with fellow teacher trainees and tutors, discussion and feedback may seem long ago. In-service teacher training provision may also be rare. Indeed, teachers are very much on their own! Teachers are also busy people with tight schedules and responsibilities for many pupils, and often find it difficult to find the time and ways to develop personally and professionally. Sometimes teachers settle into a routine and unquestioning acceptance of their day-to-day procedures. As Widdowson (1984:89) writes 'There are two phrases which are quite commonly used by teachers, as if they were in some way conclusive. One of them is: "It works". The reaction to this ought always to be: "Why?". The fact that something works is no more interesting than the fact that something does not work. What we need to do in both cases is to enquire about the conditions for success or failure, and to make them as explicit as possible so that they can be tested by other teachers in different teaching situations. The phrase "It works" should mark the beginning of enquiry, not its conclusion'.

Enquiry is the starting point for personal and professional development, as it encourages teachers to reflect on their practice by reviewing their experience in a systematic way which can lead to potential change and development. This in turn can empower teachers, lead to more effective teaching and consequently learning for our pupils, greater motivation and job satisfaction.

Before looking at specific techniques that we can use for our personal and professional development, we will first reflect on individual teaching styles.

Reflecting on your teaching style

All teachers have their own preferred teaching styles which will affect their classroom management skills and their personal and professional development. Teaching style is a very individual matter which is based on a range of factors such as the teaching/learning context, the teacher's personality, attitudes and beliefs about language learning and learning more generally and finally, the teacher's classroom experience. Different teaching styles lead to variations in matters like discipline and classroom control, the amount of noise you tolerate in your classroom or the degree of pupil independence you consider acceptable.

Task 1

This questionnaire (Fig. 52) will help you think about some aspects of your teaching style. Try to answer the questions truthfully and reflect on what this tells you about you and your teaching style. You might also like to reflect on *why* you are this way. Is it because of your training? A model teacher you admire and try to copy? Your experience? Your personality? The columns indicate how far you agree with each statement. For example, if your style lies somewhere in the middle of these statements tick the column headed by *average*. If you agree more strongly with the statement on the left tick the left column. You might like to ask

	average		
I like to have everything well planned in advance.			My best work happens spontaneously in response to something which has just happened.
I am normally well-tempered and patient.			I quickly become impatient and can easily get irritable.
I like a quiet classroom most of the time.			I don't mind noise as long as I can see the children are working.
I think children learn best when they are not given too much choice.			I believe choice is important in motivating children to learn.
I think competition in the classroom helps children to learn.			I prefer to play down the importance of competition to develop cooperation.

Fig. 52 A questionnaire about teaching style

a colleague to do this questionnaire as well and then compare your results and the implications of these for your classroom management (see chapter 16).

Setting personal and professional goals: an action plan

Now it is time to set your goals and draw up an action plan. Think about *your* goals and record them in a notebook. Review them after a month, six months and one year and see how far you have developed.

Achieving your goals

A general strategy to use in order to achieve your goals, either language or skills and techniques related, is to develop your self-awareness, in other words, to learn to judge your own language skills and teaching critically. This can be done through regular self-assessment and introspection. This involves planning what you are going to do, carrying out your plans and evaluating and reviewing your performance by applying the Plan-Do-Review model as described in chapter 5. This knowledge will enable you to identify your strong and weak points in order to make plans for your future development and self-improvement by identifying what you need to work on next. The results of your self-assessment can also help you decide whether what you are doing is effective for you.

Language development goals

It is useful to reflect on when to use the L1 and when to use English in the classroom and to consider the most effective ways of doing so. You may also feel a need to improve your English for classroom use as well as for your own personal use.

English for classroom purposes

Teachers of young learners all over the world may struggle to use English throughout their lessons or may feel uncomfortable or anxious about using the pupils' L1. This may well be because of the influence of communicative language teaching, which encourages teachers and pupils to use the target language as much as possible, or simply because there is an 'English only' rule in your school. Atkinson (1987) suggests that the use of the L1 can act as a useful tool which supports pupils' understanding and helps teachers in their teaching. This was found to be the case in Scotland where a study by Mitchell (1988), showed that teachers made very practical use of code-switching, changing from L2 to L1 when it was necessary. The sorts of factors which influenced these teachers' decisions about using the L1 included the type of task, the pupils' age and ability level, the size of the class, the competence and confidence of the teacher, the stage in the course and even the time of day! Code-switching is a frequent occurrence in classrooms everywhere, except where the teacher is a monolingual English native speaker. This is a tiny proportion of teachers of young learners. Here are four important questions to ask ourselves about this issue:

- How can we be more realistic about our own and our pupils' use of the target language?
- How can we overcome anxiety about the use of the L1 in lessons?
- How far does the L1 have an important role to play in language lessons?
- What ways are there of increasing pupils' use of the target language?

The English we use in the classroom with young learners will be very different from the English we use for general purposes and for our own personal needs. We need to think carefully about the language relevant to the needs of young learners. We saw in chapter 6 that child-centred topics such as Toys, Games, Witches, and so on, may require learning new specific vocabulary. When using English with our pupils we should also try to provide models that are as authentic and as natural as possible.

Task 2

Think of a beginners class you teach. Do you speak mainly in English, mainly in the pupils' L1, or a mixture of the two? Why? Ideally, we should aim for the first of these. However, do not feel you must use English all the time. There are certain occasions when it can be useful to use your pupils' language. How much English you use will, of course, depend on the level of your class and how long they have been learning English, the type of activity they are involved in, and your own confidence and language ability. Some reasons for attempting to use mainly English are:

- Pupils see how English is used for a variety of different purposes: giving instructions, praising, socializing, playing games, and so on, as well as providing opportunities to hear and use real, natural English.
- It encourages your pupils to reply in English. This provides practice in listening and speaking and will help them pick up words and expressions beyond the language of the coursebook.
- Pupils become aware that English is a language used for real communication and not just another school subject.

However, switching codes may be more likely to happen in certain situations. Read through the ones shown below and ask yourself if these are the times when you find yourself using the L1. Are there any others?

- Introducing a new topic or story where the context must be very clear so the pupils are interested and motivated
- Explaining the rules of a new game or task where understanding exactly what to do is crucial
- Explaining a complicated grammatical rule
- Setting homework
- Explaining the meaning of an abstract word
- Explaining cultural references and differences
- Dealing with a discipline problem
- Checking understanding with lower level pupils
- Giving instructions with lower level pupils
- Conducting review sessions with lower level pupils and other learning to learn activities which require reflection
- Comforting younger pupils and helping them feel secure. The L1 plays an affective role and initially very young learners may feel insecure

Gradually, less and less L1 will be used as pupils become familiar with classroom procedures and activities and as their English improves.

If you are not happy about the amount of code-switching you do, here are some suggestions for things you can do to increase how much English you use.

- Make a contract with yourself to gradually increase your use of English. Can you set yourself a realistic target to use a certain extra amount of classroom English each week? Monitor your progress over several weeks and in time you will be surprised how much more English you use.

- Place written prompts (e.g. lists, flashcards) in English on your desk to remind you of key language. Focus on a set of words at a time and gradually build them up. Finally, you can use older pupils to check how much English you are using. They will soon remind you if you are not doing this and it will usually have the side-effect of increasing their efforts to use English also.

- Listen to recordings of sample classroom language and rehearse before you go into the classroom. You may even like to write out a script.

- Record yourself. Make a cassette recording of part of one of your lessons (a ten minute extract is sufficient). Before listening, decide which area(s) you are going to focus on, for example, English for social chit chat, introducing the lesson, organizing the pupils, giving instructions, presenting new language, checking understanding, asking questions, setting up an activity, controlling/disciplining, praising/encouraging/giving feedback, reviewing and ending a lesson. Do not focus on more than one or two areas at a time. Listen to your recording and identify any problem areas you have in English and work on these. Think of the same class again. What problems, if any, did your pupils have? Why? Try to use this technique regularly and focus on different areas. This can also help you understand the reasons for some of the problems your pupils may be having. Label and date your cassettes to enable you to compare them later. You will hear the progress you and your pupils have made.

Encouraging pupils to use English
As we saw in chapter 2, young children are very good mimics and tend to be less inhibited about using an L2 than some older pupils. From this point of view teaching young teenagers can be a little more difficult.

Task 3
Read through the strategies below and see which ones you think you could use with your pupils. If you can find one, or two, set yourself a target of introducing it and monitoring how it works over a few weeks.

1 Make a contract with more reluctant pupils for them to use the target language for a specific amount or time (e.g. five minutes) then gradually increase this time. Make sure you always monitor this and give praise where it is clear the pupils have tried hard to do this.

2 Consider using fines and rewards (e.g. points, stars). Children usually like an element of competition which you can sometimes use to your advantage.

3　With older pupils you can try discussing with your pupils some rules for use of the target language and encourage them to ask permission when they want to use the L1.

4　If you use self-assessment techniques you may encourage pupils to monitor for themselves how much English they use so they can set themselves targets.

You may find other examples of strategies which seem to work, but these form a good starting point.

A reflective teacher will be sensitive to her pupils' needs and attempt to use English as much as possible. She will, however, be aware of the specific reasons and occasions listed above for using the L1 in order to support her pupils' learning. It is possible that a bilingual teacher may have some advantages over a teacher who does not share the same language as her pupils since she will be more aware of the kinds of difficulty pupils experience in trying to speak a foreign language. For example, she may have a much clearer idea of pronunciation difficulties they are likely to meet, understand the source of the grammatical errors they make and the reasons why they chose the wrong words. Sometimes it may even be a little demoralizing or demotivating for pupils not to be able to use their L1 at all. However, while we try to be realistic about switching between English and your pupils' L1, we must also remember that learning a foreign language means there must be a lot of exposure to it! If too much of the pupils' L1 is used in class then their opportunities for learning English successfully are reduced. It's all a question of balance.

English for general purposes
Many teachers complain that they find it difficult to maintain their level of English because they teach low-level classes, or have a lack of contact with the English language. Here are some practical suggestions for improving your English for general purposes:

- Use a dictionary to help with pronunciation and stress.
- Listen to published material on cassette and notice some of the pronunciation features referred to in chapter 6. Are there any individual sounds which you find particularly difficult? Are there any examples of linking? Is the sentence stressed in the way you would expect? Are there any examples of weak forms? How many examples of falling or rising tones can you hear? If you have any particular difficulties, practise repeating particular phrases using the model provided by the cassette.
- Organize a regular time to practise your speaking.
- Find out where you can talk to other speakers of English.
- Have blank cassettes available so you can record yourself and note your

main strengths and weaknesses. Choose one area at a time to concentrate on. You will gradually build up your confidence and develop both accuracy and fluency. See the self-assessment task in chapter 14.

- Listen to recorded versions of books and read in English.
- Listen to as much authentic English as possible such as radio programmes, films or television.
- Use the internet. Download teaching resources and lesson plans, read reviews of recent publications, read interviews with key ELT professionals and discuss teaching issues with other teachers.

Skills and techniques development goals

Teaching children requires a great deal of energy and flexibility as well as special talents. Many teachers come to teaching with special talents or develop others that will provide variety and add enjoyment to their lessons. Think about:

- Telling stories: Are you good at using expressions, mime and gestures, alternating between soft and loud speech to create dramatic effect or build up suspense by whispering or using pauses? (See chapter 14.)
- Singing or playing an instrument: These talents are excellent for making songs and rhymes an integral and enjoyable part of your lessons. (See chapter 12.)
- Drawing/creativity: Drawings are very effective in conveying the meaning of a new word or when presenting new language. Even if you are not a natural artist, your drawing techniques can be improved with practice. There are several useful books which provide guidance and ideas for the teacher (see Wright 1996). You may be good at sewing and handicrafts or lettering in which case you might like to make useful things like puppets, colourful storage boxes or eye-catching notice boards to display children's work.
- Using the computer: Make clear worksheets or flashcards, word process young children's written work to give them a sense of achievement, produce eye-catching headings for notice boards or book corners, produce large posters, help older children create professional-looking books out of their projects. (See chapter 15.)
- Acting: Being willing to experiment and have a go at drama yourself is especially encouraging if you want your pupils to take part. Enthusiasm counts for more than acting ability!

Suggestions for skills and techniques development

Once you have decided which aspect or aspects of your teaching you wish to develop you can decide how to do this. Plan what you are going to do, carry out your plans and then evaluate and review your plans using the plan-do-review model. Some suggestions are:

- Lesson planning: Take time to write out a lesson plan like the one in Fig. 46 from time to time. This will encourage you to reflect on your aims, the different stages of a lesson, the activity cycles, the timing, the materials you require, etc. Then evaluate your lesson by asking yourself the questions on page 243. For further details see chapter 17.
- Observing lessons: It is always very helpful to observe a colleague's lesson or invite a colleague to observe your lesson and discuss it afterwards. This takes time but if planned in advance can be a very rewarding exercise.
- Storytelling: use the self-assessment questionnaire (Fig. 38) to develop your storytelling skills.
- Carrying out a small action research project: this could be a small scale investigation, for example, to collect and monitor pupils' feedback on their lessons or to ask pupils what they think makes a good teacher (see Day 1999). You could also give children questionnaires on their favourite topics, games, stories, etc.
- Keeping a diary: Keep a diary of your teaching perhaps on one particular class or comparing two different classes.
- Carrying out case studies: Carry out a case study of a particular classroom, group of learners, or even a single learner. For an example, you could use a record card (see Fig. 50) for monitoring a child's progress.
- Producing materials, for example, theme-based packs of visual aids, story props, etc.
- Reading articles in magazines or journals. Try to read at least one article a month and try out any new ideas. (See References and further reading.)
- Contacting publishers and ask to be put on their mailing lists so you are informed about new publications, seminars and workshops, conferences, etc. Try to go to at least one talk or conference a year.
- Joining or starting a teacher development group.
- Joining discussion groups for example, www.tefl.net or the one available through the IATELF young learners special interest group at www.countryschool.com/younglearners.htm
- Talking to other teachers about what you are doing and what they are doing.

See Scrivener 1994 for further ideas.

References and further reading

Aitchison, J. 1987. *Words in the Mind*: Oxford: Basil Blackwell

Anning, A. 1991. *The First Years at School*: Ballmoor: Open University Press

Anning, A. 1998. 'Teachers' Theories about Children's Learning' in Calderhead, J. (ed.) *Teachers Professional Development*: Lewes: Falmer Press

Ashworth, J. Clark, J. & Ellis, G. 1996. *Play It Again!*: Harlow: Longman

Ashworth, J., Clark, J. 1993. *Longman Picture Dictionary*: Harlow: Longman

Asher, J. 1969. 'The Total Physical Response Approach to Second Language Learning' *Modern Language Journal* 56:133-139

Atkinson, D. 1987. 'The mother tongue in the classroom: a neglected resource?' in: *English Language Teaching Journal* Vol 41/4:241-247

Ausubel, D. 1964. 'Adults vs. Children in Second Language Learning: Psychological Considerations' *Modern Language Journal* 48:420-424

Baker, C. 1993. *Foundations of Bilingual Education and Bilingualism*: Clevedon: Multilingual Matters

Baker, C. 2000. *A Parents' and Teachers' Guide to Bilingualism*: Clevedon: Multilingual Matters

Batstone, R. 1994. *Grammar*: Oxford: Oxford University Press

Berman, M. 1998. *A Multiple Intelligences Road to an ELT Classroom*: Bancyfelin: Crown House

BOEN (Bulletin Officiel de l'Education Nationale) 1989. 'Experimentation contrôlée d'une langue vivante étrangère à l'école élémentaire' No 11

Bourke, K. 1996. *The Jungle Grammar Books*: Oxford: Oxford University Press

Bourke, K. 1999. *The Grammar Lab*: Oxford: Oxford University Press

Brent Language Services. 1999. *Enriching Literacy*: Stoke-on-Trent: Trentham Books

Brewster, J. 1995. 'Task-based learning: strategies for teachers and trainers' in: *Proceedings of the APAC Convention*: Barcelona: University of Barcelona

Brewster, J. 1999. 'Teaching English through content: supporting good practice' in: Kennedy, C. *Innovation and Best Practice*: Harlow: Longman

Brewster, J. 2001. 'High Hopes: creating optimal conditions for ELT in elementary schools' in: *Proceedings of the ELTeCS Conference ELT Curriculum Development for Young Learners in East Asia 2000*: Taiwan Normal University/British Council/ELTeCS East Asia

Brewster, J., Ellis, G. & Girard, D. 1992. *The Primary English Teacher's Guide*: London: Penguin

Briggs, R. & Ellis, G. 1995. *The Snowman. The original storybook with activities for young learners of English*: Oxford: Oxford University Press

Brown, K. & Brown, M. 1996. *New contexts for modern language learning. Pathfinder Series for Language Teachers* No 27: CILT

Bruner, J. 1983. *Child's Talk: Learning to Use Language*: Oxford: Oxford University Press

Bruner, J.S. (ed.) 1972. *Play*: Harmondsworth: Penguin

Cajkler, W. & Addelman, R. 2000. *The Practice of Foreign Language Teaching*: London: David Fulton

Cameron, L. 1994. 'Organising the world: children's concepts and categories, and implications for the teaching of English' *English Language Teaching Journal* Vol 48 No 1

Cameron, L. 2001. *Teaching Languages to Young Learners*: Cambridge: Cambridge University Press

Carlo, M. & Royer, J. 1999. 'Cross-language transfer of reading skills' in: Wagner, D., Venetzky, R. & Street, B. (eds) *Literacy: An International Handbook*: Oxford: Westview Press

Carter, R. & McCarthy, M. 1988. *Vocabulary and Language Teaching*: Harlow: Longman

Chamot, A. & O'Malley, J. 1994. *The CALLA Handbook: Implementing the Cognitive Academic Language Learning Approach*: Ontario: Addison-Wesley

Chomsky, C. 1969. *The Acquisition of Syntax in Children from 5 to 10*: Cambridge, Mass.: MIT Press

Chomsky, N. 1959. Review of *Verbal Behaviour Language* Language 35:26-58

Chomsky, N. 1965. *Aspects of the Theory of Syntax*: Cambridge, Mass.: MIT Press

Coyle, Y., Valcarcel, M. & Verdu, M. 1997. 'Classroom interaction and children's EFL learning strategies' in: Karavas-Doukas, K. & Rea-Dickens, P. *Evaluating Innovations and Establishing Research Priorities: Proceedings of the Conference on The Teaching of Foreign Languages in European Primary Schools*: Warwick: University of Warwick Press

Crystal, D. 1986. *Listen to your child*: London: Penguin

Cummins, J. 1979. 'Linguistic interdependence and the educational development of bilingual children' in: *Review of Educational Research* 49:222-251

Curriculum Council for Wales 1991. *Under Fives in School*: Cardiff: Curriculum Council for Wales

Day, C. 1999. *Developing Teachers*: London: Falmer Press

De Jong, E. 1986. *The Bilingual Experience A Book for Parents*: Cambridge: Cambridge University Press

Dickinson, L., Carver, D. 1980. 'Learning how to learn: steps towards self-direction in foreign language learning in schools' in: *English Language Teaching Journal* Vol.35 No 1

Djigunovic, J. & Vilke, M. 2000. 'Eight years After: Wishful Thinking vs The facts of Life' in: Moon, J. & Nikolov, M. (eds.) *Research into Teaching English to Young Learners*: Pecs: University of Pecs Press

Dlugosz, D. 2000. 'Rethinking the role of reading in teaching a foreign language to young learners' in: *English Language Teaching Journal* 54/3:284-291

Donaldson, M. 1978. *Children's Minds*: London: Fontana

Dörnyei, Z. 1998. 'Motivation in second and foreign language learning' in: *Language Teaching* 31:117-135

Doyé, P. & Hurrell, A. (eds.) 1997. *Foreign Language Learning in Primary Schools*: Strasbourg: Council of Europe

Dudeney, C. 2000. *The Internet and the Language Classroom*: Cambridge: Cambridge University Press

Dunn, O. 1994. *Help Your Child with a Foreign Language A Parents' Handbook*: London: Berlitz

Eastment, D. 1999. *The Internet and ELT*: Oxford: Summertown Publishing

Eastment, D. 2001. 'Search engines, web directories, and sites for news and current affairs' *English Language Teaching Journal* Vol 55 No 1

Ellis, G. 1997. *We're Kids in Britain*: Harlow: Longman

Ellis, G. 1999. 'Developing Children's Metacognitive Awareness' in: Kennedy, C (ed.) *Innovation and Best Practice*: Longman in association with the British Council

Ellis, G. 2000. 'Is it worth it? Convincing teachers of the value of developing metacognitive awareness in children' in: *Learner Autonomy, Teacher Autonomy: Future Directions*, edited by Sinclair, B., McGrath, I. & Lamb, T., Longman in association with the British Council

Ellis, G. & Brewster, J. 1991. *The Storytelling Handbook for Primary Teachers*: London: Penguin

Ellis, G. & Brewster, J. 2002. *Tell it Again! The New Storytelling Handbook for Primary Teachers*: London: Penguin Longman

Ellis, G. & Sinclair, B. 1989. *Learning to Learn English*: Cambridge: Cambridge University Press

Ellis, R. 1985. *Understanding Second Language Acquisition*: Oxford: Oxford University Press

Ellis, R. 1994. *The Study of Second Language Acquisition*: Oxford: Oxford University Press

Etchells, C. 1999. 'News from the Net 3: Online Safety'. In: *CATS Children and Teenagers The Young Learners SIG Newsletter*: IATEFL No 1

Fisher. R. 1990. *Teaching Children to Think*: London: Simon Schuster
Freebairn, I. 2000. 'The course book - future continuous or past?' in: *English Teaching Professional* Issue 15

Gardner, H. 1993. *Multiple Intelligences. The Theory in Practice*: London: Harper Collins
Garvie, E. 1990. *Story as Vehicle*: Clevedon: Multilingual Matters.
Gerngross, G. & Puchta, H. 1996. *Do and Understand*: Harlow: Longman
Gibbons, P. 1991. *Learning to Learn in a Second Language*: Primary English Teaching Association. NSW, Australia
Gipps, C. 1994. 'What we know about effective primary teaching' in: Bourne, J. (ed.) *Thinking Through Primary Practice*: London: Routledge/Open University
Girard, D. 1974. *Enseignement précoce des langues vivant*: National Ministry of Education, France
Graddol, D. & Meinhof, U. (eds.) 1999. 'English in a Changing World' *AILA Review* Vol 13
Graham, C. 1979. *Jazz Chants for Children*: Oxford: Oxford University Press
Gray, K. (compiler) 1996a. *Jet Primary Resources Book*: London: Mary Glasgow Magazines/Scholastic
Gray, K. (ed.) 1996b. *Fun and Games in English*: Addlestone: DELTA
Greenwood, J. 1997. *Activity Box*: Cambridge: Cambridge University Press

Halliwell, S. 1992. *Teaching English in the Primary Classroom*: Harlow: Longman
Hancock, M. 1995. *Pronunciation Games*: Cambridge: Cambridge University Press
Harding, E. & Riley, P. 1986. *The Bilingual Family A Handbook for Parents*: Cambridge: Cambridge University Press
Hawkins, E. 1984. *Awareness of Language*: Cambridge: Cambridge University Press
Heaton, J. 1990. *Classroom Testing*: Harlow: Longman
Hester, H. 1983. *Stories in the Multilingual Primary Classroom*: London: ILEA
Holderness, J. 1991. 'Activity-based teaching: approaches to topic-centred work' (ed.) Brumfit, C., Moon, J., Tongue, R. London: Collins ELT
Holderness, J. & Hughes, A. 1997. *100+ Ideas for Children*: Oxford: Macmillan Heinemann
Hooper, H. 1996. 'Integrating science with a majority of ESL learners: integrating language and content' in: Clegg, J. (ed.) Mainstreaming ESL: Clevedon: Multilingual Matters
Housen, A. 1997. 'Teaching and learning second languages in the European schools' in: Karavas–Doukas, K. & Rea-Dickens, P. 1997. *Evaluating Innovations and Establishing Research priorities* Proceedings on the Conference on The Teaching of Foreign Languages in European Primary Schools: Warwick: University of Warwick Press
Hughes, A. 2000. ' Reviews: Teaching English to young learners' in: *English Language Teaching Journal* Vol 54 No 2

Jones, B. 1995. *Exploring Otherness. Pathfinder Series for Language Teachers* No 24: CILT
Jupp, C. & Harvey, A. 1996. 'Policy Practice and Research': Dictogloss NALDIC Newsletter

Kenworthy, J. 1987. *Teaching English Pronunciation*: Harlow: Longman
Krashen, S. 1981. *Second Language Acquisition and Second Language Learning*: Oxford: Pergamon
Kroll, B. & Wells, C. 1983. *Explorations in the Development of Writing*: Chichester: John Wiley
Kubanek-German, A. 1998. Survey article 'Primary foreign language teaching in Europe - trends and issues' *Language Teaching* 31:193-205
Kubanek-German, A. 2000. 'Emerging Intercultural Awareness in a Young Learner Context: A Checklist for Research' in Moon, J. & Nikolov, M. 2000 *Research into Teaching English to Young Learners*: Pecs: University of Pecs Press

Lang, J. 2001. http://www.education.gouv.fr/discours/2001/dlangviv.htm
Lee, W. 2001. 'The National Curriculum and Textbook of primary English in Korea' in:

Proceedings of the Conference of ELT Curriculum for Young learners in East Asia 2000: National Taiwan Normal University Taiwan ROC/British Council/ELTeCS East Asia

Lenneberg, E. 1967. *Biological Foundations of Language*: New York: John Wiley & Sons

Lewis, M. 1986. *The English Verb*: Hove: Language Teaching Publications

Lightbown, P. & Spada, N. 1993. *How Languages are Learned*: Oxford: Oxford University Press

Littlewood, W. 1993. 'Cognitive principles underlying task-centred foreign language learning' in: Bird, N. et al. (eds.) *Language and Content*: Institute for Language in Education. Hong Kong

Maclennan, S. 1987. 'Integrating lesson planning and class management' in: *English Language Teaching Journal* Vol 41 No 3

Maley, A. 1999. 'Surviving the 20th century' *English Teaching Professional* Issue 10

Malmberg, B. 1997. *The STRIMS Project Conclusions – Recommendations*: Uppsala, Sweden: University of Uppsala

McConkey, R. 1985. *Working with Parents: A Practical Guide for Teachers and Therapists*: London: Croom Helm

Martin, C. 1995. *Games and Fun Activities* Young Pathfinder Series: London: CILT

Mitchell, R. 1988. *Communicative Language Teaching in Practice*: London: CILT

Mohan, B. 1986. *Language and Content*: Ontario: Addison-Wesley

Montgomery, D. & Rawlings A. 1986. *Bright Ideas: Classroom Management*: Leamington Spa: Scholastic

Nagy, W. 1997. 'On the role of context in first- and second-language vocabulary learning' in: Schmitt & McCarthy (eds.) *Vocabulary, Description, Acquisition and Pedagogy*: Cambridge: Cambridge University Press

Nelson, K. 1977. 'Cognitive development and the acquisition of concepts' in: R. C. Anderson et al. (eds.) School and the Acquisition of Knowledge. Hillsdale, N.J.: Lawrence Erlbaum Associates

Nikolov, M. 2000. 'Issues in Research into Early Foreign Language Programmes' in Moon, J. & Nikolov, M. (eds.) 2000. *Research into Teaching English to Young Learners* Pecs: University of Pecs Press

Nisbet, J. & Shucksmith, J. 1986. *Learning Strategies*: London: Routledge

Nunan, D. & Lamb, C. 1996. *The Self-Directed Teacher*: Cambridge: Cambridge University Press

Nunan, D. 1999. 'Does Younger = Better?' in: *Matters* Vol 9 No 4: TESOL

O'Malley, J.M., Chamot, A.U., Stewner-Manzanares, G., Kupper, L. & Russo, R.P. 1985. 'Learning Strategies Used by Beginning and Intermediate Students' *Language Learning* Vol 35 No 1

Opie, I. & Opie P. 1967. *The Lore and Language of Schoolchildren*: Oxford: Oxford University Press

Palim, J. & Power, P. 1990. *Jamboree Communication Communication Activities for Children*: Walton-on-Thames: Thomas Nelson and Sons

Palmer, S. 1991. *Spelling: A Teacher's Survival Kit*: Harlow: Longman

Park, J. 2001. 'Teacher Education for ELT in Korean Elementary Schools' in Proceedings of the ELTeCS Conference *ELT Curriculum Development for Young Learners in East Asia 2000* Taipei: Taiwan Normal University Taiwan/British Council/ELTeCS East Asia

Paul, D. 1996 *Songs and Games for Children*: Oxford: Macmillan Heinemann

Perrett, J. 1995. *Wordbird*: Harlow: Longman

Philpot, S. 1994. *Spotlight on Grammar*: Oxford: Macmillan Heinemann

Philpot, S. 2000. *Building Blocks for English*: Addlestone: DELTA

Rea-Dickens, P. & Rixon, S. 2000. 'Assessment of young learners' English: reasons and means' in Rixon, S. (ed.) *Young Learners of English: Some Research Perspectives*: Harlow: Longman

Read, C. 1999. *The Princess in the Tower: Activities for 3–11 year olds*, CATS, The Young Learners SIG Newsletter, IATEFL

Retter, C. & Valls, N. 1984. *Bonanza 77 English Language Games for Young Learners*: Harlow: Longman

Richardson, R. 1999. *Enriching Literacy – Text, Talk and Tales in Today's Classroom: A practical handbook for multilingual schools*: Brent Language Service: Trentham Books

Riley, P. 1985. 'Strategy: conflict or collaboration?' *Melangues Pedagogiques*: CRAPEL, Université de Nancy 11

Rivers, W. 1981. *Teaching Foreign Language Skills*: Second edition. Chicago: University of Chicago Press

Rixon, S. 1992. 'English and other languages for younger children: practice and theory in a rapidly changing world' in: *Language Teaching* Vol 25 No 2

Rixon, S. 1999. 'Introduction' in: *Young Learners of English: Some Research Perspectives*: Harlow: Longman in association with The British Council

Rixon, S. 1999. 'Where do the words in EYL textbooks come from?' in *Young Learners of English: Some Research Perspectives*: Harlow: Longman in association with The British Council

Rosen, H. 1985. *Stories and Meanings*: NATE

Roth, G.1998. *Teaching Very Young Children*: London: Richmond Publishing

Rubin, J. 1975. *What the 'Good Language Learner' can teach us*, TESOL Quarterly, Vol 9.1:41-51

Scovel, T. 1988. *A Time to Speak: A Psycholinguistic Inquiry into the Critical Period for Human Speech*: Rowley, Mass.: Newbury House/Harper & Row

Schmitt, N. 1997. 'Vocabulary learning strategies' in: Schmitt, N., McCarthy, M. (eds) *Vocabulary, Description, Acquisition and Pedagogy*: Cambridge: Cambridge University Press

Scrivener, J. 1994. *Learning Teaching*: Oxford: Macmillan Heinemann

Seidl, J. 1992. *Grammar One*: Oxford: Oxford University Press

Sharma, P. 1998. *CD-ROM: A Teacher's Handbook*: Oxford: Summertown Publishing

Sinclair, B. & Ellis, G. 1992. 'Survey: learner training in EFL course books': *English Language Teaching Journal* Vol 46 No 2

Sinclair, B. 1999. 'More than an act of faith? evaluating learner autonomy' in: Kennedy, C. (ed) *Innovation and Best Practice*: Longman in association with the British Council

Singleton, D. 1989. *Language Acquisition: the Age Factor*: Clevedon: Multilingual Matters

Skehan, P. 1998. *A Cognitive Approach to Language Learning*: Oxford: Oxford University Press

Skinner, B.F. 1957. *Verbal Behaviour*: New York: Appleton-Century-Crofts

Slattery, M., & Willis, J. 2001. *English for Primary Teachers*: Oxford: Oxford University Press

Snow, C. & Hoefnagel-Hohle, M. 1978. 'The critical period for language acquisition: evidence from second language learning' in: *Child Development* 49:1114-28

Sperling, D. 1999. *Internet Activity Workbook*: Englewood Cliffs, N.J.: Prentice Hall Regents

Stern, H. (ed.) 1969. *Languages and the Young School Child*: Oxford: Oxford University Press

Sullivan, M. 1988. *Parents and School. Bright Ideas Management Books*: London: Scholastic

Van Ek, J. 1980. *The Threshold Level*: Oxford: Pergamon

Tang, G. 1992. 'The effect of graphic representation of knowledge structures on ESL reading comprehension' in: *Studies in Second Language Acquisition* 14:177-195

Tann, S. 1991. *Developing Language in the Primary Classroom*: London: Cassell

Taylor, G. 1984. *Be Your Child's Natural Teacher*: London: Penguin

Teeler, D. & Gray, P. 2000. *Use the Internet in ELT*: Harlow: Longman

Toth, M. *Children's Games* 1995. Oxford: Macmillan Heinemann

References and further reading

Ur, P. 1985. 'Survey review: Courses for younger learners': *English Language Teaching Journal* Vol 39 No 4

Ur, P. 1988. *Grammar Practice Activities*: Cambridge: Cambridge University Press

Ur, P. 1996. *A Course in Language Teaching Practice and Theory*: Cambridge: Cambridge University Press

Valcarcel, M. 1997. 'The Spanish education reform system' in: Karavas-Doukas, K & Rea-Dickens, P. *Evaluating Innovations and Establishing Research Priorities: Proceedings of the Conference on The Teaching of Foreign Languages in European Primary Schools*: Warwick: University of Warwick Press

Vale, D. 1996. *The Cambridge Picture Dictionary*: Cambridge: Cambridge University Press

Vale, D. 1998. *Picture Grammar for Children*: Oxford: Macmillan Heinemann

van Lier, L. 1996. *Interaction in the Language Curriculum*: Harlow: Longman

Vygotsky, L. 1978. *Mind in Society*: Cambridge, Mass.: Harvard University Press

Wajnryb, R. 1990. *Grammar Dictation*: Oxford: Oxford University Press

Wallace, C. 1992. *Reading*: Oxford: Oxford University Press

Webster, D. 1989. *Muzzy Comes Back*. Parent's Notes: BBC English

Wells, G. 1986. *The Meaning Makers*: London: Hodder & Stoughton

Wenden, A. 1985. 'Facilitating learning competence: perspectives on an expanded role for second-language teachers': *The Canadian Modern Language Review* Vol 41 No 6

Wenden, A. 1987. 'Incorporating learner training in the classroom' in: Wenden, A., Rubin, J. (eds) *Learner Strategies in Language Learning*: Englewood Cliffs: Prentice Hall International

White, R. 1988. *The ELT Curriculum*: Oxford: Basil Blackwell

Whitehead, M. 1990. *Language and Literacy in the Early Years*: London: Paul Chapman

Widdowson, H. 1978. *Teaching Language as Communication*: Oxford: Oxford University Press

Widdowson, H. 1984. 'The incentive value of theory in teacher education': *English Language Teaching Journal*, Vol 38 No 2

Willes, M. 1983. *Children into Pupils*: London: Routledge & Kegan Paul

Williams, M. 1995. 'Survey review: Materials for teaching children and teenagers': *English Language Teaching Journal* Vol 49 No 2

Williams, M. 2000. 'Survey review: Materials for young learners' *English Language Teaching Journal* Vol 54 No 4

Willis, J. 1981. *Teaching English through English*: Harlow: Longman

Willis, J. 1996. *A Framework for Task-Based Learning*: Harlow: Longman

Windeatt, S., Hardisty, D. & Eastment, D. 2000 *The Internet*: Oxford: Oxford University Press

Wright, A. 1985. *Picture Dictionary for Young Learners*: Harlow: Longman

Wright, A. 1995. *Storytelling with Children*: Oxford: Oxford University Press

Wright, A. 1996. *1000+ Pictures for Teachers to Copy Revised edition*: Harlow: Longman

Wright, A. 1997. *Creating Stories with Children*: Oxford: Oxford University Press

Zaro, J.J. & Salaberi, S. 1995. *Storytelling*: Oxford: Heinemann